# Teaching Bullies

*Also by Jennifer M. Fraser*

*Be a Good Soldier: Children's Grief in English Modernist Novels*

Available from: University of Toronto Press,
Scholarly Publishing Division

*Rite of Passage in the Narratives of Dante and Joyce*

Available from: University Press of Florida

# Teaching Bullies

## Zero Tolerance on the Court or in the Classroom

Jennifer Margaret Fraser, PhD

Published by Motion Press

Library and Archives Canada Cataloguing in Publication

Fraser, Jennifer Margaret, 1966–, author

Teaching Bullies: Zero Tolerance on the Court or in the Classroom / Jennifer Margaret Fraser.

ISBN: 978-0-9940820-2-2

PS8611.R3824C78 2013    C813'.6    C2013-903305-X

Publisher: Motion Press

Front cover image: HurtWords "*Weapon of Choice*" project; see http://hurtwords.com/

# *Statements of Praise for Teaching Bullies*

Boys model the messages they receive about becoming men. When adults inculcate homophobic attitudes among children, boys learn a binary trap: they can embody the traits associated with images of traditional masculinity, or they might be labeled "sissy," "wuss," "gay" in a pejorative way, or ruder words. Many boys feel pressured to become the biggest of wheels, the sturdiest of oaks, the most virulent repudiators of femininity. The link between machismo and violence can start early for boys pushed into a gender straitjacket.

*Teaching Bullies* offers ideas that could help us create a compelling counter-narrative in part by detailing, incident after sickening incident, what happens when teachers, coaches, and school administrators misuse masculine power. *Teaching Bullies* will encourage parents, educators, and community leaders who want to foster safe and inclusive school environments where all students can thrive, both socially and academically. Jennifer Margaret Fraser's documented narrative is a powerful call to action that should galvanize us all to take a stand against homophobic bullying in our schools.

> – Barry MacDonald, founder of www.MentoringBoys.com,
> and author of *Boy Smarts: Mentoring Boys for Success at School*,
> and *Boys on Target: Raising Boys into Men of Courage and Compassion.*

Bullying by teachers is a devastating problem that can leave long lasting and deep emotional scars on its victims. These innocent children are often re-victimized by schools that seek to hide or cover-up the abuse (and it is abuse) because these administrations would rather bury the scandal rather than face the embarrassment of what was done under their jurisdiction.

For too long victims and their families have been either ignored, threatened or simply felt uncomfortable speaking out. That's why Jennifer Fraser's book is an important step forward in the battle to reclaim our schools for our children. We need to let victims know that their suffering matters and that they will be defended.

> – Stuart Chaifetz, parent advocate, Akian's Dad

This is such an important conversation that must be had in the school system and in amateur sports. As I read this book, I was consistently taken aback at the "normalizing" that seems to happen in response to bullying-type behaviors in sports. If any other teacher in the school system were to speak to students in the same way, as it appears some sports coaches may speak to students, there would be no question about the repercussions. I found that same "normalizing" in my research on blame.

The question now is how to support coaches, teachers, students, parents, politicians, policy makers, and organizations? Jennifer Fraser started this conversation and it is up to us as a community to continue the conversation as part of transforming coaching and amateur sports.

– Cheryl Mitchell, PhD

The topic of bullying is one that all schools devote considerable time and resources to investigate, monitor, and deliberate on suitable consequences. In a cyber world, the boundaries have broadened to the point where it is unclear what falls under the jurisdiction of a school and its administrators. Most cases dealt with by school administrators tend to be peer-to-peer bullying or perceived bullying. But what happens if the bully is an adult in a caregiving position?

The research Jennifer Fraser draws upon presents a disturbing picture of what can happen when students are bullied. Psychological bullying can take many forms but they all have the potential to humiliate, and damage young minds. What guidelines exist? Where is the line drawn over what is acceptable in the heat of a game or in a practice when a coach is trying to encourage athletes to push themselves harder? It is time for educators to take a closer look at this topic and develop clearer standards that need to be incorporated into all teacher-training programs across the country.

– Richard Calderwood, high school principal

Policy makers will find this book a useful introduction and guide to the reason for concern as well as to the literature and press on the issue in the North American and British context. Dr. Fraser uses her skill as a storyteller to draw the reader in with personal experiences, but she keeps us there with research and strong analysis. This book should be an essential resource for any parent or educator seeking help in learning how to avoid the harm caused by teacher bullies.

– Patricia Lane, lawyer and mediator

At professional and university level sports, and more recently, even in league play, major cracks have been appearing in the iconic mythology and armor of sport. And they are being dealt with more swiftly and directly every day.

But, ironically, in the supposed safe haven of school, many young athletes and their families continue to suffer without voice. It is on this last bastion of the 'winning culture' that Jennifer Fraser's new book, **Teaching Bullies**, stakes its claim.

Through a skillful weaving of poignant tale and full evidential analysis, Fraser offers us a picture that is all too familiar - one of abuse, emotional extortion and final dejection at the hands of those 'old school' arbiters of the 'what it takes to win' philosophy of life.

This is a world in which respect, decency and professionalism are lost in the name of 'toughness'. It is one in which manipulation and bullying rather than respect and skillful teaching are used to 'bring up' our youth.

What is most insidious in Fraser's tale is how, when voices are raised, the education system at all levels can leave the besieged without protection. **Teaching Bullies** is the touchstone, even a battle cry, for those who understand what sports in school should really be about – playing, learning and growing!

– John Baty, internationally recognized<br>Speech & Debate Coach, Consultant

For the fourteen students who spoke up

and for all others who suffer in silence

# CONTENTS

# Contents

# CHAPTER ONE

# WHEN THE BULLY IS THE TEACHER

> The logic is that these coaches give athletes the worst
> in order to get the best out of them. But at what cost?
> People excuse — or even celebrate — such behavior
> as a passion. But, let's call it by its real name: abuse.
>
> – Charles M. Blow, *New York Times*, April 2013

Our sixteen-year-old son was competing at the 2012 Provincial Basketball Championships in Kamloops, British Columbia (BC) when one of the boys on the team texted his parents to say he *"couldn't take it anymore."* The coaches were calling the team *"a bunch of pussies," "hopeless"* and *"retarded."*

For my husband and me, that was the point of no return.

When we heard those words, we knew we had to get our son away from those coaches. No matter what it took, we could not let anyone speak to our son like that. This wasn't the first time we'd seen or heard there was something wrong on the team with how the coaches were "motivating" the players, but this time, there was no going back. We could no longer excuse or forgive. The basketball court that our son loved so much was becoming a place he dreaded and hated.

In January 2012, during a game, we'd seen the young Head Coach call our son off the court and start yelling angrily at him. At six-four and close to two hundred pounds, our son towered over the coach. It was hard to understand what he could have done to incur such rage on the preceding play. Our son clearly couldn't take another second of the coach's angry rant and started to back away. The coach reached out and clenched our son's arm, pulled him in close, and then he yelled so loudly that we, along with other parents in the nearby stands heard: "*Don't walk away when I'm fucking talking to you!*" The Assistant Coach on the sidelines did nothing. Although he was a generation older and renowned for having previously coached for a year a player who was highly successful in the NBA, he took the Assistant Coach position, perhaps because his own son was on the team. We were shocked at the Head Coach's conduct and at the Assistant Coach's choice to be a bystander as this rant unfolded courtside. At home after the game we told our son we had to report the incident, but he begged us not to talk to the coaches or report their conduct to the Administration. When your son is sixteen and says if you speak up "*you'll ruin everything*" for him on the team and at school, you naturally hesitate to do what you know is the right thing.

A month later, in February, this same Head Coach called the boys "*fucking retards*" during practice in the School gym behind closed doors. Parents were discouraged from attending practices and even from staying in the same hotel or interacting with our children when they were at tournaments. All this was presented to us as important for team bonding. Our own son didn't tell us about the "fucking retards" comment, but confirmed it that night after we heard from other families whose sons had spoken up. Once again, the Assistant Coach had done nothing but, based on his silence, seemed to approve.

Again, our son begged us not to say anything. My husband and I did not know what to do. If it were his math or English teacher who had said this, we would have had him transfer classes; however, it's not so easy if it's a coach. There's only one team. It is difficult to imagine any scenario whereby a math teacher could speak to students in such a humiliating and harmful way without being held to account, let alone forcibly grab a student and physically restrain them for more in-the-face yelling. However, these coaches seemed to adhere to different standards simply because this took place on the court and not in the classroom. When our

2

son asked us not to report, we respected his wishes, setting aside our deep misgivings. The pressure on him was already more than enough. The need to secure a letter of recommendation to apply as a student athlete to universities was paramount. The need for playing time and avoiding being benched loomed in our son's mind. We knew another player's mother had expressed concerns before the start of the 2012 season and that her son, despite his skill and work ethic, spent most games on the bench. It was a powerful motivator for us to keep quiet. Nonetheless, other parents were furious and threatening to go to the School Administration. I counseled them to give these coaches yet another chance.

Besides, I told the parents, going to the Headmaster or Director of the Senior School would, if anything, make it worse. The School where I used to work was not in my experience a place where raising concerns or lodging formal complaints resulted in positive change. More often, it brought grief to those who asked for students to be protected. I am aware of two other teachers at the School who quit rather than suffer any further harassment after they reported colleagues' harmful conduct.

The coaches, who we ultimately learned from detailed student testimonies were regularly swearing, using homophobic language, yelling, grabbing, benching players whose parents spoke up, shunning players, throwing chairs or clipboards, and making many teenagers afraid, were *teachers*, and so was I. These teachers were my colleagues.

For a parent to complain about teacher conduct is difficult, for a fellow teacher to do it is *painful*. I knew these teachers. I had worked with them for eight years. I knew they had many wonderful qualities in the classroom and I knew some had children attending the School just like I did. However, that March when our son returned from the Basketball Provincials in Kamloops, BC, he was ill. He had canker sores all over his tongue and mouth and had been unable to eat and could barely drink. I took him to the doctor, and while she prescribed antibiotics, because he

3

was about to embark on a School-sponsored service trip to Kenya, she said it looked like stress. Her advice was to wait a day or two and see if the sores cleared up. She said spiking cortisol levels could have this effect on the body. Within about eight hours, his mouth improved so much that he never needed to take the medication. Since these symptoms seemed to be stress-related, we held off discussing what was clearly an untenable environment for a student-athlete to be in. He went off on his trip to Kenya and we began dealing with the crisis. It did not take much research to learn that not only did the coaches' behavior sound like emotional abuse, but also that experts depicted such treatment as having extremely harmful long-term effects on teens. When we read multiple studies that documented the ways the bullying conduct we had witnessed and heard about was very damaging and the impact could last a lifetime, we knew it was crucial to protect our son however best we could.

We made the difficult decision to transfer our son to another local independent school that had a competitive basketball program. Because he hoped to pursue the game at the university level, and according to his coaches, was capable of doing so, he needed to be at a school that gave him the maximum opportunity to develop in a high-level competitive environment. We knew he would never transfer schools otherwise. We spoke with the Head Coach at the other school and determined there was a spot for him at the school and on the basketball team. When my husband explained who our son was, the coach laughed and said he had just come from a meeting where the coaching staff had discussed strategies around containing our son's game in the hope of winning the following season. Needless to say, he seemed more than pleased at the chance to have him join their team.

However, before we could transfer our son, we needed permission from his school and from BC School Sports. In BC, when an athlete transfers to a comparably competitive school athletic program, BC

School Sports, the governing body for school sport competition, won't allow the student to compete in athletics until a year has passed. BC School Sports confirmed by phone that our son would be unable to play for the other school's basketball team; it was against their policy. My husband contacted a lawyer, who at the time also happened to be on my former school's Board of Governors, to find out if there were any legal options we could pursue – ones that would lead to our son playing basketball in a bully-free environment. When the Lawyer heard my husband's account about why we wanted to have our son transferred – the coaches' conduct – he assured us that transferring to another school would not be necessary. The Lawyer was confident that the Headmaster would address this serious situation with the coaches and the way they were treating the players. The Lawyer asked my husband and me to contact other players' parents and have them inform him about what their sons' experiences had been on the court.

So, I sent a carefully crafted email out to team parents, some whom I had never met, to write to me if they had any concerns about the coaching staff or the way the players were being treated so I could forward their messages on to the Lawyer/ Board Member. Both my husband and I were astounded at the resounding response to my email. Many parents sent back replies that expressed great concern over inarticulate screaming, swearing, homophobic slurs, humiliation, shunning, and favoritism they had witnessed or heard about from their sons. We learned that some parents had already gone to the coaches directly or to various Administrators, including the Headmaster, looking to put a stop to the behavior. One parent even described a recent meeting with the Assistant Coach and the Director of the Senior School where the coach acknowledged he had a "problem" and should go on probation. Ironically, when far more complaints came in from concerned parents about this coach, the Director of the Senior School failed to put him on probation. Even more shocking to us was the responses we received were not just about incidents during the 2012 season: apparently parents had started talking about the email and we began receiving emails with corroborating accounts from parents whose children had already graduated from the school. And it wasn't just parents from the boys' basketball team. There were similar accounts describing "bullying" by the girls' basketball coach, who was also the Director of Athletics, the very person with whom students or parents were required to express concerns or lodge formal complaints.

Parent after parent described coaching that did not have winning as its goal, but instead seemed to be much more about bullying certain players while placing others on pedestals. It wasn't just our son who was being bullied; it was multiple students. It wasn't just one season; we now heard from other parents that bullying in one form or another had been inflicted on both the Boys Junior and Senior Basketball Teams and the Girls Senior Basketball Team dating as far back as 2007.

I forwarded the email responses on to the Lawyer/ Board Member, and understood that he in turn provided them to the Headmaster for his review and immediate action. My husband and I each crafted letters outlining why we wanted permission from the school to transfer our son as required by BC School Sports. I also said I would resign if the Headmaster did not put a stop to the bullying.

We knew our son would not want to leave the school, and I didn't want to leave it either. He had been there since grade four, and had benefited from its excellent teachers and fantastic programs. He played in the orchestra; he was in the middle of an outdoor leadership program. He had many friends. I liked and respected my colleagues. I especially loved my department that was full of committed educators and creative writers. For eight years I had worked with students from all over the world who inspired me with their intelligence and desire to learn; I had no wish to resign. However, as a teacher and a mother, I would not remain working at a school that suspended or expelled students for bullying, but called comparable conduct on the court "old style coaching" when it was perpetrated by teachers who were coaching basketball.

As a society, we profess to have zero tolerance for peer-to-peer bullying. When one child bullies another on the playground, there is no internal struggle to decide if what transpired was due to a child's passionate nature. We intervene. When one child bullies another, we don't try to assess whether the behavior makes the victim feel harmed or motivates them in some way. We intervene. When peers bully, there's no talk about the fine line between harm and encouragement. Yet somehow, when a teacher bullies a student or a coach bullies a student-athlete, it's perceived differently. The behavior is rationalized as being meant to inspire the victim and stemming from an outpouring of competitive drive or passionate care for the individual's athletic success. Bullying among peers is on the rise, and one cannot help but wonder if it is due in part to this hypocritical approach – bullying is not tolerated except when it's done by adults – that must be extremely confusing for children. While it makes general sense to give a child-bully the benefit of the doubt, because he or she may *not* be aware of just how badly derogatory terms can hurt another child, it is *not* acceptable to extend that same benefit of the doubt to adults.

It would be doubly difficult to extend that benefit to those adults whose very profession as teachers requires them to understand child development.[1]

---

[1] As experts in coach abuse, Ashley Stirling and Gretchen Kerr state: "It could be argued that sport psychology consultants are in similar positions as others in cognate professions such as education. Teachers, for example, due to their 'daily experiences with students and observations of their growth and development, [have] significant

If there is one person in our child's life we should hold accountable for knowing exactly how harmful bullying is, surely it's a teacher.

Bullies on the playground use whatever advantage they have – size, popularity, intelligence – in an effort to oppress their targets. Still, when bullying happens from child to child, there is a basic equivalency. However, when a teacher bullies a student, the playing field is not remotely equal. We tend to think of teens as young adults, but legally they are "children" until the age of nineteen. While they can vote, drive a car, and hold a job, they lack power and are for the most part at the mercy of the adults who inhabit their lives. In a sixteen-year-old student's world, a teacher has nearly unlimited power and control over his or her future – over their grades, scholarships, playing time for student-athletes – so a far more intense level of bullying may occur between teachers and students and coaches and student-athletes. A significant part of a teacher's education and professional credentials revolve around reinforcing students' value – physically, mentally, and emotionally. Teachers are necessarily required to measure, rate, assess, compare, and judge children so they can gauge exactly where a child stands in terms of achievement, potential, and character relative to their peers. Teachers hold incredibly powerful positions in children's lives and their decisions can have a lasting effect on a child's future.

When a teacher says, let alone yells, "retard" or "you're not trying," it's psychologically the same as recording an "F" on a child's report card. Studies show a teacher's negative judgment of a child's

---

reasons to be involved in the identification of, prevention of, and interventions for child maltreatment' (Lowenthall, 2001, p. 6)." Ashley E. Stirling and Gretchen A. Kerr, "Sport Psychology Consultants as Agents of Child Protection," *Journal of Applied Sport Psychology* 22, 2010: 305-319.

performance not only blocks opportunities and closes doors for the student in the immediate future, but it also has the power to stay with that child for the rest of his or her life. A teacher's bullying comments can have the force of an official, public statement about a student's ability, potential, and character, especially if they are made in front of other students and teachers.

In 2012, when conservative pundit Anne Coulter tweeted in reference to US President Barack Obama that he was a "retard," *Globe and Mail* writer Cliff Lee, commented: "In a time when bullying is being seriously addressed because of its sometimes fatal results and the mental scars it can leave behind years after the fact, it's inexcusable for Coulter to behave like her words are innocently fanning the flames of political discourse." He went on to say: "Coulter is no better than an immature school-aged bully who uses words to hurt others."[2] The key word here is "hurt." As a society, we have no problem saying "zero-tolerance for bullying" when it is child to child because so many reputable studies have documented the hurt that occurs in these situations. When adults bully children, we can reasonably assume a far worse hurt occurs; however, society struggles to hold the adult accountable. Suddenly, what was zero-tolerance for a bully on the playground abruptly becomes a great deal of tolerance for a bully, especially on the court when adults are involved.

At my former school, when the School Administration minimized and dismissed concerns about bullying by coaches, when they chose not to hold teachers accountable, parents ended up fighting a losing battle to protect their children. While a bully on the playground has no real power,

---

[2] Cliff Lee, "Ann Coulter's 'retard' tweet says more about her than her politics," *The Globe and Mail* Oct. 24 2012: http://www.theglobeandmail.com/life/the-hot-button/ann-coulters-retard-tweet-says-more-about-her-than-her-politics/article4635521/

a teacher has enormous power and can more intensely and more seriously target the child whose parents speak up. Often, parents are forced to maintain a terribly conflicted code of silence – where their child's wellbeing is traded for good grades, a letter of recommendation, or a sports scholarship.

When parents responded to my initial email that the Lawyer/ Board Member asked me to write, one mother I did not know wrote me back that a full year earlier, in 2011, she had written an eleven-page document informing this Lawyer along with the Chair of the Board of Governors and the School Chaplain, that "child abuse" was occurring on the basketball teams. She provided a great deal of anecdotal evidence from students and sent the document to the Board, not only in her capacity as a player's mother, but also as a lawyer who believed there was no place for this in a school setting. She worried that reporting the abuse would mean that her son, going into grade twelve, would suffer repercussions. She asked that her document be kept strictly confidential and that the Headmaster only be informed verbally to protect the students' identities. The Lawyer wrote her an email confirming that the Headmaster had indeed been informed. She had faith that now that the Board Members, Chaplain and Headmaster were alerted, positive change would occur. Her son told her things were better and she assumed all was well in the following season until she received my email a year later in March 2012. She could not have known that concerned parents from at least five families had been meeting with the Director of the Senior School and had contacted the Headmaster to report that the coaches were bullying students and demanding that the bullying stop. The Headmaster did not tell these families that the Board of Governors had alerted him to the abuse, or tell the parent who filed the eleven-page report that others were coming forward with the same concerns.

As a *mother*, when I found out in March 2012 that these coaches had been allowed to bully my son unchecked for a full year after the report's formal submission to the Board of Governors, I was physically ill. As a *teacher* I could start to see the path unfold before me – I was legally obligated to report these events to the Teacher Regulation Branch. My teaching license would be on the line if I failed to alert the proper authorities about what I now knew.

However, the parents who had come forward with serious concerns believed the two Board members, the Chaplain and the Headmaster when now, after receiving so many parent emails and meeting with them, these officials assured us that they fully understood the harm being done and they would pay for psychological counseling and heal "emotional bruises." There would be "different coaching." In May 2012, the Headmaster brought in a fantastic basketball coach who did a six-week clinic with the students. The Headmaster informed us that he had begun negotiations to have the new coach work at the school the following year. Although we were anxious about what we had learned, we hoped the Headmaster would finally do the right thing and protect students. Our uneasy trust was indicative of how powerful the desire was to quietly remain part of the community, and allow the Administrators to address the problem.

In a recent article, "That's not Coaching, That's Child Abuse," American author Harlan Coben recounts a personal story about his child being bullied by a coach and discusses how some parents acted and continued to support the abusive coaching style:

> The coach I mentioned earlier was finally removed. There are many parents who still back and excuse him. Some simply don't know better because their child doesn't share or has become

immune to the bullying. Worse, many shrug it off. "There are a lot of parents who coach like that," they say. Wow. [3]

At my former school, the coaches had parents who fully supported them and these parents argued that their children benefited from the "old style coaching." However, what has surprised me in the three years I've been dealing with this crisis is that some of the students who were favored and who defended the coaches appear to be suffering just as much as the targeted students, if not more. Reports about students being put on suicide watch, dropping out of university, turning to hard drugs, binge drinking, suffering depression and displaying other destructive behaviors may well speak to the suffering students face when bullied by their coaches. Strikingly, similar self-destructive behavior has surfaced among those students who vociferously defended the coaches as the events at my former school unfolded. It appears that in a bullying dynamic, the situation may well be equally unhealthy for the target, the bystander, *and* the beneficiary.

Nonetheless, teachers bullying students has not received much expert attention. In a 2014 article, Ashley E. Stirling and Gretchen A. Kerr concur: "there has been no longitudinal research on the occurrence of emotionally abusive behaviors within the parent-child or pupil-teacher relations."[4] It is time this harmful dynamic received expert attention. Throughout, I will depend on the expertise of Dr. Gretchen Kerr and Dr. Ashley Stirling, sought-after sport-psychology advisors and award-winning academics who work in the University of Toronto's Faculty of

---

[3] Harlan Coben, "That's Not Coaching. It's Child Abuse," *Bloomberg View*, May 2013: http://www.bloombergview.com/articles/2013-05-30/that-s-not-coaching-it-s-child-abuse-

[4] Ashley E. Stirling and Gretchen A. Kerr, "Initiating and Sustaining Emotional Abuse in the Coach-Athlete Relationship: An Ecological Transactional Model of Vulnerability," *Journal of Aggression, Maltreatment & Trauma*, vol. 23, 2014: 116-135.

Kinesiology and Physical Education and whose area of expertise is emotional abuse in sport, harassment, and abuse in youth sport, as well as experiential education and the psychosocial aspects of high-performance athlete development.

Emotionally abusive teachers don't force students to smoke weed or snort coke, nor do they tilt the beer can or bottle to their lips; therefore the law does not hold bullying teachers accountable. Since the self-destructive behavior appears to be a "choice" made by the teenager, they are seen to be responsible for their own self-harm. However, as is well documented, bullies get into kids' heads and their humiliating, lambasting mantra may well encourage self-destructive conduct. Laws must become much more psychologically informed to hold accountable those who bully, especially when they are in positions of power over children.

Bullying is not about a teacher losing their temper in an isolated incident or saying something insensitive to a student by accident. Likewise, on the playground, bullying is not the word used when there's a conflict between two kids or a scuffle or a temper tantrum or a harsh word exchanged. In her recently updated, ground-breaking book on the subject, *The Bully, the Bullied, and the Not-So-Innocent Bystander,* Barbara Coloroso writes that bullying is "insulting activity that is intended to humiliate and harm the target." She specifies that "It can be, and often is, persistent, continual, and repeated over time, but it does not have to be. Once is enough to constitute bullying."[5] Emily Brazelon, in her book on bullying, notes that "Dan Olweus, the Scandinavian psychologist who is credited with launching the field of bullying studies back in the 1960s, has been arguing for many years, [that bullying] is a ***particular form of harmful aggression.*** And so the effort to prevent bullying isn't about

---

[5] Barbara Coloroso, *The Bully, the Bullied, and the Not-So-Innocent Bystander,* updated edition, Harper Collins: 2015 (46).

13

pretending that kids will always be nice to each other, or that they don't have to learn to weather some adversity."[6] Bullies, especially in sports, are quick to argue that their intent is to teach the targeted child a lesson about adversity or toughening up. However, this excuse is as weak as a child saying that their bullying was just meant to be "a joke."

As Barbara Coloroso explains the four markers of bullying: it requires an imbalance of power, the intent to harm, a threat of further aggression and ultimately, terror. The final marker is most interesting because as Coloroso explains: "The bullied child is rendered so powerless that he is unlikely to fight back or tell anyone about the bullying. The bully counts on bystanders becoming involved or at least doing nothing to stop the bullying."[7] As soon as a teacher refers to students as "retards" or "pussies" whether it is in math class or during a basketball practice, the conduct matches Coloroso's definition: the power imbalance between student and teacher is exponential; the intent to harm is conveyed by the insulting, humiliating, terms used; no reasonable argument can convince that these terms assist athletes on improving their skills, learning techniques, or developing confidence; the power to bench players, to ignore them, to control plays, to choose positions, to grant awards and scholarships create the ideal conditions for further aggression that may escalate until students turn a blind eye to others' suffering. One player on the senior girls' basketball team described an occurrence that demonstrates a bullying dynamic at work. She had a badly swollen knee that hurt with every step. Nonetheless, she felt pressured to keep playing during a practice. Finally, her knee gave out and she hit the floor. The

---

[6] http://www.slate.com/blogs/xx_factor/2013/02/20/new_duke_study_on_bullyi ng_childhood_victims_bullies_and_bully_victims_all.html
[7] Barbara Coloroso, *The Bully, the Bullied, and the Not-So-Innocent Bystander*, updated edition, Harper Collins: 2015 (47-8).

pain was excruciating; she was crying and unable to get up. Not a single girl on the team approached her or offered her any help. Instead, they watched the coach go over to look down at the student where she was writhing on the floor and issue a brief command: "Get up." What this coach did fits the criterion of bullying, and the girls' immobilized response suggests "terror" at work. My guess is there were girls who wanted to rush to the side of their fallen teammate who was so clearly in agony, but they were rendered powerless by a bullying dynamic. The student had torn her ACL and was done for the season. Despite being a talented player and dedicated athlete, she's never played basketball again.

In terms of bullying, Barbara Coloroso explains that, "Kids, parents, and educators need to feel more comfortable talking together about what's really going on in kids' lives. Before we can begin such a constructive conversation, two obstacles must be overcome: ignorance and apathy."[8] The goal of this book is to focus on teachers' bullying of students, and coaches' bullying of student athletes. When an adult bullies a child, their actions are called a variety of interchangeable terms: emotional abuse, verbal abuse, and psychological abuse. Ignorance is at work when the argument is made that athletes need to be toughened up and so bullying is necessary. Apathy is at work when parents, educational administrators, and teachers normalize the abusive conduct of coaches. In response to ignorance, this book provides research. In response to apathy, this book issues a call to action.

---

[8] Barbara Coloroso, *The Bully, the Bullied, and the Not-So-Innocent Bystander*, updated edition, Harper Collins: 2015 (39).

# Chapter Two

# Protecting the Abuser, not the Abused

> *I know that I will struggle with these feelings for a long time and I'm just fine with that. Dr. Goldberg continues to reiterate that those who are courageous can also be very afraid and I'm very afraid. I want to go to a school where me and my friends feel safe, where teachers stand up for students when another is out of line, where students are respected for standing up for what they believe is right.*
>
> – A letter our son wrote while suffering yet another night of insomnia

By April 2012, the Lawyer/ Board Member had sent the package of emails I had compiled from concerned parents to the Headmaster. More than thirty parents complaining in unison about coaching practices elicited a swift response. The Headmaster reviewed the materials and promised "different coaching" for the following year. Recognizing students had what he called, "emotional bruises," he offered to pay for psychological counseling for all students harmed by the coaching behavior. Based on the Headmaster's long overdue, but clear promise to protect students, my husband and I decided we no longer needed to transfer our son to another school. He could stay at his current School filled with long-time friends, benefit from the many excellent teachers he had for his other subjects, finish his outdoor leadership program, and continue to play basketball. His dream to one day make it onto a university team remained intact.

However, by late April, the Headmaster informed the involved parents that to hold the coaches accountable, it was not enough to have the written complaints from parents; he needed to hear directly from the students. Thirteen current and former students, some away at Canadian and American universities, provided detailed testimonies about their experiences, our son included. It is difficult and rare for students to speak up about peer bullying, let alone teacher bullying. Therefore, students are expected to choose whom they feel safe with in reporting on abuse. Some students gave testimonies to the Lawyer/ parent and others chose to have me record their experiences. They felt that as a trusted teacher, I was a safe adult to tell. There may have been other testimonies as well. In the ones that I took, it was startling how similar the students' accounts were, even though many of them did not know each other. However, these detailed written statements did not constitute enough evidence for the Headmaster to take decisive action. He stated that he needed now to personally interview those students still on campus who had not yet graduated, to gather further evidence that would enable him to take the action he had committed to in early April 2012.

I know of at least eight students who were asked to further share their experiences with the Headmaster, School Chaplain and the Lawyer/ parent who was working closely with the Headmaster to address the crisis. I only attended one interview, which was with the Lawyer's son. During these student-Administration sessions, the students recounted the treatment they received from their coaches: they reported being exposed to homophobic slurs, derogatory terms, yelling, and screaming. They also reported coaches swearing at the team or targeting specific players, gesturing in threatening or dismissive ways, physically manhandling players into position, asking humiliating rhetorical questions, restraining students who tried to get away from in-the-face yelling, pushing athletes to play when injured or ill, throwing objects down in apparent anger or disgust, threatening the team with not playing or benching players whose parents spoke up, ignoring certain players or excluding them from practice. Time after time during the interviews, the eight teenagers reported this conduct. Their descriptions were fully corroborated by the eleven-page document compiled in 2011 and the other five testimonies then available.

When students report that they are being abused by a teacher whether he or she is on or off-duty, whether he or she intends the harm or not, the Headmaster is required to call in the School's police liaison officer and fully inform the officer of what the students are reporting. The Headmaster informed the Lawyer/ parent and me that he had contacted the police liaison officer. After the police officer met with the Headmaster, the Lawyer/ parent and I requested a meeting with him as well. We then sent him the student testimonies to ensure he had the key information needed to conduct his assessment. The police officer reported to us and to the Headmaster that there was a "definite pattern in the complaints, all pointing to verbal and emotional abuse." If verbal and emotional abuse were included in the Criminal Code in the way physical and sexual abuse currently are, the police could have intervened and taken steps to protect these students. However, emotional abuse is not in the Criminal Code.

The police liaison officer let us and other parents know that he conferred on several occasions with Crown Counsel to determine if the physical restraint used by the coaches on players as detailed in the student testimonies met the test for physical abuse as established in the Criminal Code. Crown Council ultimately concluded that criminal charges against the coaches could not be pursued due to the difficulty of arguing "criminal intent" to harm. While an adult cannot restrain another adult in the workplace to yell derogatory comments in his face, on the court, a coach can argue the same conduct is to motivate a teenage player.

Emotional abuse, as defined by the *World Health Organization and the International Society for the Prevention of Child Abuse and Neglect*, is as follows:

> Emotional and psychological abuse involves both isolated incidents, as well as a pattern of failure over time on the part of a parent or caregiver to provide a developmentally appropriate and supportive environment. Acts in this category may have a high probability of damaging the child's physical or mental health, or its physical, mental, spiritual, moral or social development.

> Abuse of this type includes: the restriction of movement; patterns of belittling, blaming, threatening, frightening, discriminating against or ridiculing; and other non-physical forms of rejection or hostile treatment.[9]

A teacher is by definition a caregiver in an educational setting. Along with other parents we accessed the police reports and discovered that the police liaison officer communicated clearly to the Headmaster that, based on the student testimonies, there was a definite pattern of teacher-coaches abusing players at the School.

Despite receiving written complaints from at least thirty parents, at least fourteen student testimonies, at least eight in-person interviews and the police officer's assessment that a definite pattern of abuse existed, the Headmaster did not suspend the teacher-coaches, nor did he require them to be off-campus during the investigation. He also chose not to inform parents or school faculty about the serious allegations.

There soon developed an atmosphere of fear and anxiety among the students and their families, especially those who had spoken up about

---

[9] Alexander Butchart and Tony Kahane, *Preventing Child Maltreatment: A Guide to Taking Action and Generating Evidence*, World Health Organization and the International Society for the Prevention of Child Abuse and Neglect, 2006. http://whqlibdoc.who.int/publications/2006/9241594365_eng.pdf?ua=1

their negative experiences with the teacher-coaches to me, the Lawyer/parent, the Headmaster and Chaplain. While the Headmaster appeared appropriately concerned and supportive about the students and parent complaints in the privacy of his office, there were other signs throughout the school that student-safety might not actually be the priority he professed it to be. Parent and student unease turned out to be well founded. It soon came to light that the Headmaster, while reading student testimonies, was also aware that select Alumni were being contacted to defend the teachers named in the student testimonies. From within the School, unbeknownst to the students who came forward, and who trusted the Headmaster, phone calls were being placed asking specific Alumni to write in and support the teachers, as if this was a popularity contest or a dispute that the Headmaster had to quietly settle. It did not appear these Alumni were told any specifics about the allegations or the number of students and parents who had come forward in the expectation that the Administration would put a stop to the bullying behavior. The Alumni appear to have been simply told that *several* parents were complaining – further minimized by suggestions that the complaints had to do with playing-time – and that these Alumni needed to write in to provide a defense for the teachers and the School.

In an article in *The Atlantic* on bullying and narcissism, psychologist Dr. Joseph Burgo notes the parallel between adult bullying and child bullying: "Schoolyard bullies employ identical tactics, spreading vicious rumors and recruiting followers in order to persecute their victims."[10] In those cases where adults are the bully, the behavior is

---

[10] Joseph Burgo, "All Bullies Are Narcissists: Stories of bullying and hazing in the news break down to narcissism and insecurity," *The Atlantic*, November 2013: http://www.theatlantic.com/health/archive/2013/11/all-bullies-are-narcissists/281407/

virtually the same; just the age of the bullies is different. Adults by nature are also much more sophisticated in their approach. Moreover, adults can be empowered by their profession or the authoritative position they hold relative to the child they might choose to bully – much like the Headmaster, the Chaplain and the Board of Governors during the crisis that took place at my former school. The plea that went out from individuals at the school to Alumni for support was not a transparent process, nor was it an open request to all. If negative responses came in, or Alumni refused to write in to praise the teachers, no one would know one way or the other. It was done behind closed doors by those apparently invested in protecting the teachers and the school's reputation. The request to Alumni may have been motivated by a need for the Headmaster, Chaplain and certain Board members to protect themselves from questions around negligence, considering they were informed in spring 2011 of "child abuse" occurring on the basketball teams. Effective protection was not put in place for students, so that throughout the year and confirmed in the spring 2012, the Board Members, Chaplain and Headmaster were again confronted with multiple students confirming the teachers' bullying behavior, referred to by the police as "abuse."

• • •

In April 2013, at Rutgers University, a situation similar to what we faced in 2012 made headlines across the United States when basketball coach Mike Rice was exposed as being abusive toward his players. An assistant coach, Eric Murdock, spliced together practice tapes to expose his bullying behavior to the world. The several-minute-long clip was subsequently aired on ESPN, and the sports world exploded in shock and outrage. When some Rutgers Administrators were discovered to have seen the tape and Rice had not been fired, there was an even louder outcry; however, as always, there were also staunch supporters backing those exposed as bullies or enablers of bullying conduct.

22

On the one hand, many Rutgers faculty were calling for Coach Rice to be fired, for Tim Pernetti, the Athletic Director to resign for his failure to protect the student-athletes, and for Rutgers' President, Robert L. Barchi, to also resign for Coach Rice's bullying to have occurred under his tenure. As recorded in a 2013 *Star-Ledger* article: "More than 30 faculty members [. . .] signed a letter calling for Barchi's resignation based on what they called a pattern of insensitivity and disregard for diversity issues and a lack of transparency in handling the Rice situation."[11] On the other hand, those invested in Rutgers' reputation and financial wellbeing staunchly supported Pernetti and Barchi and by default Coach Rice. As the *Star-Ledger* article goes on to describe, "There were those in Pernetti's corner. William Montanaro, Director of Athletic Development — the fund-raising arm of the athletics department, sent out e-mails to boosters asking them to send letters of support to Barchi and the heads of the university's two governing boards." An enormous group took to social media in order to defend and protect Tim Pernetti from being held responsible for Rice's abusive conduct, not holding him properly accountable, nor protecting Rutgers students from the abuse. "Separately, more than 1,100 people became members of a Facebook page called 'I SUPPORT TIM PERNETTI,' within hours after the Facebook page launched." Nonetheless, Tim Pernetti still resigned from his post as Athletic Director.

At my former school, as noted, Alumni were contacted to write in and show their support for teacher-coaches; furthermore, the School website was used in subtle ways that appeared to support those teacher-coaches whom parents and students had described as bullies: select

---

[11] Ted Sherman and Kelly Heyboer, "Rutgers coaching scandal goes into overtime, as focus settles on Pernetti," *The Star-Ledger*, April 2013: http://www.nj.com/news/index.ssf/2013/04/rutgers_coaching_scandal_goes.html

students and faculty were brought in to give two minute interviews that were then posted on the School website. This suggests a conscious and deliberate decision by School Administration to use tools at their disposal to show solidarity and clear support for the teacher-coaches involved. There was no discussion about this focus on students and teachers suddenly giving two-minute interviews about athletics while students with academic and arts achievements were ignored. Nor was there any outcry when student-athletes were put in a powerless position, being asked leading questions like "who is your favorite coach?"

What if the student needed a letter of reference from the coach for university applications? It's easy to praise and flatter bullies, especially if they hold powerful positions that can affect one's future, speaking up against them is very risky and most lack the necessary courage.

The fact is that most abuse victims do not speak up at the time abuse occurs. Most often, abuse victims only find the courage to report on their abuse when they are middle-aged and far removed from the traumatizing events. This pattern suggests there is something inherently wrong with the way society handles abuse allegations. We need to move from a system that favors abusers and silences victims. A new model must be developed whereby abusive acts are not tolerated, and victims are heard and supported. Twice now, I have been told – once by the School's Chaplain, and once by a member of the Board – that if the parents were to take the School to court for not protecting their children, it would be a terrible experience for the students because it would be a lengthy process, the expected cross-examinations would be incredibly stressful for the parents – let alone the teenagers who had been abused. The Chaplain and Lawyer/ Board Member we initially went to for support and who conjured this frightening courtroom scenario might argue it was stemming from concern for the students and families involved; however, the key point is there is a problem with our legal system in that few parents would subject their child to what would be a worse experience than the actual abuse itself. The courtroom is not a place where a victim can feel safe or supported in recounting their experience, but it should be if we want an equal playing field between adult abusers and child victims. The present system appears to protect and favor the former and re-victimizes the latter.

If bullying were treated more as a medical problem that required medical intervention, remedy, and community support, I believe it would not be so endemic in our society. If bullies were able to see themselves as inflicting on others that suffering they once endured, then perhaps there would not be so much denial, shame, or secrecy surrounding this bullying behavior. If bullies were able to seek support, then they would be less likely to deny or cover up their conduct. In the testimonies submitted to the Headmaster at my former school, many students comment on how the teachers wouldn't look at them, or couldn't meet their eyes. The students do not understand their teachers' odd behavior, but they recognize that it is uncomfortable and unusual. As one student remarks in his testimony, *"He would never meet eyes with me or talk to me."* Another says, *"[The teacher] wouldn't look at me. He's not big on eye-contact."* And still another says, *"She never looks me in the eye. Her hips are toward the court when she talks to you."*

It's uncanny reading the testimonies to find how many students comment on this.[12]

---

[12] One alumnus from the 1980s notes this inability to meet eyes: "[The teacher] and I never saw eye to eye. My first experience with him was when he simply 'cut' me from the basketball team, and only me. Guys like [Bill, John, and Eric] (all of whom I could out shoot, outrun and out-jump) were left on the team. When I asked [the teacher] 'why,' he didn't even look me in the eye, and mumbled something about [Andrew and Harold] being the forwards that he wanted to 'focus on.' I was left scratching my head, and never played b-ball again." This information came to me by

It is possible that the teachers reveal, based on the bullying behavior described in the student testimonies, in conjunction with their inability to meet the players eye to eye, that they themselves may be dealing with longstanding issues. Avoiding eye contact is one of the symptoms of PTSD.[13] Bullying is a perpetual cycle where the victim becomes the bully, who in turns bullies a new victim and that victim becomes the bully - and so on. As Barbara Coloroso explains:

> Kids who bully have an air of superiority that is sometimes a mask to cover up deep hurt and a feeling of inadequacy. They rationalize that their supposed superiority entitles them to hurt someone they hold in contempt, when in reality it is often an excuse to put someone down so they can feel "up."[14]

Until this cycle can be broken and the behavior and damage stopped, regardless whether one is the bully or the victim, it will continue to be rampant in our society.

The statistics on bullying from teachers to students, and coaches to athletes, are staggering. According to Dr. John Schinnerer:

> We know that 45% of teachers admit to having bullied a student in the past. On average, teachers have more training (1 to 2 years post graduate) in areas such as child development and educational and motivational theories than the average coach of youth athletics. So it appears safe to assume that teachers are less likely than the average coach to engage in bullying behavior. Assuming that's the case, it seems safe to assume that roughly 45 - 50% of coaches have bullied an athlete in their past.

---

happenstance; it would be interesting if Alumni were properly canvassed about their experiences playing sports for this teacher.
[13] http://www.hiddenhurt.co.uk/PTSD.html
[14] Barbara Coloroso, *The Bully, the Bullied, and the not-so-innocent Bystander*, updated edition, Harper Collins: 2015 (44).

According to the National Center for Chronic Disease Prevention and Health Promotion, there are approximately 2.5 million adults in the United States who volunteer their time to coach each year. Using our tentative number of 50% would mean that there are roughly 1.25 million adult coaches who have bullied a child athlete in the past. And this number does not even take into account coaches who are paid for their services and who may be more likely to bully due to the pressures and expectations placed upon them.[15]

Even in light of significant evidence documenting bullying as exceedingly harmful and damaging to bullies, bystanders and victims, it continues to flourish. Significant change must happen for it to stop.

At my former school, the parents who were asking that the Headmaster shield their children from the teachers involved did not see them only as harmful people; in fact, the parents as a rule saw these teachers as key contributors to the school community, despite their bullying approach to coaching. Thus, it was discussed among the parent group that the teachers needed to take appropriate steps to heal from their tendency or "addiction" to systemic bullying toward student-athletes. At the same time, it was crucial to parents that the teachers were not in contact with children during this time. The parents whose children had spoken up began conferring together; we asked the Headmaster for the teachers to be sent off campus, on salary, to have time to get the assistance they apparently needed before they returned to their coaching positions. The Lawyer/ parent was working closely with the Headmaster representing the concerned parents. She conveyed that parents were explicitly clear that no child should be put at further risk from these

---

[15] John Schinnerer, PhD, "'Help, My Coach is a Bully!': The Consequences of Verbally Abusive Coaching": http://www.selfgrowth.com/articles/Help_My_Coach_is_a_Bully_The_Consequences_of_Verbally_Abusive_Coaching.html

teachers until a psychologist assessed them and approved their return to educational duties.

Experts reveal bullying to be a destructive and compulsive behavior comparable to a drug or alcohol addiction. Psychologist and author Dr. John Burgo explains the bullying cycle:

> Bullies, like narcissists, don't emerge from happy childhoods, secure in their parents' love and imbued with a sense of their own worth. As they grow, they find ways to compensate: they shed fear, shame, and self-doubts, forcing them onto the losers they persecute.[16]

Bullying and narcissism are psychological conditions that require professional intervention; however, society continues to cover up or condone this behavior. The more we empower the cycle each successive generation of bullies will project the "fear, shame, and self-doubts" from their past onto new victims. It becomes an endless and destructive cycle. Teachers or coaches who bully should be given the time and opportunity to seek treatment and heal, but they also need to be kept away from students and athletes while the recovery process is underway.

I believe emotional, verbal, and psychological abuse must be included in the Criminal Code, especially since many studies document that emotional abuse experienced in childhood produces more anxiety and depression, presently rampant in our youth populations, than does physical and sexual abuse. In their work on emotional abuse in sports, University of Toronto experts, Gretchen Kerr and Ashley Stirling discovered the following:

---

[16] Joseph Burgo, "All Bullies Are Narcissists: Stories of bullying and hazing in the news break down to narcissism and insecurity," *The Atlantic*, November 2013: http://www.theatlantic.com/health/archive/2013/11/all-bullies-are-narcissists/281407/

Previous research on emotional abuse in the parent–child relationship has reported that emotional abuse can be harmful to a child's wellbeing due to the debilitating developmental effects and life-long implications (Jellen, McCarroll, & Thayer, 2001). The experience of emotional abuse from parents in childhood has been found to have serious implications for the child's mental health and psychosocial functioning (Jellen et al., 2001), and has been suggested to correlate more strongly with depression and anxiety compared with other childhood traumas including physical abuse, sexual abuse, and neglect (Kent & Waller, 1998).[17]

Despite multiple studies dating back to the 1990s, it is surprising that emotional abuse (referred to interchangeably with psychological abuse and verbal abuse) is still not in the Criminal Code.

In Britain, the *National Society for the Prevention of Cruelty to Children* states that, "[e]motional abuse is the second most common reason for a child to be put on the child protection register or made subject to a child protection plan."[18] Perhaps intervention occurs for children in the home; however, based on my experience at my former school, there are not nearly enough protections in place for students or student-athletes when faced with an emotionally abusive teacher or coach.

In BC, the Ministry of Children and Family Development does not have jurisdiction over abuse in public schools, and the Representative for Children and Youth does not appear to have jurisdiction over independent schools. There is no School District or Board of Education to

---

[17] Ashley E. Stirling and Gretchen A. Kerr, "The perceived effects of elite athletes' experiences of emotional abuse in the coach–athlete relationship." *The International Journal of Sport and Exercise Psychology* 11.1, 2013: 87-100.

[18] Statistic as of August 2013 from the National Society for the Prevention of Cruelty to Children: http://www.nspcc.org.uk/Inform/research/briefings/emotional_abuse_wda48215.html

turn to as there is when problems arise in the public school system. Independent schools are subject to oversight from the Office of the Inspector of Independent Schools. I contacted the Inspector's Office seeking support to protect students from, not only the teacher bullying they reported, but also the defamatory and hostile environment that subsequently emerged around them. I hoped the Inspector would help to resolve the ongoing situation. I spoke at length to the Inspector and Deputy on the phone and at their request sent a sampling of student testimonies in July 2012. The Deputy informed another involved parent that the conduct the students reported was "serious" and had to be reported to educational authorities. However, when I wrote the Inspector again in August 2012 about the escalating situation, he did not respond. I was surprised on a number of levels at the lack of response; however, most worrying was that my former school was an international boarding school and three teachers identified in the student testimonies as being abusive toward their players were also "house-parents." I would have expected the Inspector for Independent Schools to monitor students in residence very closely and have a process whereby they could be confidentially interviewed as to their situation. However, this does not appear to be something the Inspector of Independent Schools does.

In contrast, Hilary Moriarty of the British Boarding Schools' Association assures that safety for students is paramount and regularly assessed:

> Moriarty is adamant – as is St Benedict's – that the safeguarding of children at British public schools has been transformed in recent years. Moriarty points to the fact that boarding schools are subject to three yearly inspections by the Independent Schools Inspectorate, in which children are asked directly about their experience of being educated in that setting.

> "One of the ways the world is different now is that we live in a climate where allegations are more likely to be made by a child,

and properly received, and properly investigated," she says. "No -one can ever say that this is watertight, but we have robust systems. The security of schools now comes from the fact that you can't be complacent. They are alert, and that very alertness is your defense."[19]

In the fall of 2012, at my former school, faculty were informed that the school was going to be assessed by the Inspector of Independent Schools as part of a routine check. In September 2012, the school replaced the Director of the Senior School as the previous Director went on to pursue other work. Along with other parents, I did my best to inform the new Director about the seriousness of the teacher bullying as recorded in student testimonies and assessed as such by the police and the Inspector of Independent Schools. However, the Director would not listen, saying the issue had been dealt with. He informed the faculty in September 2012 that the Inspector of Independent Schools was investigating and I believed it was due to the students' testimonies. However, the Director announced to faculty in October that the school had passed the inspection with flying colors. There was no talk of students being asked directly about their experiences, as is standard practice in Britain, or about how their allegations might be received properly or investigated independently. There was no mandate from the Inspector's Office about suspending teachers to allow students to speak up in a safe environment.

While teacher /student bullying has received little expert study or public attention, university coaches verbally abusing student-athletes has been a much more newsworthy topic and subject of research. The student-athletes at my former school who came forward in 2012 with written

---

[19] Louise Tickle, "Britain's Elite Boarding Schools Are Facing an Explosion of Abuse Allegations," *Newsweek*, September 2014: http://www.newsweek.com/britain-elite-boarding-schools-facing-explosion-abuse-allegations-267201

allegations of verbal, emotional and some physical abuse by their teacher-coaches, did so a full year before the video of Rutgers' University basketball coach Mike Rice made international news. When the video went viral and the full story broke, it appears to have impacted the way in which abusive coaching is now understood and handled. The Rutgers story reveals that there is an emerging zero tolerance for coaches who bully their student-athletes.

In April 2013, Rutgers Assistant Coach, Eric Murdock, released a short video on ESPN showing Scarlet Knights' basketball coach, Mike Rice, screaming at players, apparently enraged at them, using homophobic slurs, putting them down, shoving them and hurling basketballs at them during practices. Multiple articles during the following weeks recorded that "Shock and revulsion to Rice's actions have reverberated through all levels of sports"[20] as the scenes hit TV and computer screens around the world. Eric Murdock spliced together hours of practice tapes to highlight Rice's abusive conduct. Outrage ranged from the Governor of New Jersey who described the coach as an "animal" to professional athletes, sportscasters and reporters who deplored his conduct in the strongest terms.[21] The vast majority acknowledged that Mike Rice's behavior was brutally harmful to his student-athletes.[22] When it became known that Rutgers University Administration was previously aware of his bullying practices and allowed Rice to continue coaching, the public was simultaneously disgusted and furious. Rice was

---

[20] Joe Drape and Nate Taylor, "Question Arises as Scandal Unfolds: Where's the Line?" April 2013: http://natetaylorsports.wordpress.com/2014/07/10/question-arises-as-scandal-unfolds-wheres-the-line/

[21] http://www.theguardian.com/world/2013/apr/09/chris-christie-rutgers-mike-rice-animal

[22] http://www.nytimes.com/2013/04/04/opinion/upon-further-review-at-rutgers.html?_r=0

instantly fired and those who knew what he had done were pressured to resign. As one *New York Times* writer records, "At least 10 faculty members, including the Dean of the Graduate School at Rutgers in Newark, signed a letter calling for Dr. Robert L. Barchi [Rutger's President], to resign his position for his 'inexcusable handling of Coach Mike Rice's homophobic and misogynist abuse of our students.'" At Rutgers, the list of faculty members who wanted those Administrators who were the "enablers of a vile bully to be held accountable"[23] quickly grew to twenty-eight. Assistant Coach, Jimmy Martelli, who modeled his coaching style after Rice, resigned shortly after when he too was exposed for treating players in a similar manner. Media outlets reported how Scarlet Knights' player Tyree Graham described Assistant Coach Martelli: "He used to belittle players by the way he talked,' Graham said, adding that Martelli called players 'b-----s' and 'p-----s.'"[24]

A year earlier, at my former school, student-athletes had reported being called homophobic and misogynistic terms by their teacher-coaches; phrases such as you're *"soft as butter," "grow some balls," "that's fucking soft,"* and *"fucking pussy."* At the basketball try-outs in September 2011, an assistant house parent, who was also involved with the rugby team, pointed out a player and asked our son who he was. Our son told him the boy's name and the man replied, "He looks like a faggot." Our son did not even tell us this story until the boys started speaking up about what had happened to them. With the exception of

---

[23] Ian O'Connor, "Professors are right in Rice scandal: Unafraid of powerful sports machine, group wants Rutgers president to go," *ESPN*, April 2013: http://espn.go.com/new-york/story/_/id/9136488/mike-rice-scandal-rutgers-professors-right-ask-ouster-president

[24] Angela Delli Santi and Katie Zezima, "Rutgers Reviewing All Practice Tapes," *Associated Press*, April 2013 http://bigstory.ap.org/article/rutgers-president-hold-town-hall-newark

throwing basketballs directly at student-players and kicking them, the testimonies from the student-athletes at my former school recorded behavior nearly identical to that displayed by Mike Rice. The student testimonies also brought to light a longstanding culture of homophobia, screaming, swearing, shunning, personal attacks, and favoritism.

According to ESPN, "Gov. Chris Christie, a Republican, said he supported Mr. Rice's dismissal, adding, '[t]he way these young men were treated by the head coach was completely unacceptable and violates the trust those parents put in Rutgers University.'" When students are abused in educational institutions, not only is the students' trust violated but so is the parents' trust. Rutgers' President Barchi announced, "I have now reached the conclusion that Coach Rice cannot continue to serve effectively in a position that demands the highest levels of leadership, responsibility and public accountability."[25] If a university basketball coach is considered to hold such a position, what role do high school coaches have in relation to their students? These players are fifteen to eighteen year olds; some living away from home for the first time. According to neurologists, their brains are still developing and they are therefore very vulnerable to stress and verbal abuse. Yet the teachers at my former school have not to this point been held responsible for their conduct, let alone publicly disciplined.

In a 2012 report, paid for by the School, the lawyer who wrote it explains away one basketball coach's behavior by quoting him as saying, "I guess sometimes I get carried away because I care too much for the kids." After the Mike Rice scandal at Rutgers University, it's hard to hear this phrase without wincing. It's like hearing Jerry Sandusky, the

---

[25] Charles M. Blow, "Calm Down, Coaches," *New York Times*, April 2013, http://www.nytimes.com/2013/04/04/opinion/blow-is-coach-rices-behavior-typical.html?_r=1&

imprisoned Penn State University legendary football coach, and long-time sexual abuser, declare his "love" for his victims.[26] Sports Columnist, Cathal Kelly wrote that Mike Rice "is plainly deranged. Were he to work in any other environment, he'd be in jail. But this is college sport, where frothing sadism can be mistaken for caring too much."[27] The teacher at my former school, quoted by the lawyer to convey his "passion and care" for his student-athletes, used to bite down on a towel as he paced the sidelines during basketball games, such was the frothing passion he could barely seem to contain. At this school, his conduct was somehow deemed acceptable. He was never suspended and parents were never informed about the bullying reported by student-athletes in 2012.

In June 2012, a month after students came forward with their testimonies, the Headmaster asked students and their parents to attend a meeting where he promised to issue a formal apology for what had gone on in the athletics department and hold those coaches accountable. The day before the meeting, the famous NBA player who, twenty years before, had been coached for a year by the Assistant Coach, showed up unannounced at the school. He made himself visible shooting hoops with the Assistant Coach during lunch. Parents whose children had given testimonies were very upset at what appeared to be an intimidating show of power. Reports went into the Headmaster at this inappropriate display. The next lunch hour, on the day of the long-awaited meeting, the NBA

---

[26] Susan Snyder and Jeff Gammage, "Alleged victim testifies Sandusky threatened him, then professed love," *The Inquirer*, June 2012: http://articles.philly.com/2012-06-14/news/32216170_1_second-mile-charity-jerry-sandusky-young-boy Or: http://www.dailymail.co.uk/news/article-2155148/Jerry-Sandusky-Former-Penn-State-coach-wrote-victims-creepy-love-letters.html

[27] Cathall Kelly, "Rutgers scandal reveals perverse nature of U.S. college sports," *The Star*, April 2013: http://www.thestar.com/sports/basketball/2013/04/08/rutgers_scandal_reveals_perverse_nature_of_us_college_sports.html

player showed up again for another visible lunch session of one on one time with the Assistant Coach. It may well have communicated the following to awestruck teenagers: support the Assistant Coach and you get access to the NBA player; report on his conduct, and you will lose this incredible opportunity. It was never made clear to parents and students whether the Headmaster supported the coach's flaunting of his connections or was unable to control his conduct.

At the meeting in the later afternoon, convened by the Headmaster, the Assistant Coach's wife openly wept and told the students that her husband "loved all the boys." To my mind, this was possibly the unhealthiest moment of this entire nightmare for our son. Other parents felt the same. There are few things worse for a bullied child to hear than what they endured was the result of the adult perpetrator's "love." This belief system can take years of therapy to undo. For students who had come forward with testimonies of emotionally abusive conduct, the wife's statement suggested that "love" is the emotion behind the abuses students had reported: screaming in apparent contempt or disgust, berating, using homophobic slurs, belittling, swearing, shunning, and humiliating.

The Assistant Coach's son was on the basketball team and also at the meeting in tears. Multiple students comment in their testimonies about how much they thought the son suffered and how much he cried during the 2012 season. Unable to score, he was nonetheless kept out on the court in what the students saw as public humiliation. While this may have brought tears of shame to any adult athlete, it would be hard to imagine it not having a devastating impact on a seventeen year old. In his grade twelve year, at the 2012 Provincials, his father in his capacity as Assistant Coach kept him on the court so long, even though he couldn't sink a basket that he was openly crying. It got to the point that players on the opposing team were clamoring for the referee to get him off the court. This is not "love" as I understand the term and it's definitely not the kind

36

of "love" I want directed at my son from a teacher acting under the auspices of a high school basketball coach. It seems that bullying can still be mistaken in sports as "love" for the players, passion for the game, and motivation to win.

In the Mike Rice scandal, the Rutgers University faculty identified this double standard that still seems to operate with coaches when it comes to how they treat student-athletes. The faculty at Rutgers were reported to be furious with the double standard that Administrators used for Rice because he was a coach and they argued that, "if *they* had ever laid hands on a student and yelled homophobic slurs at them, they would have been instantly terminated and rightly so."[28]

The coaches at my former school were also teachers and therefore, the Supreme Court of Canada holds them to a much higher code of conduct. As an English teacher, if I called a group of students "retards" and if I grabbed a student's arm, held him close, pointed my finger in his chest and said "*that's fucking soft,*" I doubt the Headmaster would need to hire a lawyer to determine if I had breached the conduct standards that govern me as a teacher. Even if one student reported bullying conduct done by a teacher, and another student witnessed it, it is highly probably that it would constitute grounds for a principal to suspend and/or discipline that teacher. However, the teachers identified by multiple student-athletes at my former school were not required to adhere to clearly articulated standards of conduct. According to student testimonies, not only did their behavior seemingly violate the code of conduct set out for teachers by the Teacher Regulation Branch, it appeared also to violate codes of conduct set out for coaches by BC School Sports: it paralleled the very behavior that led to Mike Rice and

---

[28] http://www.cbsnews.com/news/some-faculty-demand-rutgers-president-quit-over-handling-of-mike-rice-video/

Jimmy Martelli being summarily fired from their coaching positions at Rutgers.

Throughout, I will draw on the work of Dr. Alan Goldberg who is one of the leading international experts on coaching abuse. After earning his doctorate in Counseling Psychology, a retired Division I athlete himself, he coached for twenty years and has produced over thirty-five mental toughness programs and books. He has counseled university teams and individual athletes from the Olympic level all the way down to high school. Dr. Goldberg was the sport psychology consultant to the 1999 NCAA Men's Basketball National Champion University of Connecticut Huskies, and the 2000 men's soccer NCAA champions. Dr. Goldberg specializes in helping athletes overcome fears and blocks, snap out of slumps, and perform to their potential. We credit his counseling with our son's psychological survival through the bullying he spoke up about and the re-victimization he and the other students suffered from the Headmaster, Chaplain, Board, lawyers, and educational authorities.

Over the course of three years dealing with the crisis at my former school, people wondered why more student-athletes did not speak up beyond fourteen. One lawyer the school hired even tried to discredit the students by suggesting that their minority status indicated that the problem lay with them. Dr. Goldberg exposes the techniques abusive coaches use to keep athletes silent. He examined the conduct of a university tennis coach at a Division I College in the States after a student-athlete spoke up about his bullying: "[The coach] punished [the student-athlete] further by pushing her down in the lineup to the #3 singles spot. He continued to verbally demean her and question her commitment to the team and sport. At other times he would try to turn

[her] teammates against her."[29] Very similar conduct was recorded in the fourteen student testimonies from my former school; one student on the Senior Girls basketball team recounts in her testimony (names changed for confidentiality):

> *The first time I knew something was wrong was when Louisa quit mid-season. I remember [the coach] bashing her behind her back. She was 6.2 and a great athlete. And she would bash Louisa in front of the team while we were practicing. She'd say "Louisa is a quitter. She's the reason we won't do well." If [the coach] saw Louisa in the hall, she would throw dirty looks. [The coach] acted like she was disgusted by her. She egged the team on to not like Louisa. If she passed her at school, she wouldn't say hi; she would act like Louisa didn't exist.*

Dr. Goldberg provides clear insight into why it is so difficult for abuse victims to come forward. For students on the boys' basketball team, added to the fundamental difficulty of speaking up as a student-athlete, when the coach continues to have power over you and you can be penalized, was the Assistant Coach's connection to the NBA player, as well as his son being on the team. Under these circumstances it was incredibly challenging for students to come forward.

Considering the barriers to student-athletes reporting abuse, it is critical that all school administrators and authorities educate themselves about emotional abuse, and specifically coaching abuse. University of Toronto experts in sport abuse, Ashley Stirling and Gretchen Kerr articulate the intense power imbalance that occurs in sports: "the coach-athlete relationship has been shown to be an unbalanced one, with the coach having power over the athlete by virtue of his or her age, expertise,

---

[29] Dr. Alan Goldberg, "Coaching ABUSE: The dirty, not-so-little secret in sports." http://gazette.teachers.net/gazette/wordpress/dr-alan-goldberg/coaching-abuse-the-dirty-not-so-little-secret-in-sports-by-dr-alan-goldberg/

experience, and access to resources and rewards (Thomlinson & Strachan, 1996)."[30] Ten years earlier another research initiative argued that the coach-athlete relationship could be likened to a "master-slave relationship."[31] In the Mike Rice video footage, Rice's conduct toward his mostly African-American athletes sadly appears to validate the Stirling and Kerr findings.

Rather than turning to experts in the psychology of coaching abuse for a professional assessment of the behaviors articulated in the student testimonies, the Headmaster at my former school instead appealed to students who had had "happy experiences." And not surprisingly, he found some on the Senior Boys team who spoke up to defend the coaches; however, this is no way to actually establish whether or not teachers were bullying their players. The following definition by author and psychotherapist Beverley Engle illustrates that victims of emotional abuse, whether directly targeted or simply bystanders, have in effect been "brainwashed" by the abusers in ways that render them incapable of properly assessing the events that transpired:

> Emotional abuse is like brain washing in that it systematically wears away at the victim's self-confidence, sense of self-worth, trust in their own perceptions, and self-concept. Whether it is done by constant berating and belittling, by intimidation, or under the guise of 'guidance,' 'teaching,' or 'advice,' the results are similar. Eventually, the recipient of the abuse loses all sense of self and remnants of personal value. Emotional abuse cuts to the

---

[30] Ashley E. Stirling and Gretchen A. Kerr, "Defining and categorizing emotional abuse in sport," *European Journal of Sport Science*, July 2008: 8 (4): 173-181.
[31] Ashley E. Stirling and Gretchen A. Kerr, "Defining and categorizing emotional abuse in sport," *European Journal of Sport Science*, July 2008: 8 (4): 173-181.

very core of a person, creating scars that may be far deeper and more lasting than physical ones.[32]

Teenagers exposed to the berating and belittling, reported on by students at my former school, cannot be trusted to advocate for themselves and identify that those in power over them have been abusive. By the very fact that they've been bullied, they struggle to "trust their own perceptions." The student-athletes at my former school had been exposed for at least two years, some for three, probably long enough for some to have normalized the conduct so that they believed they or others on the team deserved to be humiliated, berated, and screamed at by their coaches and that it would help them be better athletes. It was meant to guide and teach. Others may have been too afraid to incur any more bullying from coaches who controlled the sport they loved and were apparently supported by the Headmaster.

Research has shown that athletes fall into two camps when they're being abused: they either fear the coach or normalize the conduct.[33] At my former school, the Headmaster did not create a safe environment for those who were afraid; instead, the Headmaster appealed to students who may have normalized the coaches' conduct. The Headmaster's approach was very worrisome in the light of research that demonstrates emotional abuse damages the victim's sense of self, and along with serious psychological damage, is also linked to chronic disease in adulthood. According to the *World Health Organization's* Preventing Child Maltreatment – a guide to taking action and generating evidence published in 2006, "one of the most important scientific developments of

---

[32] See Beverley Engle, *The Emotionally Abused Woman: Overcoming Destructive Patterns and Reclaiming Yourself*, New York: Fawcett Columbine, 1992.

[33] Ashley E. Stirling and Gretchen A. Kerr, "Abused Athletes' Perceptions of the Coach-Athlete Relationship," *Sport in Society* Vol.12.2, March 2009: 227-239.

the past decade has been proof of the links between child maltreatment, health-risk behaviors and certain chronic diseases." In the *Adverse Childhood Experiences Study*, the questionnaire used by researchers asks students this: "Did a parent or other adult in the household often or very often swear at, insult or put you down?" Notably, in the *Adverse Childhood Experiences Study*, the questionnaire is directed at parents without mention of teachers or coaches; however, teacher and coaches arguably have as much, if not more, impact on an adolescent's life.[34]

It's time to hold teaching bullies accountable for the damage they inflict on students when we are more aware than ever that verbal and emotional abuse may well lead to such devastating impacts in adulthood, not only psychological, but also physical. According to their testimonies, students at my former school were regularly sworn at, insulted and put down by their teacher-coaches. However, the students could not possibly know just how detrimental such treatment was. We can no longer allow those whose perceptions, and self-concepts have been skewed by bullying behavior defend abusive teachers or coaches and thereby silence or otherwise bring into question the voices of those who come forward to stop abuse.

In their March 2009 research paper "Abused Athletes' Perceptions of the Coach-Athlete Relationship," published in *Sport in Society*, Ashley Stirling and Gretchen Kerr found that athletes characterized their coach as "godlike": "The athletes described having

---

[34] See Felitti VJ et al. Relationship of childhood abuse and household dysfunction to many of the leading causes of death in adults: the Adverse Childhood Experiences (ACE) study. *American Journal of Preventive Medicine*, 1998, 14:245–258. Alexander Butchart and Tony Kahane, *Preventing Child Maltreatment: A Guide to Taking Action and Generating Evidence*, World Health Organization and the International Society for the Prevention of Child Abuse and Neglect, 2006.
http://whqlibdoc.who.int/publications/2006/9241594365_eng.pdf?ua=1

feelings of admiration, respect and fear for their coach, and felt their coach was omniscient." According to one athlete who reflected on her feelings toward her coach, "I idolized her." Stirling and Kerr comment on the way in which the "athletes admired their coaches' knowledge and opinions, thus reinforcing the authority of the coach in this relationship."[35] A twenty-three-year-old male hockey player describes the same dynamic of worshipping an abusive coach: "It becomes kind of like a cult because this person is both the source of demeaning [comments] as well as praise."[36] This is exactly why when some athletes praise a coach this should not discredit those who report on his or her abuse. This is exactly why when cult members come forward to report on a cult leader's abuses, the authorities do not discount what they are saying because the rest of the cult still worships their leader.

While perhaps not achieving "godlike" status, Mike Rice had defenders on the Rutgers team. He was talented enough and charismatic enough to be earning millions in a highly public position. The Associated Press Sports Editor, Tom Canavan comments on Rice's dual personality: first he presents him as the abuser, "Rice could be heard yelling obscenities at players and using gay slurs." Then he reveals him as perfectly emulating the "charismatic bully" profile, characterized by the chameleon-like ability to fit seamlessly into new circumstances: "He quickly became part of the fabric of that community, often attending church functions and youth games that his children played in." Canavan reminds his readers not to fall for this version of Mike Rice because "on the practice floor, some 30 miles away, obviously, a different person

---

[35] Ashley E. Stirling and Gretchen A. Kerr, "Abused Athletes' Perceptions of the Coach-Athlete Relationship," *Sport in Society* Vol.12.2, March 2009: 227-239.
[36] Ashley E. Stirling and Gretchen A. Kerr, "Initiating and Sustaining Emotional Abuse in the Coach-Athlete Relationship: An Ecological Transactional Model of Vulnerability," *Journal of Aggression, Maltreatment & Trauma*, vol. 23, 2014: 116-135.

surfaced."[37] Rice's conduct, both his abusive side on the court and his charming side within the community, seems to parallel that of the bullying teacher-coaches as students reported in their testimonies at my former school:

> *. . .they make it confusing and stressful because they are different in the classroom than they are with the players. This makes it stressful all day for all the players because you don't know if they are going to be nice or nasty when you run into them off the court. It would be better if they were nasty all the time really.*

> *If you know you are going to run into someone who is nasty then when you see them you prepare yourself inside in a different way than if you can count on them to be nice. It's like they've got a personality split and that makes all of school more stressful than it should be.*

Charismatic bullies master the personality split that allows them to get away with their conduct year after year. It's part of the brainwashing pattern described by Engle and largely the reason why there is so much shock when people in powerful positions like Mike Rice and Jerry Sandusky are found to be abusive behind closed doors. As one elite athlete describes this dynamic with her coach, "He would swear at me and yell 'You disgust me. You're worthless' . . . At night he would never say anything though because the parents were there. He would do it when there was nobody around to prove otherwise."[38] This is comparable to the bully who mutters obscenities and insults so that only the targeted student-athletes hear, and not referees or parents.

---

[37] http://thegrio.com/2013/04/03/rutgers-fires-basketball-coach-mike-rice-after-player-abuse-exposed/

[38] Ashley E. Stirling and Gretchen A. Kerr, "Abused Athletes' Perceptions of the Coach-Athlete Relationship," *Sport in Society* Vol.12.2, March 2009: 227-239.

In a 2014 article in *Newsweek* about teacher abuse in British private schools, an abuse victim reflected back on the devastating effect of one isolated, humiliating incident thirty years earlier:

> He remains conflicted about the close relationship he subsequently developed with the teacher, who, he says, took pains to nurture his enthusiasms and helped shape his deep appreciation of the arts. The confusion for a teenager was agonising, he says, and, as a man, the shame remains.[39]

If a single incident involving a teacher with a dual personality could have a lifelong impact on a student, imagine the damage caused by multiple abusive incidents.

In a 2012 *New Yorker* article written about Penn State's football coach, Jerry Sandusky, Malcolm Gladwell examines the dual personality type and the way school administrators regularly protect abusers. He discusses the case of the Canadian teacher, "Mr. Clay," who ultimately was not charged with sexual abuse because the principal, Superintendent, and union supervisor were keen to protect his reputation:

> The parents were at a loss. Mr. Clay was beloved. He had started a popular gym club at the school. He was married and was a role model to the boys. He would come to their after-school games. Could he really have abused them? The answer to this question is 'no': the teacher is innocent; the children are exaggerating.[40]

Notably, just like at my former school, the concern shifted to the teachers and the need to protect them, rather than the victims. Even the parents,

---

[39] Louise Tickle, "Britain's Elite Boarding Schools Are Facing an Explosion of Abuse Allegations," *Newsweek*, September 2014: http://www.newsweek.com/britain-elite-boarding-schools-facing-explosion-abuse-allegations-267201
[40] Malcolm Gladwell, "In Plain View: How Child Molesters Get Away With It," *The New Yorker*, September 2012: http://www.newyorker.com/magazine/2012/09/24/in-plain-view

whose children came forward to report on the bullying, felt a strong desire to ensure the teachers did not get into "trouble." In his article, Gladwell quotes one of the parents in the "Mr. Clay" case who explains, "We were all still trying to protect Mr. Clay's reputation, and the possibility this was all blown up out of proportion and there was a mistake."[41] It's the classic *reversal* whereby the abuser becomes the victim and everyone worries about how they might fare. The reality is however, if a teacher's reputation suffers, it's *not* because children reported they were being abused, it was because of the teacher's actions. Somehow the abuser's "reputation" becomes the responsibility of the children or parents or teachers who act as whistleblowers on abuse. However, a reputation is built on one's actions, and if teachers bully students, then they can expect to suffer a blow to their reputations. The child, parent or teacher who reports what they have seen and heard to administrators or law enforcement must not be held responsible for the teacher's reputation or whatever consequences that follow.

In Maya Roy's 2014 article in the *Huffington Post*, "Three Items on Any Abuser's To-Do List," she discusses the pattern that she sees repeated when dealing with men who bully women: "Label Yourself as the Victim," "Make Sure you Undermine the Credibility of the Women," and finally, "Use Your Brand to Create a Better Story."[42] At my former school, the teachers were portrayed as victims of whiny kids and complaining parents. Based on her experience, Roy refers to this *reversal*, whereby the abuser labels himself as a victim, saying, "Politically

---

[41] Malcolm Gladwell, "In Plain View: How Child Molesters Get Away With It," *The New Yorker*, September 2012: http://www.newyorker.com/magazine/2012/09/24/in-plain-view
[42] Maya Roy, "Three Items on Any Abuser's To-Do List," *The Huffington Post*, November 2014: http://www.huffingtonpost.ca/maya-roy/abusive-men_b_6077840.html

inoculate yourself against accusations [. . . ] by pointing out first how you are in fact being persecuted."[43] To treat teachers as if they are being "persecuted" by students is a long stretch that in order to be believable surely requires evidence of motivation or conspiracy. Speaking up is hard to do for students because there is much to lose and little to gain, except protection. When hearing reports of abusive conduct over the course of a year from multiple sources, school administrators *must* consider the possibility that the coach or teacher might actually be abusive and take appropriate steps to protect students. Throughout the crisis at my former school, the Headmaster has communicated with faculty and parents as if the teachers have been very professional while weathering persecution from students and their parents.

• • •

At my former school, the students that came forward had their credibility and their reputations undermined: they were not only positioned as the ones harming the teachers, they were also portrayed as liars in a report written by a lawyer and paid for by the school. My credibility was undermined as well in this same report. As a teacher acting as whistleblower, I was treated like a parent causing trouble. This was undeserved as my son had attended the school since grade four and I had never approached the Headmaster to complain about his school experience before. I had worked at the school for eight years and in that time had registered complaints against one other teacher whose conduct was abusive as described by multiple students and faculty at the school. My son had no involvement with this teacher and this teacher was "retired" prematurely. This teacher was not a coach so the argument that me and other parents were invested in our children's sport success and

---

[43] Ibid.

47

that's what motivated us to report the coaches' bullying conduct was also unfair. Of course I wanted to protect my son; as a mother, I lacked a history of complaints; as a teacher, I had a track record of speaking up when I heard from students that they were being harmed.

The students who provided written testimonies and attended in-person meetings with the Headmaster and School Chaplain did not have any track record of lying. In many cases these children had literally grown up at the School, many having attended since kindergarten or grade one. The lawyer's report that positioned the students as liars did not offer any explanation as to why they would suddenly start telling falsehoods about their teachers in their final years at the school.

It could be argued that the School "Brand" was foremost in some minds when decisions about addressing the concerns expressed by students and parents surfaced. The Assistant Coach's connection to an NBA athlete, combined with an appeal to Alumni, were used to undermine the students' request for protection. Maya Roy describes the abuser's technique as a way to "Solidify [his] base of power and go directly to [his] allies."[44] Abusers' techniques might be obvious to an expert like Maya Roy; however, in general, most people do not know how to recognize an abuser's tactics and can be fooled into excusing away the behavior.

In a 2013 article in the *New York Times*, American basketball sports caster and radio host, Dan Dakich records his surprise at Mike Rice's dual personality in clarifying terms: "he knew and liked Rice, who had been a call-in guest on Dakich's Indianapolis radio show. When he saw the video, however, he was stunned, he said. 'I was sickened,' he

---

[44] Maya Roy, "Three Items on Any Abuser's To-Do List," *The Huffington Post*, November 2014: http://www.huffingtonpost.ca/maya-roy/abusive-men_b_6077840.html

added. 'I wanted to hit him.'"[45] At my former school, Alumni had written emails of support and praise for the coaches involved without perhaps knowing the full extent of the abusive practices recorded in the students' testimonies and backed up during the in-person interviews with School Administrators. These emails and letters of support have been used to argue these teachers should not be held accountable because parents did not inform coaches that their abusive coaching style was causing their children harm. Given no corrective or disciplinary action was taken to address the verbal abuse hurled at players, it could be concluded that educational authorities currently favor the abuser rather than the abused.

Was it the responsibility of Mike Rice's victims, or their parents, to tell him that enraged yelling, using homophobic slurs, shoving and grabbing players, humiliating and swearing was harmful to their children? Surely there are standards of conduct or laws in place to protect student-athletes so that when a teacher or a coach breaches these standards, they are held accountable. However, the teachers' bullying conduct, as reported in student testimonies, at my former school was not publicly disciplined. There was seemingly little attempt to have their behavior measured against a code of conduct, legislation, regulations, nor was much weight given to multiple players from different teams reporting similar negative coaching experiences. Instead, responsibility miraculously shifted from those who were accused to those who reported they were being bullied. In these scenarios, it appears that an enormous amount of accountability is laid at the feet of students, while little accountability is expected of the teacher or coach. This needs to change.

---

[45] Joe Drape and Nate Taylor, "Question Arises as Scandal Unfolds: Where's the Line?" April 2013: http://natetaylorsports.wordpress.com/2014/07/10/question-arises-as-scandal-unfolds-wheres-the-line/

Ed Runyan in his 2014 article published in the *Youngstown News* about an abusive coach turns to Judy Jones, Associate Director of the Midwest Region for SNAP, the Survivors Network of those Abused by Priests, to explain the way in which abusers get away with the harm they do to children. She specifically addresses sexual predators; however, emotional predators or bullies often fit the same profile and use comparable techniques to keep their abusive acts hidden:

> [Abusers] also appear to do a lot of good things, they can be very charismatic and you may think they would never harm a child. They have to be this way, in order to not get caught and to continue to abuse. They devote lots of time and energy building trust with their victims by giving them money and gifts. They tend to make the child feel that they are special and loved.
>
> Sexual predators are often powerful and well loved, we must overcome the dangerous myth that because someone is successful or warm or caring, he or she couldn't have done that! It would be comforting if those who preyed on the vulnerable were obvious social misfits whose appearance would somehow set off alarm bells and give us the willies or the creeps. They rarely do.
>
> Usually, predators are among the last people we would suspect of sexually violating others. At a party, the predator isn't some oddball sitting alone in a corner because others feel uncomfortable with him. Most often, the predator is the guy throwing the party.[46]

The teachers at my former school took the students on wonderful trips, spent one-on-one time coaching players during lunch hours, gave them fun t-shirts with nicknames printed on the back. We didn't know that

---

[46] Ed Runyan, "100 Interviewed in Sexual Abuse Probe of Ex-Coach," *Youngstown News, vindy.com*, September 2014: http://www.vindy.com/news/2014/sep/14/sexual-abuse-probe-of-ex-coach-widenssfl/

overtures such as these were entwined with the humiliating and homophobic terms that multiple players spoke up about in their testimonies. The Administration, Board of Governors and the lawyers they hired were right on one level: students struggled to sort out their perceptions of these teachers. On the one hand these coaches seemed so wonderful or "god-like" like the coaches described by athletes interviewed by Stirling and Kerr and, on the other hand, their behavior was also incredibly destructive according to student testimonies. Still, the student-athletes finally spoke up about the harm they endured, only to be treated as if they were the ones somehow out of line.

Parents and students, caught in a bullying cycle with a teacher or coach, are the least likely to communicate their concerns. They may respond to the charisma of the coach, normalize abusive conduct they witness or hear about, and as a result, not be able to process or comprehend the dual persona, as seen with Jerry Sandusky, Mike Rice and other recently fired university coaches. Dr. Alan Goldberg discusses a student-athlete who was bullied by her coach, but didn't report on it: "Perhaps [the athlete's] reluctance to tell anyone was partially related to the 'brain washing' that [the coach] regularly engaged in with [the athlete] and her teammates."[47] After being through the experience myself, I think the "brainwashing" both Engle and Goldberg speak about is an apt way to describe what happens to parents as well. It's a fine line parents must walk, like student-athletes, because high-school students *depend* on their teachers for playing time, positions, letters of reference, awards, and positive report card comments scrutinized by university admissions. If a parent files a complaint or fails to write supportive emails, their child may

---

[47] Dr. Alan Goldberg, "Coaching ABUSE: The dirty, not-so-little secret in sports." http://gazette.teachers.net/gazette/wordpress/dr-alan-goldberg/coaching-abuse-the-dirty-not-so-little-secret-in-sports-by-dr-alan-goldberg/

be even more limited, targeted, and ostracized. As author Harlan Coben explains in his article about coaching abuse in the *BloombergView* in 2013:

> We've all seen these guys on the sidelines. We parents may not condone it, but we've learned to accept it. We put up with this behavior because we worry that if we question it, there will be repercussions for our kid. He'll get less playing time, we fear. She will be moved down from the A to the B team. He will be the brunt of even more abuse. We see our choices as putting up with it or denying our kid the sports experience. We start to justify it in our minds.[48]

At my former school, this may be why parents and students wrote supportive emails to the coaches; this could be why the students begged their parents not to speak up on their behalf. Charismatic bullies are by their nature very popular, and anyone who questions their conduct or expresses concerns is made to feel like they are the only one with a problem because other parents and students appear to accept the behavior as normal.

It is not just adults in positions of power that fit into the charismatic bully category; studies show that such a bully is highly popular even in childhood. As Dr. John Schinnerer, discusses in an article about coaching abuse:

> Many bullies are relatively popular and have 'henchmen' who help with their bullying behaviors. And so it was with the swim team where the coach's bullying is supported and endorsed by the woman in charge of the team. Bullying does not take place in a

---

[48] Harlan Coben, "That's Not Coaching. It's Child Abuse," *BloombergView*, May 2013: http://www.bloombergview.com/articles/2013-05-30/that-s-not-coaching-it-s-child-abuse-

vacuum. There has to be an environment around bullying behavior which allows it and enables it to survive.[49]

When the Headmaster at my former school was alerted, by the eleven-page document filed by the Lawyer/ parent, to "child abuse" occurring on the School basketball teams in 2011, a year before we came forward, he was surprised there was a problem, because as he put it one teacher in particular, the Head Coach, was so "popular." Dr. Schinnerer explains why this is a concerning response from a person who by their very position is responsible for the safety of the children in their care:

> Psychological research has debunked several myths associated with bullying, including one that states bullies are usually the most unpopular students in school. A 2000 study by psychologist Philip Rodkin, PhD, and colleagues involving fourth-through-sixth-grade boys found that highly aggressive boys may be among the most popular and socially connected children in elementary classrooms, as seen by their peers and teachers.[50]

Teachers and administrators need to educate themselves as to the characteristics of the charismatic bully to be in a position to recognize the signs and thereby protect students be that on the court or in the classroom. Educators need the training to be able to cut through the emotional confusion generated by the split personality in adult-bullies in the same manner they have been trained to recognize it in a child-bully. In an article entitled, "What Happens When Bullies Become Adults?" staff writer, Devyne Lloyd discusses research conducted by journalism students at Michigan State University that they ultimately published in a

---

[49] John Schinnerer, Ph.D, '"Help, My Coach is a Bully!': The Consequences of Verbally Abusive Coaching": http://www.selfgrowth.com/articles/Help_My_Coach_is_a_Bully_The_Consequences_of_Verbally_Abusive_Coaching.html
[50] Ibid.

book. The journalism students found that "most bullies are intelligent, popular and highly charismatic."[51] School administrators must exercise caution when students report abusive teacher conduct and not assume that if the teacher is popular, bullying cannot be happening.

Studies about charismatic bullies show that the driving force behind their abusive behavior may be narcissism. In a 2013 article in *The Atlantic* psychologist, Dr. Joseph Burgo studies the power of *reversal* whereby the abuser positions himself as the victim and he uses cyclist Lance Armstrong's conduct as an example. Witnesses who first spoke up about Armstrong's performance enhancing drug-use were humiliated by the cyclist in the press: "To shore up his winner status, Armstrong wanted to make his detractors appear like contemptible losers; he tried to turn public opinion against them, enlisting the support of his many fans." In Canada, disgraced Canadian musician, writer, and former CBC radio broadcaster, Jian Ghomeshi presented himself on Facebook as being the victim after being accused of sexual assault: "I've been fired from the CBC because of the risk of my private sex life being made public as a result of a campaign of false allegations pursued by a jilted ex girlfriend and a freelance writer."[52] He has since been charged with multiple counts of sexual assault.

Notably, this dual personality type or charismatic bully appears to be especially attracted to competitive sports because of the win-lose dynamic. Dr. Burgo explains:

---

[51] Devyne Lloyd, "What Happens when Bullies Become Adults?," *Michigan State University, School of Journalism* blog "The New Bullying," April 2012: http://news.jrn.msu.edu/ bullying/2012/04/01/bullies-as-adults/
[52] Staff, "Full Text: Jian Ghomeshi's Facebook Post Why He Believes CBC Fired Him," *Global News*, Oct 2014: http://globalnews.ca/news/1637310/full-text-jian-ghomeshis-post-on-why-he-believes-cbc-fired-him/

It helps to view the bully as a kind of competitor on the social playing field, one who strives not only to win but to triumph over the social losers and destroy their sense of self. As in competitive sport, where winners and losers exist in a binary relation to one another, the bully is yoked in identity to his victims. To a significant degree, his self-image depends upon having those losers to persecute: *"I am a winner because you are a loser."*

At my former school, the Headmaster and Board of Governors responded to students and parent reports of abusive behavior by teacher-coaches by publicly discrediting them in a report written by a lawyer that insinuated they were telling "nasty lies" and "manufacturing evidence." When the Headmaster didn't find the first lawyer's report he commissioned useful, and therefore did not allow families to read it, the Chair of the Board and the Lawyer/ Board Member we initially contacted hired a second lawyer. Parents, believing the School officials had protecting students as their goal, were included in choosing the lawyer and in setting the terms of reference that would govern his investigation into emotional abuse reported by students. However, two months later, the lawyer's report further humiliated the students and their parents; before they could even read it, the Headmaster published it widely throughout the School community. The Headmaster and Board of Governors thereby transformed the accused teachers, identified in the student testimonies, into "winners" triumphing over the "loser" students and their parents in a competition that went far beyond the basketball court. Dr. Burgo describes this competitive technique used by bullies and often by those who support them:

> All bullies are narcissists, with an inflated sense of self-importance and a marked lack of empathy for their victims' suffering, while many narcissists turn out to be powerful bullies. In defending his winner-status against detractors, for example, Lance Armstrong made extensive use of the legal system and his access to media in order to bully and intimidate anyone who

challenged him. In particular, he tried to destroy their reputations.[53]

It was a remarkably painful experience for students going into grade eleven and twelve to have come forward at the Headmaster's request, provide detailed written testimonies, and later in-person interviews about what they suffered at the hands of their teachers, only then to have the Headmaster turn around and publicly attack *their* character and their parents' reputations by widely disseminating a lawyer's report that positioned them as being weak and as lying. In a 2008 article on workplace bullying, Thomas Hoffman, quotes from Jean Ritala's book, *Narcissism in the Workplace* where she compiles a list of behaviors exhibited by bullies at work. Based on the written accounts from the fourteen students who came forward at my former school, the teacher-coaches involved exhibited most if not all these behaviors. According to Ritala, narcissists often display the following traits at work:

- Arrogant and self-centered, they expect special treatment and privileges.
- They can be charismatic, articulate and funny.
- They are likely to disrespect boundaries and the privacy of others.
- They can be patronizing and critical of others but unwilling or unable to accept criticism or disagreement.
- Likely to be anxiety-stricken or paranoid, they may exhibit violent, rage-like reactions when they can't control a situation or their behaviors have been exposed.

---

[53] Joseph Burgo, "All Bullies Are Narcissists: Stories of bullying and hazing in the news break down to narcissism and insecurity," *The Atlantic*, November 2013: http://www.theatlantic.com/health/archive/2013/11/all-bullies-are-narcissists/281407/

- They are apt to set others up for failure or pit co-workers against one another.
- They can be cruel and abusive to some co-workers, often targeting one person at a time until he quits.
- They may need an ongoing "narcissist supply" of people who they can easily manipulate and who will do whatever they suggest – including targeting a co-worker – without question.
- They are often charming and innocent in front of managers.[54]

The fourteen separate testimonies when reviewed collectively paint portraits of charismatic coaches flying into rages, targeting certain players until the student quits – even if it means giving up a full-scholarship – pitting players against one another so there isn't any sense of "team" left, drawing on new students year after year to fuel the narcissism. According to student testimonies, they appear as individuals who are charming and innocent when required, articulate and funny, and yet who are also cruel, abusive and disrespectful when other adults are not present.

In a 2014 investigative report by lawyer Christy R. Fargnoli regarding Charleston Cougars' basketball coach, Doug Wojcik which led to the termination of his contract for alleged verbal abuse, again the dual personality type appears. Fargnoli writes, "The players describe Coach Wojcik, generally, as having a 'Jekyll and Hyde' personality in that he can be both very nice and very mean – and this can switch at a moment's notice."[55] The fifty-page Fargnoli report forms a keen contrast with the one written by the second lawyer and published by the Headmaster at my

---

[54] Thomas Hoffman, "Narcissists at work: How to deal with arrogant, controlling, manipulative bullies," *Computer World*, June 2008: http://www.computerworld.com/article/2535227/it-management/narcissists-at-work--how-to-deal-with-arrogant--controlling--manipulative-bullies.html

[55] Christy R. Fargnoli, "Investigative Summary and Report, Re: Doug Wojcik Investigation," June 2014: http://www.postandcourier.com/assets/pdf/Investigative%20Report%20-%20Wojcik%202014%2006%2026.pdf

former school. Fargnoli's report includes detailed statements given by employees who claim they worked closely with the team, but never witnessed the coach crossing the line into abuse. It also includes detailed statements from employees and players who record witnessing or suffering the coach's abuse. The coach's swearing, demeaning, insulting, screaming, humiliating terms are recorded and the investigator states in her conclusions it is "likely" that these personal insults, raging behaviors, and regular use of obscenities happened despite those who said they had not seen them.[56] In contrast, the report at my former school was only ten pages and presented the conclusions without including the findings. It devoted over a page to those who praised the coaches, but only a brief quote to those who came forward with written testimonies that detailed the bullying. This kind of lopsided report fails to account for the dual-personality so often seen in charismatic bullies.

In an article by Vinay Menon, Jian Ghomeshi, is also described as a "Jekyll and Hyde." Ghomeshi, who was fired by the CBC in the spring of 2014, may also fit the profile of a charismatic bully. In public, he appeared as a very charming and charismatic man; yet in October 2014 he was charged with four counts of sexual assault and one count of overcoming resistance by choking; followed in January 2015 by three additional counts of sexual assault. A great deal of discussion arose around the reason why his victims did not file police reports over the years. *Toronto Star* Columnist, Vinay Menon explains:

> There's a reason women are reluctant to report sexual assaults. The real system, built upon a presumption of innocence, is stacked in favor of the accused. Most assaults involve a known assailant. A case often devolves into a "he said, she said" impasse. The problem is *she* needs to say so much more than *he*.

---

[56] Ibid.

She has to share intimate and painful details with strangers. She has to relive the attack. She has to endure skepticism and, often, outright hostility. She may be stigmatized. She may be subjected to a cross-examination so heartless and invasive, it feels like a second, third and fourth assault.[57]

Much like Menon's depiction of an unjust court system for abuse victims, I too felt concerned about the wellbeing of the students, particularly in light of an email I received from the school Chaplain basically suggesting that reporting to the Commissioner for Teacher Regulation would result in more suffering for the students as they would be cross-examined. If it's painful for an adult woman, a victim of sexual assault, to be on the stand, imagine how it would be for a teenager who has been bullied for years by a teacher. In our case, the teenagers would have to relive the humiliation, yelling, homophobia, shunning and grabbing they recorded in their testimonies just as they did in the four accounts of what they went through, which they were asked to give: one to a teacher or lawyer, the second to the Chaplain and Headmaster, the third to another lawyer, the fourth to a former RCMP officer who was also a lawyer. The students had already endured enough skepticism and outright hostility based on the way information was released and/or "messaged" by School Administrators. And if we turned to the Commissioner for Teacher Regulation or to the justice system, these students would be subjected to cross-examination and it would be invasive, at least according to the way the Chaplain phrased the email I received which will be discussed in detail in chapter seven. The legal system needs to review the way in which child-abuse victims and also victims of sexual violence are treated

---

[57] Vinay Menon, *The Star*, November 2014: http://www.thestar.com/entertainment/2014/11/01/in_praise_of_the_court_of_public_opinion_menon.html?app=noRedirect

in court. If we as a society want victims to report and we want to actually achieve a fair result, the system needs to change from being, to use Menon's words, "stacked in favor of the accused."

In Associated Press Sports Editor, Tom Canavan's portrayal of the "two Mike Rices," another Jekyll and Hyde-like coach, he stresses that it is important to understand that emotional abusers are very strategic. They do not constantly bully, only in certain situations and perhaps maybe even infrequently, but it's still happening. An abuser's good deeds, caring gestures, and "popularity" should therefore be irrelevant and should never be used as a way to explain away abusive conduct. In another article, a player on the Rutgers team is quoted defending Mike Rice's coaching style: "'He did a lot for us off the court, academically, socially,' Johnson said during a separate telephone conversation. 'I have to say I enjoyed my time, even if it was an emotional rollercoaster.'"[58] This is the same argument that can be made about Jerry Sandusky with the way he established his foster-care for boys, his seemingly wonderful, award-winning charity *The Second Mile*, his exceptional knowledge of football. This is the same argument that can be made for Jian Ghomeshi with his significant fan-base and highly popular radio show. If we use the talent or goodness abusers have as a way to cancel out the damage they do, then we enable them to continue abusing.

According to BC's Ministry of Education, emotional abuse is not measured by the intentions or good qualities of the abusers; it is measured by the reactions of students: "When emotional abuse is chronic and persistent, it can result in emotional harm to the child. Under the *Child, Family and Community Service Act*, a child is defined as emotionally

---

[58] Prim Siripipat, "Players Defend Mike Rice," *Associated Press*, April 2013: http://espn.go.com/mens-college-basketball/story/_/id/9135440/two-rutgers-players-defend-fired-coach-mike-rice

harmed if they demonstrate severe: anxiety, depression, withdrawal, or self-destructive or aggressive behavior."[59] These symptoms appear in the students' testimonies and were reiterated by their concerned parents. The Ministry of Education addresses abuse done by parents, as opposed to teachers or coaches, and therefore it appears they expect the Ministry of Children and Families to step in and protect, but *their* jurisdiction only extends to families, not schools. Thus, the Ministry of Education does not appear to address the fact that it may well be the teacher or coach who is causing emotional harm.

Unlike physical and sexual abuse, psychological abuse does not leave an identifiable physical mark and continues to be more permissible in our society. Emotional bullies are therefore not as careful to cover up their behavior in the way a sexual or physical abuser does. Coach Rice can be seen on nationally televised games raging courtside, but it is still not as brutal as how he acted during practices. No one matched the public raging with the homophobic slurs until Eric Murdock showed the world the video montage of Coach Rice on ESPN. Likewise with the teachers at my former school, they raged during competition, but the mostly inarticulate yelling seemed to be about the game, rather than homophobic or derogatory put downs directed at individual players or the team as a whole. While there were exceptions, they were few and far between. In the intensity of athletic competition, it was easy for parents to misread the coaches' conduct. However, when parents got a clear glimpse from their son or daughter's testimony, into what happened behind closed doors at practices, and what was said during half time talks or after tournaments, they were as horrified as the world was at Mike Rice's behavior at practices.

---

[59] http://www.mcf.gov.bc.ca/child_protection/pdf/handbook_action_child_abuse.pdf

While the court of public opinion had no problem concluding Mike Rice's behavior was highly abusive, there is a perpetual refrain from educational administrators that trying to identify "emotional abuse" is complex and difficult. The following 2013 article based on a study conducted at the University of Toronto is as clear in its definition of emotional abuse as it might be for physical or sexual abuse. Moreover, the study documents research into emotional abuse that dates back more than twenty-years. Emotional abuse in sports is not a new concept nor is it difficult to define:

> Emotional abuse is defined as a pattern of deliberate non-contact behaviors within a critical relationship between an individual and caregiver that has the potential to be a harmful critical relationship, also referred to as a caregiving relationship, is a relationship that has significant influence over an individual's sense of safety, trust, and fulfillment of needs (Crooks & Wolfe, 2007). An example of a critical relationship in sport is the relationship between the coach and the athlete. In the sport environment, the coach may play the role of the caregiver, as he/she may be entrusted with ensuring the safety and fulfillment of many of the athlete's physical and emotional needs. This is especially true at the higher levels of sport, where athletes may spend more time with their coach than their own family (Donnelly, 1993). Ways in which athletes may experience emotional abuse within the coach–athlete relationship include: through physical behaviors (e.g. throwing objects, punching walls), verbal behaviors (e.g. ridicule, belittlement, name-calling, humiliation), and the denial of attention and support (e.g. intentionally ignoring the athlete or refusing to provide adequate feedback) (Stirling & Kerr, 2008). Previous research has indicated that emotionally abusive coaching practices exist in sport (Gervis & Dunn, 2004; Stirling & Kerr, 2007, 2008). And investigations of abuse in the coach–athlete relationship suggest that emotional abuse may be the most frequently occurring form

of abuse in the sport environment (Kirby, Greaves, & Hankivsky, 2000).[60]

Emotional abuse of student-athletes by coaches was being studied and defined as far back as 1993; to argue this type of abuse is a contentious, ill-understood phenomenon, twenty-odd years later, is simply not a defense. Administrators and educators must be well versed in how to protect children from all forms of abuse – be it physical, sexual, or emotional. It is incumbent on high-school teachers and administrators to be informed, and educated, about all aspects of child development.

In the *BloombergView*, author Harlan Coben puts emotional abuse by coaches into more straightforward terms:

> When you call a kid a name or belittle him, that's abuse. Plain and simple. It should be treated as such. If you cannot coach without screaming, don't coach. I appreciate how much time and effort it takes. I've coached kids, too. But if you can't do it without tantrums, find something else to do. This is abuse. Parents may not be aware of the long-term effect coaches like these have on their child. Study after study has shown that verbally aggressive language doesn't motivate. In fact, it harms.[61]

What struck me in Coben's article was that he begins his article with the same term used by the teachers at my former school, according to student testimonies. As Coben explains, "The coach called one player a 'f*****g retard' in front of his teammates."[62] The word "retard" shows up so often

---

[60] Ashley E. Stirling and Gretchen A. Kerr, "The perceived effects of elite athletes' experiences of emotional abuse in the coach–athlete relationship." *The International Journal of Sport and Exercise Psychology* 11.1, 2013: 87-100.
[61] Harlan Coben, "That's Not Coaching. It's Child Abuse," *BloombergView*, May 2013: http://www.bloombergview.com/articles/2013-05-30/that-s-not-coaching-it-s-child-abuse-
[62] Ibid.

in discussions around coaching abuse that it appears to be as tried and true as homophobia in its ability to shame and silence athletes.

Another way experts assess emotional abuse is by the targets' perceptions and feelings. Dr. John Schinnerer explains that emotional abuse by coaches isn't only what they *say*; it's what they *do*: gesture and facial expression and the tone in which words are said. Echoing the BC Ministry of Education's defining terms, Schinnerer argues the subjective experience of victims is the measuring stick of emotional abuse. When he poses the question, "What does verbal and emotional abuse look like in athletics?" the answer is striking:

> Usually, this involves a coach telling an athlete or making them feel that he or she is worthless, despised, inadequate, or valued only as a result of their athletic performance. And here's the catch, such messages are not conveyed merely with the spoken word. They are conveyed by tone of voice, body language, facial expression and withdrawal of physical or emotional support. This is a large part of the reason why the problem of bullying in athletics is so hard to quantify – a clear definition of bullying is somewhat elusive. Even if we can define it, as above, it's highly difficult to measure.
>
> Bullying is partly defined by the subjective experience of the athlete. In other words, if the athlete feels shamed, frightened, or anxious around the coach due to his or her constant shouting, name-calling or threatening, then the label "emotional abuse" is warranted.[63]

Schinnerer's point is that no one should tell the athlete what it felt like to be screamed at, be called a retard, or be exposed to gestures of disgust.

---

[63] John Schinnerer, PhD, "'Help, My Coach is a Bully!': The Consequences of Verbally Abusive Coaching": http://www.selfgrowth.com/articles/Help_My_Coach_is_a_Bully_The_Consequences_of_Verbally_Abusive_Coaching.html

The students at my former school recorded in their testimonies how the coaches' gestures, facial expressions, and silences made them feel humiliated, worthless and threatened; their subjective experience, however, was dismissed by the Headmaster, the lawyers he hired, and ultimately by the Commissioner for Teacher Regulation as will be discussed in more detail in further chapters. Administrators and teachers tell students to report, to speak up, to never be a bystander, but in this case, when students actually did find the courage to give verbal and written testimonies about their teachers, their accounts were minimized and then they were publicly humiliated by the same Headmaster who asked for them to give testimonies and interviews in the first place.

Only one player on the Rutgers University Scarlet Knights risked speaking up against Coach Rice before the video was played on ESPN. Again, the parallels between Rutgers University and my former school are striking: student-athletes likely remained silent, not only because of the psychology behind abuse, but more practically because they did not want to risk opportunities for playing time, chances to develop as athletes, not to mention letters of reference and scholarships to colleges and universities. They could not risk asking to play their sport without being bullied. As T. F. Charlton writes in response to the Mike Rice scandal in *Salon.com*:

> Instead of teaching young athletes to accept and shoulder abusive coaching as being 'for their good,' let's teach them — and remind ourselves — that they have a right to not have their emotional and physical boundaries violated. Let's provide an institutional structure that is proactive about preventing and addressing abuse and protects athletes and staff who speak out about it.[64]

---

[64] T. F. Charlton: "Why do athletes tolerate abusive coaches? In locker rooms, insubordination is a worse crime than abuse of authority. Unless that changes,

As a society, we will never eradicate bullying until we create a culture of support and remedy for those who find themselves in a cycle over which they have little or no control. Narcissism is understood as a personality disorder; it is an illness. We need to start developing effective remedies. That said, teachers or coaches who bully need to be removed instantly from their positions until they are able to stop, get a clean bill of health from a psychologist, and hopefully return to their job. We would never let a teacher with a highly contagious disease near students. Likewise, we should never let a coach or teacher who suffers from a bullying or other psychological disorder to interact with students as their tendencies may well be passed on. As a student recounted in his testimony, *"I worry that I might become like [the coaches]. I'm scared I will snap and coach like them. It's a really big worry for me. I have the fear that being abused, I'll abuse others."* Another student reports that when coaching his little brother's team, he found himself resorting to the same abusive practices to which he had been subjected. When the adult with whom he was coaching pointed out his behavior to him, he felt terrible. Nevertheless, it was still a struggle for this bullied player to stop emulating the abusive coaching style he had learned as a younger player.

This honest admission by teenagers about how they have been negatively impacted is extremely concerning especially in terms of the students who normalized the bullying behavior, did not speak up against it, or turned a blind eye when they witnessed it happen. Perhaps this is why there is a bullying epidemic, not only in schools, but also in the workplace.

---

nothing else will." *Salon.com*: http://www.salon.com/2013/04/05/why_do_athletes_tolerate_abusive_coaches/

# CHAPTER THREE

# PSYCHOLOGICAL ABUSE AND STUDENT TESTIMONIES

> I have never seen such detailed, well-documented, and consistent testimony from so many athletes (combined with my own observations from work with one such student) that confirm and validate the existence of a very serious and damaging problem.
>
> – Dr. Alan Goldberg, after assessing six of fourteen testimonies at my former school

When teachers bully students, the official terms used to describe their behavior are verbal, psychological, or emotional abuse. Bullying becomes abuse particularly when an adult is in a "caregiver" role such as a coach or teacher. The *Public Health Agency of Canada* published a report that defines bullying "as psychological abuse when inflicted on children by adults." Authors of the 2008 report, psychologists Deborah Doherty and Dorothy Berglund state that "Generally, researchers and front line service providers define [psychological abuse] as the systemic destruction of a person's self-esteem and/or sense of safety, often occurring in relationships where there are differences in power and control (Follingstand and Dehart 2000)."[65]

---

[65] Deborah Doherty and Dorothy Berglund, "Psychological Abuse: A Discussion Paper," Ottawa: Public Health Agency of Canada, 2008. http://publications.gc.ca/collections/collection_2009/aspc-phac/HP20-12-2008E.pdf

The teacher-student and coach-athlete relationship have an inherent power and control imbalance. Generally the teacher or coach has all the power and control, while the student or athlete has little to none. Children have been trained since early childhood, and throughout their school years, to adhere and submit to this power differential; from the age four or five, students and athletes are taught to listen to and respect their teachers and coaches. It seems that this early childhood training has the potential to set the stage for a child's submission to adult bullying. Psychologist Mike Edger explains this in the following way:

> Bullied kids think there is something the matter with them. This deflates them and creates a lack of comfort and security in sports. It is possible young athletes are afraid to talk about being bullied by coaches. Often, young athletes' first reaction to being treated this way is shame. They feel as if they somehow caused the coach to treat them badly. Bullying can hurt an athlete's confidence—in and out of sports. When athletes are being bullied, and singled out by coaches they begin to have doubts about their ability to perform which cause them to question their role in sports. [66]

The student-athlete has been trained from his or her earliest years that the teacher/ coach has the right, and the credentials, to assess them and assign a value to them. So great is their power and control, researchers have likened the influence of a coach on a player to that of a priest over a congregation:

> Athletes require the coach's specialized knowledge and skills in order to succeed and, as a result, an athlete develops some level of dependency on his or her coach. Tofler et al. contended that, "In general, they [elite athletes] are in awe of coaches and other

---

[66] Mike Edger, "How Bully Coaching Affects Athletes," September 2012. http://www.sportpsychologytoday.com/youth-sports-psychology/how-bully-coaches-affect-athletes-mental-game/

authorities, who hold the key to potential success." Tofler and colleagues also stated that the power of the coach is considerable and should not be underestimated, and Brackenridge likened the power of the coach to that of a priest whose absolute knowledge is not questioned or challenged. Brackenridge further explained that this power is sustained and reinforced because of the coaches' abilities to develop and maintain success in athletes.[67]

When adults abuse their position or power and bully those in their care, the damage to the child-victim can be extreme.

Louise Tickle, a British lawyer specializing in child abuse cases, comments on the silence that usually persists among abuse victims: "We haven't got any modern day institutional abuse cases on our books. Experience shows that kids can't deal with the abuse while it's going on. They bury it till later."[68] For high school or university students, to speak up against their teacher for any reason would be highly unusual; they have literally been trained not to at this relatively young age. This reveals a failure in the school system and perhaps even in the way children are raised when it comes to speaking out against what they know to be inappropriate behavior on the part of the adults in their lives. There needs to be more effective ways to support children who are being bullied by teachers or coaches. Students should be taught from early on what their rights are and what emotional abuse looks and sounds like. Just as we teach children how to say "no" to unwanted sexual advances, we also need to teach them how to say "no" to those who might psychologically, emotionally, and verbally abuse them.

---

[67] Ashley E. Stirling and Gretchen A. Kerr, "Abused Athletes' Perceptions of the Coach-Athlete Relationship," *Sport in Society* Vol.12.2, March 2009: 227-239.
[68] Louise Tickle, "Britain's Elite Boarding Schools Are Facing an Explosion of Abuse Allegations," *Newsweek*, September 2014: http://www.newsweek.com/britain-elite-boarding-schools-facing-explosion-abuse-allegations-267201

Student-athletes rarely if ever speak up about abuse at the hands of a coach or a teacher, and often they will defend a coach whose conduct is being questioned. This is a well-recognized phase in the abuse cycle. According to Dr. Alan Goldberg, "one of the common dynamics in any abusive relationship is that the victim begins to feel like she is directly responsible for the abuse. This guilt-fueled illusion is encouraged by the abuser who continuously feeds this distortion to the victim."[69] In their article for the *Public Health Agency of Canada*, Doherty and Berglund created a chart that sets out psychologically abusive behaviors and the following ones were reported in the student testimonies at my former school. I have used fictional names to protect the students' identities and most passages stated in one student testimony were consistently found in the testimonies of other student-athletes across a five year span. These descriptions about coaching conduct are strikingly similar to those submitted by the Lawyer/ parent in her communication with Board, Chaplain, and ultimately Headmaster in 2011.

In certain testimonies, students report that teachers may have not personally bullied student-athletes; instead they acted as the "supportive" bystander. According to the testimonies, these bystanders witnessed the events, but did nothing stop them. The students report that these bystanders took no steps to prevent the incidents from happening again and by all accounts never reported what they saw to parents, School Administrators, or the authorities. Equally disturbing was a student account about how one teacher regularly comforted students after watching them being abused by colleagues; and yet did not, to my

---

[69] Dr. Alan Goldberg, "Coaching ABUSE: The dirty, not-so-little secret in sports." http://gazette.teachers.net/gazette/wordpress/dr-alan-goldberg/coaching-abuse-the-dirty-not-so-little-secret-in-sports-by-dr-alan-goldberg/

knowledge, report these matters to the School Administration. As one student describes the abuse:

> [The Coach] will yell technical stuff, but he'd say "be tougher" "fucking soft" "this is a fucking shambles" "look before you pass" "Horrible, fucking horrible" or "lazy" "hopeless" "you're embarrassing." He yells this multiple times. [The other coach] would comfort us. Bill would cry.

Imagine how confusing it would be for students in this situation – when a teacher condones the abuse witnessed only moments earlier. Clearly the abuse is acknowledged as harmful and students therefore required comforting, yet no material steps are taken to stop it from being repeated. It's so painful to read about a young man reduced to tears during a basketball practice or during a game. Crying is a natural response to humiliation and ridicule yelled by a caregiver. The other teacher's impulse to comfort demonstrates compassion, but bottom line, students expressed in their testimonies that he did not take steps to stop the bullying.

We have a tendency to be more protective of students when they are younger and until recently believed them to be more vulnerable; however, as the next chapter discusses, neuroscientists are only now realizing that the adolescent brain is in just as vital a stage of development as the brain of an infant to three year old. It is highly fragile at this time and great losses or gains can occur during the teenaged years. Also important to understand is that in the intense power imbalance between coaches and athletes, bullying is categorized as "abuse" whether it is adult to child or adult to adult. According to experts, Gretchen Kerr and Ashley Stirling, "The criterion of 'critical relationship role' does not include an age restriction. Many of the athletes in this study experienced abuse both as a child and as an adult, thus demonstrating that the experience of emotional abuse is not limited solely to children."[70] Workplace bullying is adult to adult as well.

Even when victims are adults, reporting on bullies still poses almost insurmountable challenges. It would appear that regardless of greater maturity and experience, those in a power imbalance struggle to speak up about their suffering. Therefore, whether in schools, in universities, on sports teams or in the workplace we need to create opportunities for reporting on bullies in order to ensure abuse is not occurring. As Stirling and Kerr argue, based on their study, "The finding that athletes were unwilling and/ or unable to report their experiences of abuse suggests that athlete advocates are needed."[71] Children need advocates too.

In the spring of 2012, at the request of the Headmaster, and with their parents' consent, students gave in-person testimonies that were transcribed. Each student statement about what he or she had experienced took approximately two hours. Each student approved the transcribed statement, taken by a lawyer (one player's parent) or taken by me in my capacity as teacher. Neither of us took our own child's testimony. After typing up the students' testimonies, we sent each one back to the respective student and asked them to change anything inaccurate, and if they wanted, to give consent for the approved testimony to be sent to the Headmaster.[72] Every student consented to their testimony being forwarded on to the Headmaster in the belief that he would fulfill his

---

[70] Ashley E. Stirling and Gretchen A. Kerr, "Defining and categorizing emotional abuse in sport," *European Journal of Sport Science*, July 2008: 8 (4): 173-181.
[71] Ashley E. Stirling and Gretchen A. Kerr, "Abused Athletes' Perceptions of the Coach-Athlete Relationship," *Sport in Society* Vol.12.2, March 2009: 227-239.
[72] The lawyer who took testimonies followed the "Voice of the Child" protocol used in the court system and I followed the *Independent School Guide on Child Abuse* guidelines.

promise to have different coaching, pay for psychological counseling and heal students' emotional bruises.

Teacher-coaches are caregivers and in a trusted position with student-athletes. They coach, mentor, have closed door practices and even travel with children. The relationship is necessarily comparable to a parent and child. As critical as trust is in the student-athlete to coach relationship, imagine the impact when the relationship is also between a school "house-parent" and a student-athlete living in residence. Three of the teacher-coaches were also house-parents. We did not ask any students in residence if they would like to give testimonies about their experience because they were in such a significant loyalty-bind. With parents far away and being from different countries and cultures, often not well-versed in English, trying to explain the situation or ask for informed consent was not feasible. These students were the most at risk and yet we could not ask them if they wanted to speak up.

Coach abuse experts Ashley Stirling and Gretchen Kerr stress how critical even the coach to student-athlete relationship is, let alone house-parent to resident student:

> In the sport environment, the coach may play the role of the caregiver, as he/she may be entrusted with ensuring the safety and fulfillment of many of the athlete's physical and emotional needs. This is especially true at the higher levels of sport, where athletes may spend more time with their coach than their own family (Donnelly, 1993).

In this context, it bears quoting once again their clear description of what constitutes abusive coach conduct:

> Ways in which athletes may experience emotional abuse within the coach–athlete relationship include: through physical behaviors (e.g. throwing objects, punching walls), verbal behaviors (e.g. ridicule, belittlement, name-calling, humiliation), and the denial

of attention and support (e.g. intentionally ignoring the athlete or refusing to provide adequate feedback) (Stirling & Kerr, 2008).

The students at my former school described all three categories in their testimonies: physical, throwing down objects; verbal, name-calling, humiliation, ridicule; and denial of attention and support, both ignoring and refusing to provide adequate feedback. Being teenagers they would not have known that each behavior exhibited by their coaches was a documented form of what constitutes "emotional abuse." Regarding the students at my former school, the administrators, lawyers and educational authorities did not appear to consult experts or refer to research in order to assess the students' experiences.

Previous research has indicated that emotionally abusive coaching practices have existed in sport for quite some time (Gervis & Dunn, 2004; Stirling & Kerr, 2007, 2008). And investigations into the coach–athlete relationship suggest that emotional abuse may be the most frequently occurring form of abuse in the sport environment (Kirby, Greaves, & Hankivsky, 2000).[73] With there now being at least twenty years of research available, it is surprising that educational authorities, school, and university administrators argue they need new guidelines, or argue that emotional abuse is difficult to identify, or they were unaware harm was being done to the students in their care. Surely it is incumbent on all institutions that are responsible for students' wellbeing that staff are informed and educated about abuse. It is even more vital that, as is the case in the United Kingdom, boarding schools in North America have inspectors, with the authority to create safe environments or a safe process

---

[73] Ashley E. Stirling and Gretchen A. Kerr, "The perceived effects of elite athletes' experiences of emotional abuse in the coach–athlete relationship." *The International Journal of Sport and Exercise Psychology* 11.1, 2013: 87-100.

through which students can confidentially share any negative experiences at the hands of their caregivers.

In the *Public Health Agency of Canada's* report, Doherty and Berglund explain that psychological abusers use "accusing and blaming" strategies such as "telling a person repeatedly that he or she has caused the abuse." In other words, the fault lies with the child; the abuse is somehow deserved. Doherty and Berglund also speak about bullies, "blaming the person unfairly."[74] At my former school, these tactics show up repeatedly in the student testimonies:

> *If we lost we were an embarrassment to them- they told us that at the Provincials. That we had embarrassed them and the School. Then they took the Grade 11s aside and told us that the reason that some of us didn't get much court time was that we were not disciplined and we were soft and we hadn't tried hard or worked hard. This was ridiculous because we had been to so many practices and worked so hard.*

Another student states the following: "*They constantly told us we were disappointing them as coaches. Only Andrea was okay, everyone else 'wasn't trying.' But we're so obviously trying our hardest. This makes me angry; instead of wanting to win, I didn't want to even play.*"

Students began basketball training at the School in September 2011 (even though it is considered by BC School Sports to be against the rules) and they played right through – generally six days a week – until March 2012; however, most players wouldn't see playing basketball as a chore or burden because they loved the game more than anything. To turn these facts around and lambaste students, making them feel as if they

---

[74] Deborah Doherty and Dorothy Berglund, "Psychological Abuse: A Discussion Paper," Ottawa: Public Health Agency of Canada, 2008. http://publications.gc.ca/collections/collection_2009/aspc-phac/HP20-12-2008E.pdf

deserved to be cursed at, yelled at, and humiliated because they "didn't try" fits into the category of "psychological abuse." Another student explained what it was like to be blamed all the time:

> *Sometimes the coaches rage at me saying "this is your fault" or "you're not putting effort in" or "you need to fix this." Now, Don is questioning whether he could even play at [a local college]. Before grade 11 and 12 at [my former school], he could have played a bunch of places with Canadian Interuniversity Sport (CIS). Of all the players, he plays the strongest when confident. He can do anything, take any shot. But here, he was so scared of being taken off and yelled at. So yeah, they broke him.*

Almost all the students who spoke up commented on their powerless position and how painful it was to watch their teammates being bullied:

> *It's the kind of department where you don't speak up to defend yourself or another player. If you do you might not play. You are constantly bombarded with what you did wrong. I felt badly when [the Assistant Coach] would be so bad to Phil. He said "Phil you are the softest player in the province. You are as soft as butter." [The Assistant Coach] is so negative all the time that I just shrugged it off but now I can see that it hurt Phil a lot.*

Almost universally the boys' testimonies talk about "another player," a "teammate" being hurt. This may be a safer way to describe how the teachers' behavior hurt them as well. I came to learn it is very difficult for a teenage boy, especially one constantly denigrated by homophobic slurs, to speak about his own suffering. For generations, men have been taught to believe that, if they hurt or admit to being hurt, it's somehow a weakness. To admit their feelings means they could be viewed as being "soft." As one student recounted, *"[The Head Coach] would yell in my face at practice until I couldn't take it and I would try to get away from his anger and then he'd grab my jersey or arm."* This same student stated that despite his efforts to tune out the bullying language, he was nonetheless subject to the message that the players were to blame:

> *I decided once it started happening that I was not going to let them get to me. I zoned out of every after game meeting and lots of huddles especially if I wasn't playing. I just couldn't let the swearing and the negative stuff in me. So I don't remember half the things they said to me and about me or to the other players. I do remember the main message that we were to blame.*

In Doherty and Berglund's definition of psychological abuse, they say beyond faulting and blaming the victims, another technique used by bullies is "criticizing behavior and ridiculing traits" the victims may have. They explain that this behavior involves "continuously finding fault with the other person or making the person feel nothing he or she does is ever right." These abusive tactics in turn diminish "the identity, dignity and self-worth of the person."[75] As one student explains, *"They used fear all the time. You made one mistake, they would yell or call you down or call another player down – it's the same thing – it isn't happening to you, but you know it can."* Another student recounts how *"[the Assistant Coach] swears under his breath a lot saying 'are you fucking kidding me' or 'Jesus fucking Christ' or 'we're so fucking bad.'"* He adds that, *"They yell all the time. This is why we're afraid."* The students fear being ridiculed and criticized. One student tells just how personal the ridicule was:

> *"Once in Grade 9, I made an around the back pass, not to be fancy, but because it was the only thing to do in that situation. It worked well. After that [the Assistant Coach] took me aside and said 'I don't want to see any of that Harlem Globetrotters shit*

---

[75] Ibid.

*any more.' It felt bad because I was being successfully creative and having fun."*

The teacher pulled this student aside, not for a skill-based explanation or comment, but apparently to humiliate and limit the player's on court behavior. This harmful "teaching" method is reported throughout all fourteen testimonies.

Several student testimonies speak to the teachers' control over the game: any unscripted plays resulted for the target students in punishment, regardless whether or not the play improved the team's chance to win. It's unusual for a basketball player to be criticized for scoring a three-pointer yet, according to the testimonies that was a common occurrence. One female player recounted the following:

*At the Police Tournament, I started hitting threes; they pulled me off and said my defense wasn't good. Everything I did was not good enough. They never communicated or played us to our strengths. [The coach] never really spoke to me. Only [the other coach] did. They swear so we hear it on the bench, but not loud enough that the parents can hear it. [The coach] will say to [the other coach]: "She's so fucking stupid." "She's not playing d." "She looks like a chicken with her fucking head cut off."*

If a coach was using this language toward a student-athlete, one could reasonably expect the assistant coach to report the verbal abuse, or at least for the assistant coach to protect the player and make the coach stop; in this case however, the assistant was the coach's father. It is difficult to imagine that a high school sports team would be coached by a teacher and her father, but at my former school this was considered acceptable.

Likewise, it is hard to imagine that fifteen- to eighteen-year-old boys would be truly afraid of their coaches, but the fear described in the testimonies illustrates just how powerful humiliation coming from a respected authority figure could be. The following quote captures what it was like to play for these coaches:

78

> *I see Malcolm with [the Head Coach] up in his face yelling,*
> *pointing his finger, swearing as far as I can remember, the*
> *messaging is like this: You need to…You can't….You're*
> *sloppy…what you're doing is wrong…you're killing the*
> *team…you're responsible.*

The student who described the scene above goes on to tell what happened repeatedly to another player and how he felt witnessing it and being powerless to make it stop.

> *[The other coach] said I needed to be more aggressive and I was*
> *"playing like a robot." That was a damaging comment like [the*
> *Head Coach] saying under his breath "fucking retard" about*
> *Scott and [the Head Coach] in Malcolm's face yelling "fucking*
> *soft" and maybe "grow some balls."*

As researchers document, the trauma for adolescents, considering their stage of brain development, from such an experience parallels those experiences recorded by psychologists from children who witness domestic abuse or the trauma experienced by combat soldiers.[76]

After having read all fourteen testimonies, it became clear that certain specific students for unknown reasons had become targets. While critical and ridiculing comments were hurled at the entire team, during practices in particular, students recount in their testimonies that specific players were singled out for additional bullying by the teachers. The relentless focus on particular targeted students is described in the following quote:

---

[76] http://www.goodtherapy.org/blog/bystanders-to-violence-the-child-witness-1018125 and also see John Schinnerer, Ph.D, "'Help, My Coach is a Bully!': The Consequences of Verbally Abusive Coaching": http://www.selfgrowth.com/articles/Help_My_Coach_is_a_Bully_The_Consequences_of_Verbally_Abusive_Co aching.html

*[The Head Coach] was very threatening with Malcolm. He was incredibly aggressive. He would pull him to the side while we watched and he was overwhelmingly aggressive and angry. This happened multiple times. It got to the point where Malcolm would try and turn away which appeared to make [the Head Coach] even angrier. It was all rhetorical questions with very obvious answers like "do you want to play?" "what were you thinking?" "do you deserve to play?" But when [this coach] gets super angry, you think he's going to start throwing chairs like he did at the game when the ref made a call he didn't like. He threw a chair. It's really demoralizing because we get a technical foul and they get a point. The closest I came to speaking up was to say "don't do that" (get another foul). He got one in every game in the Provincials when I was in grade 11.*

None of the parents I spoke with, or heard from, had any idea that the conduct described by students was occurring at practices, half-time talks, and tournaments. Yes, there was talk among the parents in the stands about the teachers' swearing, yelling, out of control behavior and technical fouls assigned to the coaches during games for their irate behavior. Nonetheless, very few parents had the confidence to raise any concerns over this conduct with School Administrators. The parents who did bring their concerns forward were stonewalled and so it appeared for all intents and purposes that nothing effective was done to stop the coaches' behavior.

The student's description above is about our son. My husband and I witnessed comparable behavior once at a game and thought it was a misstep by the coach and one never to be repeated. Our son did not tell us such abusive conduct was happening over and over again in practice. We didn't know. This is a key takeaway for all parents: students bullied by teachers are unlikely to tell anyone, especially their parents, about what is happening. They may offer oblique statements to test the waters in an attempt to get a parent's attention indirectly, but they worry about further repercussions and they may well have been brainwashed into thinking they are somehow *in trouble* with their teachers. Students don't want their parents to see a bad report card. Likewise, they don't want their parents to know that the teacher has called them a "retard" or an "embarrassment." In a child's mind, when a *teacher* makes that comment, it just might be *true* since it's the teacher's job to assess and grade students for post-secondary institutions. Understandably teenagers would be very anxious about sharing with their parents that the teacher holds a negative view about them.

When our son was just a Junior player, the Senior Boys Head Coach would contact him to come and shoot hoops one on one with him during lunch. He told us our son was going to be the "X-Factor" and he said on his report card he would be "sought after" by colleges. This coach made it seem as though he wanted to develop our son's significant potential. But when practices began in September 2011, our son informed us he was the "focus of relentless criticism." We told him he was lucky, that the coaches were trying to take his game to the next level. We didn't know what was really going on until we read the student testimonies in May 2012 where boys describe our son being subjected to in the face yelling, being grabbed, and then restrained when he couldn't bear anymore of the in-the-face humiliating diatribes or the yelling and shaming in front of the other players.

This teacher had been my colleague for several years and all our interactions led me to believe him to be easygoing, fun, kind and supportive. I would never have guessed that he had a completely different persona that came out during basketball practices. At games, we normalized his behavior as "intense" and attributable to being competitive and wanting the team to succeed. We later learned that at least a year previous to our son's experience on the Senior Team, other parents had been expressing significant concerns about the coaches' bullying conduct directly to the coaches, the Athletic Director, the Chaplain, the Director of the Senior School, the Headmaster and the Board of Governors.

A key challenge faced by students and parents at my former school who wanted to lodge a complaint was that one of the bullying coaches identified in student testimonies was *also* the Director of Athletics. In other words, according to student testimonies the very person to whom students or parents were expected to raise or report issues or concerns was herself a bully. Parents assumed incorrectly that the Headmaster would have her step down from her position considering the detailed testimonies from multiple players spanning four years on the team; however, she remained in her position throughout all investigations into her conduct. This made it likely that no other girl on the team would speak up as the Headmaster made clear with this decision that he fully supported her and her conduct. It's hard enough to go up against a teacher, coach, house-parent, Director, let alone the Headmaster himself. The following description is a female player's account of the coach and Director of Athletics' treatment of a basketball player who was also a talented rugby player:

> You've got to listen to what she says and just take it like Angela, so you get to play, "you're an athlete and you're not trying"; "You're a fucking rugby player, play like one"; "you're fucking soft," and Angela cries, but she likes Angela a lot so if she just takes it, she gets playing time. [The coach] doesn't understand what she's doing to us.

Another student describes the way in which the Athletic Director, under the guise of coaching, went after other players:

> [The coach] treated Norine horribly. Norine had no confidence in life or basketball by the end of it. Always sworn at and pulled off
>
> the court. [The coach] would yell at her "You're playing horrible defense." She would bring the whole team around and use "we"

82

> *to humiliate Norine because it would obviously refer to an error*
> *she might have made in the moment:*
> "*I can't believe we are jumping at fake shots.*"
> "*I can't believe we don't know fundamentals.*"
> "*I can't believe we didn't learn that in grade 5.*"
> *We are gathered around and we all know this is targeted at*
> *Norine, but she says "we."*

It makes sense that reports about bullying are falling on deaf ears when the player testimonies reveal that the Athletic Director herself regularly inflicted verbal abuse on the players. However, it does not explain why the other Administrators at the School also failed to address the "child abuse" that was clearly detailed in the eleven-page document filed with the Board and Chaplain and communicated to the Headmaster in 2011, or the fourteen student testimonies provided in 2012.

In defining psychologically abusive behavior, Doherty and Berglund document how the behavior moves from "ridiculing and criticizing" the victim, to "degrading the victim." This degrading behavior includes "insulting, ridiculing, name calling" and it is accompanied by "yelling, swearing, publicly humiliating or labeling the other person as stupid." According to one female student's testimony, the Athletic Director lectured the players in one outburst that they had "learned to be losers" during their time at the School; this would be a highly charged phrase given it came from a teacher who by all accounts is criticizing her colleagues and the very School ethos itself:

> *She gave us a big speech about how from the Junior School on at*
> *[the school], the teachers develop in us a losing attitude. She*
> *said, "it's because you guys don't want to win." She accused us*
> *of being losers. You've been taught your whole lives to lose. She*
> *starts to cry when she gives these speeches. It's the most insulting*
> *thing for me. She cries when we lose important games. You feel*
> *you've made someone cry so you feel horrible. She cries and*

*says, "I wanted to win." Then she leaves. It puts huge pressure on me.*

Teachers who call students "retards, losers, embarrassments" may believe that they are somehow toughening them up for a harsh world; however, according to the research, it has the opposite effect. Few would argue that a child that bullies other children on the playground, and makes them fearful and anxious, is in *any way* helping them become stronger people. If we all believed that, then there would be no demand for "zero tolerance" polices around bullying in our schools; there would be no need for educational initiatives directed at children to address bullying behavior nor would there be a need for constant encouragement not to be bystanders when children see bullying occur. There would be no suicides as a result of bullying. Yet, when it's a teacher or a coach yelling degrading or insulting words at a student, some argue it is an effective way to motivate a child; it is intended to make a student-athlete more competitive and to prepare him or her to "win." This is comparable to arguing that when a student steals something from another student, it is unacceptable, but if a coach steals something from a student, it is meant to motivate him or her.

In the student testimonies, degrading, yelling, swearing, and name-calling by coaches were the most frequently recorded psychologically abusive behaviors that the students said they endured. As one player recounts:

> *[The coaches] would call us names, sometimes as a group and sometimes one on one. Fucking retards, fucking stupid, a waste of a player, these were common. They would be yelled or spoken quietly or said under their breath.*

During games these abusive terms would be muttered, apparently so that the other team's coaches, referees, or parents who were watching would not hear. Often, the students commented in their testimonies about how the Assistant Coach in particular had several "favorites" who were exempt from bullying; however, for the other players, the negative messaging directed at them was relentless.

Several player testimonies described a preference for the Assistant Coach who consistently criticized them over the young Head Coach, who half the time was fun and laid back, a good friend, and then suddenly during practices or games became viciously aggressive and insulting toward those same players. Multiple testimonies spoke to the abrupt change in this coach from a friendly, joking person into a raging, humiliating tyrant; in their testimonies, the students say they never knew what to expect from the young Head Coach and found it more stressful than the Assistant who was consistent in his degrading and humiliating. According to one testimony, *"[the Head Coach] had two ways of operating – super chill – and – when coaching he's pointing in your face and yelling at you. When he coaches, sometimes when he's angry, the impression is it's your fault."* Likewise, according to student testimonies, the coach of the Senior Girls' team also had this Jekyll and Hyde split that journalists used to describe Mike Rice, Doug Wojcik and Jian Ghomeshi:

> *[The coach] would blur the line between being your friend. She would play mind games. She'd joke around about boys. She would ask after girls and their boyfriends. She'd look at a guy and say, "he's so cute. You should go talk to him" She was your buddy; then two minutes later, she's screaming at you, swearing at you, saying, "we lost because of you." Now I'm worthless on the court and it's all my fault we lost.*

Many testimonies described what are understood to be grooming behaviors: the coach would draw a player into a close relationship, only to then abruptly transform it into one where the student was subjected to insulting, humiliating, aggressive behavior and verbal attacks. In our son's case, he was called to shoot hoops with the Senior Coach when he was a Junior player. He'd be asked to sit with the Coach on trips and was sent many text messages about how to improve. But, as recounted in the boys' testimonies, he was also the focus of humiliating tirades from the Coach while the team was made to watch.

The student testimonies describe the "charismatic bully" persona discussed by journalists and psychologists for instance, Canavan, Gladwell, Jones and Schinnerer. According to the testimonies, the students found this dual personality extremely confusing. Although my husband and I had witnessed the one abusive incident that targeted our son at a game, I would never have believed that these teachers, these coaches I respected would transform from the fun, gentle, calm, intelligent people I observed in their classrooms, saw joking with students in hallways, shared stories with in the staff room and laughed with at staff social events into people who, according to student testimonies, hurled insults, yelled up in their faces, restrained them and humiliated them once their feet hit the basketball court. The students expressed similar surprise and confusion: *"He was really nice when I was in grade 10, but then it changed when I was in grade 11 and on the team. I was shocked at the change."* Another student states:

> *Before [the Head Coach] was my coach he was like my pal, my best friend kind of guy. In the scrimmages in the past he would always be in there telling you tips and be fun. When he was the team coach he was totally different. It was confusing. I remember after a practice we were all happy and in the huddle and me and Dirk were fooling around and bumping into each other and out of the blue he said "Stop fucking touching each other." That was a shock. It might have been the first one. It got worse as the games started.*

The students were unaware that what they were describing in textbook terms were the acts of a "charismatic bully" or an "abusive narcissist."

Administrators far too often respond to the discovery that abuse has occurred at their institutions with doubt, disbelief and shock that those teachers they oversee have bullied students. Based on faulty reasoning that children should speak up immediately when they are subjected to abusive behavior, administrators tend to be perplexed and fall back to logic as a basis for moving forward. The base argument is that if abuse was happening then no child would tolerate it. Administrators ask questions such as 'why are the children speaking up now when this has gone on for a long time?' They fail to recognize how it is nearly impossible for children to understand that what they are experiencing is in fact abuse and that they have the right to speak up and stop it. To expect child abuse victims to identify, name, and categorize their experiences, as if they are psychologists, psychiatrists and neuroscientists, is ridiculous. It would be like an oncologist saying a cancer patient doesn't have a malignant tumor because the patient can't see it and name it. It would compare to an oncologist suggesting that the tumor is not really there because the patient did not report it the moment it began its cancerous growth.

While the students at my former school did not have the correct vocabulary or informed assessment of what they were being subjected to, they were very aware and articulate about what it felt like to have teachers screaming, blaming, and insulting them and their peers under the guise of coaching. In their testimonies, the students were clear that the teachers' bullying did not result in increased self-assurance that further prepared them for the "real world"; in fact, it resulted in the exact opposite. In their testimonies, players described feeling threatened, afraid, miserable, less confident and less self-assured. The players go on to describe feeling powerless to save their friends and recounted that they were often fearful: "*Dirk's super confident one on one. I love playing one on one with him because nobody is yelling. Yelling stuff like 'that was a terrible shot' 'can't have that.' It made me afraid to shoot.*" These serious athletes expressed great frustration that they were not learning to play the game better, instead their individual and team development was being stunted because their teachers' focus appeared to be on personal attacks rather than on skill development and training in order to win.

This belief is captured by one player who explained, "*[The Assistant Coach] knows a lot about basketball, but I'm not a big fan. I never saw his knowledge.*" And regarding the girls' coach, another says, "*She ignored me. No feedback at all. She gets angry all the time, pulls you off and doesn't speak to you. Physically you have to go to her and say what can I do better? She's not clear or specific about what you can do.*" Repeatedly the players lament that they never knew what it was they had done "wrong." More important, the testimonies reveal that the critique from their coaches was not about the game, or about techniques or their growth as players; rather, it appeared to be bullying without any developmentally related purpose:

> *But she could never put into words what I had done wrong. It was always "fucking retarded" and "you guys are lazy" and "you're not trying." At half time she'd be raging. I couldn't fit into their idea of a team. She was always saying stuff like "I'm really disappointed in you" "You should be embarrassed" "you weren't trying" "You looked lazy."*

A psychologically abusive person attacks the victim's character; he or she doesn't teach what to do better because that's not what's at stake. The behavior isn't intended to improve the player. Just like the playground bully doesn't call another kid a "retard" to help him or her do better at school; likewise, a teacher who calls students "retards" is in no way helping develop them. That teacher is instead showing a complete disregard for the most fundamental educational and child development principles. What is so tragic is that student testimonies describe confusion over how they are "responsible" for the tirades. Repeatedly in the testimonies, students struggle with "taking responsibility" for their "mistakes" and how if only they had been given some tangible instructions or direction, they would have fixed whatever they did "wrong."

> [The Head Coach] and [the Assistant Coach] both just ignored Bill the whole year. That was hard to watch. That's how you know if you have played badly – they ignore you unless they swear at you or call you down in front of the team or off to one side. If you play well you get a high five. If you play badly they don't meet your eyes and ignore you. They never even looked at Bill all year.

Students struggle to understand what Bill has done "wrong" because they cannot recognize that it's likely Bill is simply a target: ostracizing is a textbook bullying technique to ruin a person's sense of self. Bill was a committed, passionate player. By the end of a humiliating second season, according to student testimonies, he wouldn't even join in during practices; he'd simply shoot hoops at the other end of the gym. The coaches did not approach him to see what was wrong.

Statements very similar to the one above are given in multiple testimonies from students who report that they "could do nothing right," and had to play alongside favored students who could apparently do no wrong. And still, these targeted students tried to learn to do better, ultimately holding themselves to account for making "mistakes" – such as "scoring three-pointers" or pulling down multiple rebounds in a single game. Confusion about the coaches' conduct is rife throughout all the fourteen testimonies; the players struggle time and again to understand what is happening to them. As a female player explained, "I would get yelled at, but I didn't know what she wanted me to do. It was how she said things like rubbing her head and throwing her arms up like she was disgusted with you. Her facial expressions [said] 'Oh my God Nadine, what are you doing?' I was made to feel like a failure, that nothing was good enough." Yet another student's description of the same coach, again

89

speaks to a lack of coaching instructions intended to develop skills replaced with personal, humiliating attacks on the student's character:

> *We always have an assistant who used to play for the [school] team. This year it was Nancy. When Lisa got stressed out one time, she went to Nancy and said, "I don't know what they want me to do?" There's so many mixed messages. Nancy just said, "it sucks, they're being mean to you."*
> *[The Coach] to Lisa:*
> *"I'm watching you play basketball and can't believe you play rugby"*
> *"They'd kick your ass there too"*
> *"You're letting us down."*
> *"You're not trying."*
> *"You're not tough."*
> *"You couldn't play rugby."*
>
> *This whole thing about how we're not trying became a joke with us because it's so unfair. If we're not trying why are we at basketball practices and games six days a week?*

In addition to the yelling, personal attacks, and gesturing their disgust, coaches would also shun targeted students as recorded in the student testimonies. Disgust or contempt, in teacher-student interactions, should be a red flag that emotional abuse is at work. As Jim Thompson, founder and chief executive of the *Positive Coaching Alliance* comments, after seeing the video in which Mike Rice screams at his basketball players, "I was struck by the contempt that Coach Rice had for his players – the way he treated and talked to them."[77] As a registered Clinical Counselor, educator, sought-after speaker and authority on boys and learning, author

---

[77] Joe Drape and Nate Taylor, "Question Arises as Scandal Unfolds: Where's the Line?" April 2013: http://natetaylorsports.wordpress.com/2014/07/10/question-arises-as-scandal-unfolds-wheres-the-line/

Barry Macdonald advises that, "We should never shame boys by showing contempt."[78]

In the *Public Health Agency of Canada* report, Doherty and Berglund include "ignoring" as one weapon in the psychologically abusive person's arsenal. They define ignoring as "purposely not acknowledging the presence, value or contribution of the other" and even "acting as though the other person were not there."[79] In the student testimonies, one student comments on how painful it was to witness the coaches ignoring another player: "*I was frustrated with Bill's treatment. He's put in a huge effort and he always sat on the bench except for the last minute. By the end, they weren't even practicing him. He would go off on his own in the gym taking shots on a hoop. It was uncomfortable for me.*" Many times parents watched in shock as a player, who had not seen any court time, would be put on for the last minute. The player would appear awkward from having sat for so long and would not have even a remote chance to contribute in any way during their sixty seconds. It certainly did not seem like an effective strategy if winning was the goal. As students describe in their testimonies, it was felt to be nothing but public humiliation. In contrast, other players would be on the court so long, they would appear exhausted, almost ill with fatigue. Again, it wasn't a winning strategy.

The students struggled to understand why the coaches were shunning certain players. In one of the testimonies, a student offers the explanation that Bill was penalized for taking part in an international School trip which interfered with basketball practices set over the

---

[78] Barry Macdonald, *Boy Smarts: Mentoring Boys for Success at School*, Mentoring Press, Surrey, 2005: 86.

[79] Deborah Doherty and Dorothy Berglund, "Psychological Abuse: A Discussion Paper," Ottawa: Public Health Agency of Canada, 2008. http://publications.gc.ca/collections/collection_2009/aspc-phac/HP20-12-2008E.pdf

holidays: "*After that, Bill didn't play as much. By the end, Bill is unemotional. He had been rejected so many times.*" When I took the boys' testimonies, I found this reaction over and over again. They appeared neutral, unemotional, withdrawn. It is important not to mistake this for not caring. Instead, as the student puts it so effectively "he had been rejected so many times." It is expressive of someone who does not trust; it is expressive of someone in pain.

A female player records in her testimony the same story about not being able to attend practices set during the holidays because she was away with her family – she was penalized upon her return by no longer being a starter. Being ignored by a peer can lead to feelings of rejection and shame. However, it cannot be compared to the experience where a teacher purposely does not acknowledge a student's presence or value. As another student on the Senior Girls' Basketball team recounted, "*She always ignored me. She wouldn't talk to me or tell me what I was doing wrong. It would have been easier if she yelled at me. Then I could yell back. If she could have put into words what I was doing wrong, but it was always swearing. Parents from other schools even were cringing.*" Ignoring is readily found in most articles that examine abusive coaching and is well-documented bullying behavior. At this age, students have no frame of reference or means to identify, label or understand how harmful in the long-term bullying by a coach or teacher can be. Instead, they simply believe that if they speak up it will only get worse. That's why student-athletes so often quit the team when a bully is the coach.

This is in part why it is so important for school administrators and authorities to educate themselves to recognize psychologically abusive behavior both on the court and in the classroom. Dr. Carl Pickhardt in his *Psychology Today* article, entitled "Adolescents and Bullying Coaches" writes the following:

Bullying behaviors from coaches include intimidation (using yelling and threats to scare into obedience), insulting (name calling to demean appearance, toughness, or worth), ridicule (making fun of bad play or lack of skill), humiliation (singling out a player for public embarrassment or blame), and benching (refusing to let a student play.) The impact of these kinds of actions on adolescent age players can be performance anxiety about making mistakes, hesitant play because of unsure decision-making, loss of confidence in one's capacity to perform, believing mistreatment is deserved, losing enjoyment of the sport one once enjoyed, even quitting the sport to avoid any coaching at all.[80]

Basketball was like breathing for our son, but in his final high school year he quit the team along with five other senior players and he has not played competitively since.

"Rejecting" is yet another psychologically abusive practice used by bullies. Doherty and Berglund, define "rejecting" as when a bully systematically refuses to "acknowledge a person's presence, value or worth" and "communicates to a person that he or she is useless or inferior."[81] In the student testimonies, there were frequent detailed references to the way in which some students would be "broken down," while others would be "built up," very much in keeping with how Doherty and Berglund describe the technique of rejection where instead of *all* the children being treated equally, the caregiver expresses rejection

[80] Carl Pickhardt, PhD, "Adolescents and Bullying Coaches: When secondary school coaches bully players, parents must step in," *Psychology Today*, January 2012. http://www.psychologytoday.com/blog/surviving-your-childs-adolescence/201201/adolescents-and-bullying-coaches
[81] Deborah Doherty and Dorothy Berglund, "Psychological Abuse: A Discussion Paper," Ottawa: Public Health Agency of Canada, 2008. http://publications.gc.ca/collections/collection_2009/aspc-phac/HP20-12-2008E.pdf

and dislike to one child and inclusion and kindness to another. As one student described it:

> In grade 11, we had a team wide three point shooting competition. Dirk won, I came second. But when we played, if he took a shot and missed, they would pull him off and yell at him. If James and Paul took a shot and missed they would not be pulled off [. . .] James got star treatment. He was confident and aggressive. Dirk was not allowed to shoot. [The coach] didn't believe in his ability. For Dirk, it showed that [the coach] didn't have confidence in him and that totally affected his game. He used to be obsessed with basketball. He would play in the winter, in the snow in his yard. Now with all our facilities he won't go near the gym. He blames our coaches for that.

It is noteworthy that the student quoted above, and even Dirk himself, do not recognize the tactic being used by the coaches to apparently favor certain players and to reject or devalue others. Both students seem to try and rationalize and understand the coaches' actions from a skills-based perspective, without seeing the facts: Dirk is the best shooter on the team, as the contest proved; however, he has been told he's not allowed to shoot. It's a vicious circle: the more he is "not allowed" to shoot, the less confidence he has. He goes from being the best shooter on the team to missing shots; the coach pulls him off and yells at him further eroding his confidence. He stops wanting to play; he stops loving the game. In contrast, the favored student develops his "confidence" because he can miss shots and know that he won't be pulled off the court and yelled at.

What is surprising is that a coach would sacrifice winning a game or even a championship by hemming in and rejecting the team's best three-point shooter. Yet multiple testimonies comment on how the plays were designed so that only the favored players were allowed to shoot; the others had to pass to these players rather than take their own shots. One student records in his testimony that the teacher's approach did not allow the team to reach its potential and how frustrating that was for the players:

> *When thinking of how [the Assistant] coached, in comparison to our Gr. 9 coach, the difference is huge. I found that [the teacher who coached in grade 9] was very fair and very supportive of the team, and even in the most stressful situations he held his composure. We also went much farther with [the grade 9 teacher] coaching, placing 12th in the provincials when we didn't even get to the islands under [the Assistant Coach]. Also with [the Assistant Coach] constantly yelling it was very hard to stay calm and play with confidence. Consciously I started to block [him] out and when he would yell and scream about the things I did wrong I would just nod my head and brush him off. But my confidence definitely dropped this year. In Gr. 9 I think that I was quite a consistent 3-point shooter, but due to the change in position and me not being allowed to shoot 3-pointers, my shooting ability immediately dropped.*

This student suggests some reasons that the team did *not* do well or fulfill its potential; clearly in this instance, yelling did *not* motivate players; it demoralized them and made them insecure. Only letting the favored players shoot, while targeting others with bullying, did *not* make a winning team. Allowing coaches to swear and scream did *not* toughen players up; it upset them, demoralized them and eroded their confidence. If abusive coaching was the way to win then the Junior Boys, Senior Boys, and Senior Girls Teams should have been repeat Provincial Champions; instead, they have lost to other teams for over twenty years.

The student testimonies describe a bullying culture of fear, favoritism and humiliation. While this culture has been sanctioned by the Headmaster and Board of Governors at the School, as well as excused away by lawyers paid for by the School, and even condoned by the Commissioner for Teacher Regulation, multiple news stories since April 2013 have demonstrated that bullying by university-level coaches is no

95

longer tolerated. At the University of Indiana at Purdue, "Interviews with eight former basketball players revealed a culture of fear, favoritism, humiliation."[82]

These interviews were enough to require women's basketball coach Shann Hart to resign; however, the fourteen testimonies from students at my former school, that revealed a comparable culture, were not seen as sufficient to issue any reprimands let alone suspensions or firings. Yet as one player on the girls' team describes the culture:

> ...there's blatant favoritism. I don't want to be sour grapes, but I was the one who mostly heard "fuck that" or "fucking get it together" or "holy fuck Marissa" over and over again "What the fuck are you doing Marissa." She would never give you concrete criticism. It wasn't helpful [. . . ] It was never positive. There's tons of communication with Julie, Michelle and Andrea and the rest of us were left out. There wasn't consistency so you didn't know what to do. In a pre-game talk, they would talk to Julie, Michelle and Andrea. People were scared to shoot. We were down by ten and I was put in. I scored two three pointers and [the coach] said that was good and all I could think was, I could do that all the time if you'd let me. Mostly they yelled at me for doing stuff like that. We weren't allowed to play like that.

As recorded in their testimonies, students clearly express how the treatment feels unfair, but no one will speak up in case they are benched or become the next target. As another player on the team described how this coach, also the School's Director of Athletics treated them and why the players wouldn't speak up when they witnessed a teammate being bullied: "*A lot of girls are scared of her because they worry they won't*

---

[82] Alan Petersime, "Ex-players say IUPUI women's coach Shann Hart 'did it again'," Indianapolis Star, August 2010: http://indianabasketballdigest.com/index.php/topic/7676-usa-today-ex-players-say-iupui-womens-coach-shann-hart-did-it-again/

*get playing time.*" The students describe coaching conduct that shifts between overt humiliation and subtle rejection, bullying techniques recorded in multiple studies. Instilling a sense of fear in players over coveted "playing time" helps to sustain the bullying culture and is a key component in maintaining the abuse cycle year after year.

School City of Mishawaka High School basketball coach Robb Berger was sued in 2011 for humiliating and then shunning one of the school's players. The suit claimed senior Jim Ross' minutes were among the fewest on the team – despite his apparent skill and height advantage.

> At 6 feet 9 inches, senior Jim Ross was Mishawaka High School's tallest basketball player this past season. But his minutes played were among the shortest. His parents, Don and Shirley Ross, are so angry at coach Robb Berger that they are suing him and School City of Mishawaka in St. Joseph Circuit Court.

Their lawsuit makes no mention of playing time. Instead, they claim that beginning in 2005, Berger "harassed, berated, humiliated, intimidated and psychologically abused" the youth. In a court filing, Berger has denied the lawsuit's substantive allegations. Examples of the verbal abuse, according to the lawsuit, include the following:

> "You are eight (f——) feet tall, why can't you make a lay up?"
> "You were almost competitive and got a god(d—) rebound."
> "You can't run, you can't jump, you can't play."

And this, from a harassment complaint letter the Rosses sent to School City of Mishawaka Superintendent R. Steven Mills:

> "My grandmother is faster than you and my kid has more heart."

As a result, Jim Ross suffered emotional distress, withdrew and shut down, the lawsuit claims. After the couple complained to Mills, Berger "switched his method of abuse to ignoring Jim Ross and acting as if he did not exist, as if he were not present," the suit claims.[83]

According to the fourteen testimonies, the abusive language Jim Ross was subjected to was not nearly as harsh or humiliating as that regularly shouted at players at my former school. On our son's 2012 report card, the Head Coach wrote that he was on the cusp of being one of the best athletes to ever play basketball for the school and that he would be sought after by college teams – yet he wasn't a starter, spent little time on the court, and found himself harassed, berated, humiliated, and intimidated during practices. In keeping with Jim Ross's experience, our son suffered emotional distress, withdrew and shutdown. However, we cannot afford to fight for his rights in court nor would we subject him to further bullying by lawyers. As a teenager diagnosed with PTSD, our son is not safe in a courtroom. This allows bullies and abusers, especially those protected by wealthy private schools, to get away with their conduct. If as a society we truly want to stop bullying and emotional abuse, this needs to change. Legal processes should protect victims and hold perpetrators to account.

• • •

The recent heightened awareness about abuse in sport has resulted from a number of courageous disclosures from athletes who experienced abuse. This has led to a new drive within the sport community to protect children, adolescents, and young adults for whom sport has become an important part of life. Protecting participants from all forms of bullying, harassment and abuse is a crucial element of safety. *Hockey Canada*

---

[83] Jeff Parrott, "Parents Sue Hoops Coach, Mishawaka Schools," *South Bend Tribune*, September 2011: http://articles.southbendtribune.com/2007-03-20/news/26788195_1_coach-berger-claims-shirley-ross

considers any form of bullying, harassment or abuse to be unacceptable and will do all it can to prevent this intolerable social problem within its ranks. In *Hockey Canada's Coach Stream Pre Task Readings* guide where the "ten leading tactics used by bullies to control their target" are identified, the list provides further evidence that the coaching style described by the student-athletes at my former school was harmful and has no place in sports:

- Unwarranted yelling and screaming directed at the target
- Continually criticizing the target's abilities
- Blaming the target of the bullying for mistakes
- Making unreasonable demands relating to performance
- Inconsistently applying the rules so that some individuals are adversely affected while others are not, thus further diminishing and alienating the target
- Repeated insults or put-downs of the target
- Repeated threats to remove or restrict opportunities or privileges
- Denying or discounting the target's accomplishments
- Excluding or ostracising the target from group or team activities
- Taking credit falsely for someone else's accomplishments[84]

The student testimonies describe every single one of these bullying tactics used against them by their coaches. As one player's parent put it, the teachers appear to display *"favoritism in its most extreme and destructive form, where targeted players are singled-out and blamed for the inability of the chosen ones to perform."*

Students don't normally complain about being treated unfairly. I can only recall one other teacher at any school I have worked at in twenty

---

[84] http://cdn.agilitycms.com/hockey-canada/Hockey-Programs/Coaching/NCCP/Downloads/coachingnccp_pretaskreading_e.pdf

years who was seen as favoring certain students. When multiple students say that the teachers do not operate based on a student's merit, but instead treat students according to a bullied-versus-favored student system, chances are good there might be a problem with the teacher. When administrators hear from three or four students and their parents reporting favoritism – of any kind – it should cause concern. Seven or eight students describing favoritism and being yelled at should set alarm bells ringing. Fourteen students, of varying ages, from different teams, over different years, providing written testimonies that describe a culture of fear, favoritism, and humiliation, followed up by in-person interviews with Administrators, should set off a firestorm.

Despite favoritism being a well-documented psychologically abusive technique used by bullies, it was minimized and dismissed by the Administration at my former school. However, favoritism is insidious and dangerous: it underpins racism, anti-Semitism, sexism; it is the cycle that blocks women from promotions or equal pay for equal work, it causes misogynist and homophobic or racially inspired hate crimes, it underpins systems of abuse like apartheid. It creates bystanders who witness bullying, but remain quiet because they do not want to suffer similar consequences. It creates a group of supporters who defend bullies and drown out the cries when the victims speak up. As Barbara Coloroso's work on bullying reveals:

> Sadly, even when the four markers of bullying are clearly in evidence, adults have been known to incorrectly label, minimize, or dismiss the bullying, underestimate its seriousness, blame the bullied child, and/or heap on additional insult to injury by simply failing to properly identify what is going on.[85]

---

[85] Barbara Coloroso, *The Bully, the Bullied, and the not-so-innocent Bystander*, updated edition, Harper Collins: 2015 (77).

While Coloroso depicts exactly the reversal that happened at my former school, whereby the students were held accountable and the teachers were excused, it is also apparent that this is not an exclusive or unusual crisis; it is a widespread one.

The fourteen students at my former school, who had the courage to see put down on paper descriptions of their repeated bullying by coaches, have shone a spotlight on an athlete's right to play their sport based on meritocracy and in a respectful arena free from teaching bullies.

The Headmaster at my former school begins each academic year with a talk about Rosa Parks and her quiet, but powerful heroism. In Montgomery, Alabama in 1955, when buses were segregated, the driver asked Ms. Parks to give up her seat in the "colored section" for a white passenger. Sick of the injustice, Parks did not give up her seat on the bus; she was arrested and her act of defiance became a catalyst for the Montgomery Bus Boycott and a key symbolic gesture of the Civil Rights Movement. Likewise, the students who gave testimonies will hopefully set in motion a *Students' Rights Movement* that will one day result in changes to how educational institutions are managed, how teachers are trained, and how laws are written to protect students' rights to learn in a safe, healthy, and fair environment. At present, the way abuse allegations and their assessment are handled seems to favor adult abusers rather than child victims. This needs to change. It's not an equal playing field. At a book talk given in April 2014, Barbara Coloroso not only spoke about her books on bullying, she also discussed her book *Extraordinary Evil: A Brief History of Genocide*, inspired by her work with children orphaned by the Rwandan genocide. She comments about this book that the "premise is that it is a short walk from schoolyard bullying to hate crimes to genocide."[86] The dehumanizing that occurs in bullying parallels the more extreme forms of dehumanizing that fuel hate crimes and genocide. And yet, over and over again, as Coloroso documents, bullying and hazing in schools, at universities, and even in the workplace continue to be minimized and dismissed as bonding or joking. Likewise, adult bullying in a sports context is minimized and dismissed as old-style coaching or as passion and motivation.[87] This has to change.

A 2014 article in the *Washington Post* discusses a new civil rights movement that is all about students and their educational rights. Campbell Brown, a former CNN anchor who has become an educational activist combined forces with lawyer, David Boies, in order to change tenure laws in the US, laws they argue protect weak teachers and thereby violate a fundamental right of children to have equal educational opportunities. In this bid for the civil rights of students, they are returning to the Civil Rights Movement case that overturned segregated schools:

> "Our initial approach is state law," he said. "And we'll see how much progress we can make using state law."
>
> The U.S. Constitution does not include the right to education. But civil rights activists used the equal protection clause of the Fourteenth Amendment — which says that no state shall deny to any person "the equal protection of the laws" — as the basis for

---

[86] Steve Kidd, "Author Makes Penticton Book Lecture Count," *Penticton Western News*, April 2014: http://www.pentictonwesternnews.com/entertainment/299923111.html

[87] Barbara Coloroso, *The Bully, the Bullied, and the not-so-innocent Bystander*, updated edition, Harper Collins: 2015 (57).

Brown v. Board of Education, the 1954 Supreme Court decision that put an end to racially segregated schools.[88]

It is time for parents to assert their children's rights to a safe, healthy, equal-opportunity educational experience whether in the classroom or on the court.

In a *Toronto Star* article about abusive coaching, award-winning investigative journalist Robert Cribb states that the rights of the child must be maintained within competitive sports:

> In addition to being mere bad form, abusive behind-the-bench conduct is also in breach of the UN Convention on the Rights of the Child, say researchers.
>
> The Convention's provisions require respect for the "physical, sexual and psychological integrity of the child," "sound and appropriate training, advice and guidance from competent individuals" and assurance that "sport is practised in a culture of understanding, peace, tolerance, equality of sexes, friendship and fair play."
>
> There is a "rich intersection between the rights of the child in general and the rights of the child in sports," says LaVoi.
>
> "Because we see sports in a play context, we think human rights concepts don't apply because they're so serious but, in fact, it is very applicable."[89]

---

[88] Lyndsey Layton, "David Boies: Eying Education Through a Civil Rights Lens," *Washington Post*, September 2014: http://www.campbellbrown.com/2014/09/washington-post-david-boies-eyeing-education-through-a-civil-rights-lens/
[89] Robert Cribb, "Out of Control Amateur Coaches Mentally Abuse Players," *The Toronto Star*, July 2010: http://www.thestar.com/sports/hockey/2010/07/08/outofcontrol_amateur_coaches_mentally_abuse_players.html

# CHAPTER FOUR

## BULLYING CAUSES BRAIN DAMAGE

A new wave of research into bullying's effects [shows] bullying can leave an indelible imprint on a teen's brain at a time when it is still growing and developing. Being ostracized by one's peers, it seems, can throw adolescent hormones even further out of whack, lead to reduced connectivity in the brain, and even sabotage the growth of new neurons.

These neurological scars, it turns out, closely resemble those borne by children who are physically and sexually abused in early childhood. Neuroscientists now know that the human brain continues to grow and change long after the first few years of life. By revealing the internal physiological damage that bullying can do, researchers are recasting it not as merely an unfortunate rite of passage but as a serious form of childhood trauma.[90]

– Emily Anthes for *The Boston Globe*

---

[90] Emily Anthes, "Inside the Bullies Brain: the Alarming Neuroscience of Taunting," *The Boston Globe*, 2010: http://www.boston.com/bostonglobe/ideas/articles/2010/11/28/inside_the_bullied_brain/

For any parent of a bullied child, Emily Anthes' article "Inside the Bullied Brain: The Alarming Neuroscience of Taunting" is extremely disturbing to read. The research it draws from specifies and documents in no uncertain terms that bullying causes physical brain damage. Although the article was written in 2010, the research stretches back to the late 1980s. There are few parents that would tolerate physical or sexual abuse of their child; these same parents should rise up against bullying, or even worse emotional abuse from adult to child, as according to neuroscientists bullying does the same damage.

  Despite substantial research, emotional abuse from teacher to child, or coach to student-athlete continues to be minimized and dismissed as less serious than physical or sexual abuse. This dismissal is impossible to understand considering the neuroscience that chronicles the scars bullying from peers, let alone emotional abuse by teachers or coaches, leaves on the brain. Dr. David Walsh, one of the world's leading authorities on children and teens, stresses the way in which "Brain science lends even more urgency to confronting the scourge of bullying" exactly because there are "studies suggesting that the brain changes are long-term and therefore can create emotional scars that last for a lifetime."[91] I doubt that when parents insist that "old-style coaching" is okay because it gets results and toughens kids up, they are informed about what is being done to their child's developing brain. Few parents would argue that winning high-school games excuses physical or sexual abuse by coaches. If emotional abuse does the same damage, then it too should never be tolerated or excused. However, parents may not know what the experts

---

[91] David Walsh with Erin Walsh, *Why do They Act that Way?: A Survival Guide to the Adolescent Brain for You and Your Teen*, 2nd edition, New York: Simon & Schuster, 2014 (254).

say about emotional abuse, but it is the job of teachers, school administrators and educational authorities to know.

The RCMP, Canada's federal police force, defines emotional abuse as "Verbal attacks or demeaning actions that impact on a child's self esteem and self worth."[92] More specific than "self esteem" and "self worth" are a series of significant studies that document the harm that bullying does to the developing brain, which has been shown to parallel the harm done by sexual and physical abuse, and yet it is allowed, in far too many cases, to do its harm without consequences. In the *Public Health Agency of Canada's* paper on psychological abuse by Deborah Doherty and Dorothy Berglund, they provide a variety of studies that put emotional abuse in the same category, or in an even worse one, than physical abuse: "Researchers (Dutton, Goodman and Bennett 2001, 180) have confirmed that psychological abuse is a common and significant form of interpersonal violence in terms of its frequency, and its short and long-term effects (Tomison and Tucci 1997). Moreover, several researchers have argued that victims experience greater trauma from ongoing, severe psychological abuse than from experiencing infrequent physical assault (Davis and Frieze 2002; Duncan 1999, 45-55; Guthrie 2001; Hildyard and Wolfe 2002, 679; Martin and Mohr 2002, 472-495; Sackett and Saunders 1999, 105)."[93] In a recent ground-breaking study by Duke University that followed almost two thousand students into adulthood, researchers such as William E. Copeland, Professor of Psychiatry concluded the following: "If the results of this study are dismaying because they indicate that bullying is permanently scarring, the findings also strengthen the argument for prevention. Copeland

---

[92] http://www.rcmp-grc.gc.ca/pubs/ccaps-spcca/chi-enf-eng.htm#Emotional
[93] http://www.phac-aspc.gc.ca/ncfv-cnivf/sources/fv/fv-psych-abus/index-eng.php

underscores this idea. 'Consider me a reluctant convert, but I'm starting to view bullying the same way I do abuse in the home,' he said. 'I honestly think the effects we're observing here are just as potent.'"[94] The focus of the Duke Study is peer bullying, which raises the concerning question: How permanently scarring is it when it involves a teacher bullying a student or a coach bullying a student-athlete?

The research Dr. Martin Teicher, Associate Professor of Psychiatry at Harvard Medical School conducted in 2002 found that "verbal abuse by parents was as psychologically damaging as physical abuse." More surprising, his research has shown that "kids suffered more depression, anxiety and other psychiatric disorders when bullied by peers than by parents."[95] If bullying in the school setting causes more harm than the home setting, and verbal abuse is just as damaging as physical abuse, what happens when teachers or coaches are doing the bullying at school?

Dr. Laurence Steinberg, a developmental psychologist specializing in adolescence, turns to neuroscience to describe the way school environments shape students' experiences:

> As neuroscientists are fond of saying, plasticity cuts both ways. By this they mean that the brain's malleability makes adolescence a period of tremendous opportunity – and great risk. If we expose our young people to positive, supportive environments, they will flourish. But if the environments are toxic, they will suffer in powerful and enduring ways.[96]

---

[94] http://www.slate.com/blogs/xx_factor/2013/02/20/new_duke_study_on_bullying_childhood_victims_bullies_and_bully_victims_all.html
[95] See Amy Anthes, "Inside the Bullied Brain: the Alarming Neuroscience of Taunting," *The Boston Globe*, November 28, 2010: http://www.boston.com/bostonglobe/ideas/articles/2010/11/28/inside_the_bullied_brain/?page=2
[96] Laurence Steinberg, *Age of Opportunity: Lessons from the New Science of Adolescence*, Boston and New York: Houghton, Mifflin, Harcourt, 2014.

Students at my former school were clear in their testimonies that the environment they had to endure to play their sport was toxic. They were clear that they were suffering. Only time will tell how long their suffering will endure. The Headmaster did not consult neuroscientists or emotional abuse experts when he received the student testimonies and interviewed them. Instead, he hired a lawyer. However, our legal system is out of touch with years of psychological, psychiatric, and neuroscientific studies that conclude bullying damages individuals, especially teenagers, in terrible and lasting ways. We know the police will press charges if a teacher or coach causes a physical bruise, but the police cannot intervene if a teacher or coach is causing neurological bruises that may lead to depression, anxiety, and in far too many cases, suicide. It used to be that we categorized these expressions of harm as "feelings" and considered them part of an emotional realm. However, research has shown that loss of concentration, anxiety, and depression result from *physical* changes to the brain and thus one is left wondering why we attribute seriousness to a bruise or welt on an arm, but do not accord the same concern when it's a bruise or welt done to a child's developing brain. Dr. David Walsh explains in his *Survival Guide to the Adolescent Brain* that neurological studies are "showing us how serious and long-term the damage can be. Studies reveal that there are long-lasting chemical and structural brain changes that account for the cognitive and emotional damage that can be as severe as the harm done by child abuse."[97]

In her book, *The Teenage Brain*, neuroscientist, Frances Jensen explains the correlation between mental illness in adolescence and stress:

---

[97] David Walsh with Erin Walsh, *Why do They Act that Way?: A Survival Guide to the Adolescent Brain for You and Your Teen*, 2nd edition, New York: Simon & Schuster, 2014 (252).

As adolescents' brains are maturing, their HPA axis, the hypothalamic-pituitary-adrenal axis, the body's chief stress-response mechanism, gets a workout. Researchers have found that clinical depression seems to emerge from a gradual dysregulation of the HPA axis from childhood into adolescence caused by greater-than-normal release of cortisol in the brain.[98]

Studies have now shown that stress from peer bullying produces high levels of cortisol in victims. I am not aware of any studies that test the levels of cortisol in children verbally abused by teachers or coaches. I do know that when our son returned from the Basketball Provincials in March 2012, his mouth was covered in sores that the doctor believed were due to cortisol. He could barely drink water for the pain.

In 2010, Dr. Teicher's MRI study provided further evidence of physical brain damage done by bullying: the study revealed "differences in myelination of the corpus callosum (the tissue connecting the two brain hemispheres) for kids abused by peers." He explains how this affects a student's ability to learn:

[Students] who reported having been mistreated by their peers had observable abnormalities in a part of the brain known as the corpus callosum — a thick bundle of fibers that connects the right and left hemispheres of the brain, and which is vital in visual processing, memory, and more. The neurons in their corpus callosums had less myelin, a coating that speeds communication between the cells — vital in an organ like the brain where milliseconds matter.[99]

---

[98] Frances E. Jensen with Amy Ellis Nutt, *The Teenage Brain: A Neuroscientist's Survival Guide to Raising Adolescents and Young Adults*, Toronto: Harper Collins, 2015.
[99] http://www.boston.com/bostonglobe/ideas/articles/2010/11/28/inside_the_bullied_brain/?page=2

Bullying in a school setting clearly does serious harm. Bullying does brain damage when it is by peers; one can reasonably conclude it also results in brain damage when teachers and coaches bully. In an earlier 2002 *Scientific American* article, Dr. Teicher explained that stress "sculpts the brain to exhibit various antisocial, though adaptive, behaviors. Whether it comes in the form of physical, emotional or sexual trauma [...] stress can set off a ripple of hormonal changes that permanently wire a child's brain to cope with a malevolent world." [100] Dr. Laurence Steinberg corroborates Teicher's findings when it comes to the effects bullying has on teenagers: "The adolescent brain is extraordinarily sensitive to stress." [101] We know emotional trauma can harm a child's brain in ways that parallel physical abuse, yet emotional abuse is not in the Criminal Code.

In a position paper for her Education Law Master's Program in Florida, *Extreme to Stop the Mean*, Mindy K. Reyes addresses our present failure to address the bullying epidemic that affects our world: "Research is there, examples are there, resources are there, but the shifting in responsibility is what will be pivotal in necessitating change to the current failing approach to this dilemma." [102] At present, the responsibility seems to lie with the victim while the bully, especially the adult bully, suffers little to no consequences. Reyes argues that we must face our failure to stop peer-bullying by putting it in the Criminal Code: "Just as our criminal justice system with the ability to impose sanctions, deters crime, so will bullying be deterred." I believe this applies even more powerfully when adults bully children, especially since, as Reyes states: "Since

---

[100] http://www.workplacebullying.org/2010/11/29/neuroscience_bullying/
[101] Laurence Steinberg, *Age of Opportunity: Lessons from the New Science of Adolescence*, Boston and New York: Houghton, Mifflin, Harcourt, 2014 (37).
[102] https://docs.google.com/document/d/1ZnJIKF2tzni_rxFBeJOfViSParyylvb bHJQlD3-M0X4/edit?usp=sharing

bullying overwhelmingly is classified as a learned behavior, we have to then conclude that it is not generally innate." If we can deter adults from bullying, it follows that children won't be *taught* to bully.

Dr. Teicher's findings that bullying harms the brain are comparable to research results published by Dr. Tracy Vaillancourt, Professor and Canada Research Chair of Children's Mental Health and Violence Prevention at the University of Ottawa. Vaillancourt found "higher levels of cortisol in boys bullied by peers. Too much cortisol can damage brain structures such as the hippocampus that is involved with learning and memory."[103] As Dr. Tracy Vaillancourt discovered in her 2008 research "cortisol may, in fact, underlie many of the adverse effects of bullying: It can weaken the functioning of the immune system, and at high levels can damage and even kill neurons in the hippocampus, potentially leading to memory problems that could make academics more difficult."[104] While we were worried about the painful damage cortisol appeared to have done to our son's mouth while at the basketball Provincials in 2012, we did not know that his shocking decline as a learner at the same time may well have been due to the harmful effects of spiking cortisol affecting his brain.

Dr. David Walsh addresses Dr. Teicher's research findings and further explains the physical impact that bullying has on the brain: "The amygdala is the brain's alarm center. When it is repeatedly activated the

---

[103] Dr. Tracy Vaillancourt is a Professor and Canada Research Chair in Children's Mental Health and Violence Prevention at the University of Ottawa in the Faculty of Education and the School of Psychology. She is also an adjunct professor in the Department of Psychology, Neuroscience & Behaviour at McMaster University and a core member of the Offord Centre for Child Studies. Dr. Vaillancourt's research examines the links between aggression and bio-psychosocial functioning and mental health, with particular focus on bully-victim relations.
[104] http://www.boston.com/bostonglobe/ideas/articles/2010/11/28/inside_the_bullied_brain/?page=3

brain is in a constant state of arousal. It's as if the radar is finely tuned, always ready to pick up the slightest hint of a threat. It is very difficult to concentrate, remember and learn when the brain is in survival mode, always scanning for danger." Dr. Walsh describes the specific impact of bullying on student learning: "[it] causes cognitive problems including impaired memory, attention, and concentration. It's hard for the bullied brain to learn when it's always in a state of high alert, prepared for the next attack."[105] If bullying from a peer harms the brain in multiple ways, imagine how much more severe the consequences would be when that bullying behavior is inflicted by a teacher on a student, or by a coach on a student-athlete. The abuse might occur on the court, but its impact is also felt in the classroom when the brain is harmed.

Our son had struggled with academics in Junior School and so we had an assessment done for him by an educational psychologist in grade six. With a diagnosis of dysgraphia and the accommodations of being able to use a computer, as well as have extra time for tests, our son worked hard to fulfill his academic potential. In grades seven, eight and nine, our son excelled. He earned major awards as a learner in grades seven and eight and in grades eight and nine he earned a place on the Headmaster's Honor Roll. However, in grade ten, everything changed. Now that we've read the student testimonies, we wonder if the drop in his marks was as a result of the bullying the team suffered from their coach who was the Assistant Coach on the Senior Team the following year. Our son had a second assessment done by the same educational psychologist that was completed after seven months of playing for the coach students reported on in their testimonies a year later. The psychologist's assessment showed

---

[105] David Walsh with Erin Walsh, *Why do They Act that Way?: A Survival Guide to the Adolescent Brain for You and Your Teen*, 2nd edition, New York: Simon & Schuster, 2014 (252).

shocking decline in our son's ability to process and recall information, to concentrate and to focus. At the time, our son did not tell the psychologist or us that he was suffering at the hands of his coach. The psychologist diagnosed him with Attention Deficit Disorder (ADD) and recommended medication to help him concentrate. The coach in grade ten was partially kept in check by another coach, but when he went on to be the Assistant Coach of the Senior Team, according to student testimonies, the emotional abuse not only continued the following year, it intensified greatly, as the Head Coach was even worse.

Although we supplied the lawyers hired by the School, as well as educational authorities with the psych-ed assessments that documented our son's decline in his ability to learn and the unexpected onset of ADD at age fifteen, none of them made reference to these documents. It appears that psych-ed assessments were not considered evidence of bullying or its impact on student learning. We watched our son decline from a student on the Headmaster's Honor Roll to a student who could not even write his exams in grades eleven and twelve. It is likely, based on research into the effects of emotional abuse in the coach-athlete relationship, that the inability of our son to process information, concentrate, or recall, resulting in the sudden and dramatic drop in his grades and the ADD diagnosis could be attributed to the emotional abuse he suffered as documented in student testimonies.

• • •

By all accounts our son was a very skilled basketball player. At my former school, a former university player, coaching intern and basketball coach described him in 2013:

> Best suited playing the off-guard position, [he] plays the game
> with a high basketball IQ, making quick decisions with excellent
> court vision. Very careful with the ball, he rarely commits
> turnovers or settles for bad shots. He does an excellent job

114

feeding the post, making cross-court skip passes, and starting the break with a firm outlet pass. Plus, he possesses an absolutely lethal first step. His face up/ triple threat / jab step game is far beyond his years and his mid range/ pull up/ back to the basket game is developing at an exponential rate. Lastly, [his] greatest strength lies in a high arcing shot that he is comfortable shooting coming off screens, off the dribble, or spotting up in transition. Being aware of basketball at all levels, with complete confidence I can say [he] is the best shooter in the entire province of British Columbia, and may just be the best shooter in the Country.

Coach of nationally ranked teams and former Assistant Director of Athletics at University of Victoria also described our son in 2013:

Playing guard and wing, this young man is 6'4," 200 pounds and is still maturing physically. He is strong and exceptionally smart both athletically as well as intuitively. [He] has the ability to move both with the ball and away from the ball. He can create opportunities for himself and others. While comfortable driving to the basket and sharing his elbows, he is equally able to step back gracefully and consistently deliver three point shots one after another while under pressure.

In 2012, before he quit the team, on his grade eleven report card, the School's Head Coach wrote that he would be "a much sought after player" by university teams. He positioned him on the "cusp of being one of the best ever performers [at this School]." This comment carries considerable weight because one of the student-athletes who played on the team in grade twelve went on to be a legend in the NBA. *HoopLife Forums* identified our son in 2012 as one of two "key players" to watch on his team. The other key player *HoopLife* identified barely saw court time the following season, despite his skill. After his mom complained about alcohol being left visible in the coaches' hotel room in front of the team, this key player sat on the bench for almost the whole season.

When a student has a learning disability, it often means they've had to work twice as hard as a regular student to do well in school. It also may mean they felt "stupid" until learning assessments revealed they were in fact bright, but just didn't process information in the same way as other students. Accommodations such as computer use and extra time allow them to show their potential, as they did for our son. Nonetheless, since a learning disability can be a barrier to a student successfully applying to their university of choice, our son planned to leverage his talents on the basketball court and apply as a student-athlete, hoping to play ball at the university level. The BC Ministry of Education's *Supporting Our Students: A Guide for Independent School Personnel Responding to Child Abuse* specifies that students with disabilities need particular vigilance:

> While all children are vulnerable, some are more vulnerable than others. Children with disabilities and very young children may not be able to protect themselves, and are particularly dependent on adults for their safety and wellbeing. As a service provider, you should be especially vigilant in cases of suspected abuse or neglect involving such children.[106]

A student-athlete with learning disabilities launched a lawsuit against Rutgers' coach Mike Rice; Rutgers was also named in the suit for keeping Coach Rice in his position even though the Administration had prior knowledge that he was an abusive coach. "[Derrick] Randall's lawsuit, filed Friday and made public Monday, claims he suffers from learning disabilities and experienced emotional trauma from Rice's behavior. Randall left Rutgers this year because: 'Defendants, directly and/or through their agents, willfully, recklessly, negligently and with deliberate indifference, placed Derrick in a hostile environment in which he was

---

[106] http://www.bced.gov.bc.ca/independentschools/is_resources/SOS_guide.pdf

regularly and continuously subjected to physical, mental, verbal and emotional abuse of the most outrageous nature,' the suit claims."[107]

Several student testimonies describe our son having been treated similarly by his coaches: yelled at, humiliated, sworn at, grabbed and held in close for the teacher to yell in his face, and being physically stopped when he attempted to break away from the coach's grip on his arm or jersey. According to student testimonies, our son was lambasted with homophobic slurs and berated repeatedly as part of the team, and singled out for specifically targeted outbursts in front of the team. Informed of our son's learning disability, this was particularly cruel since, as teachers in particular should know, students with learning disabilities are especially vulnerable to bullying from peers, let alone from teachers or coaches.

As a parent explains in a *Globe and Mail* article on the effects of peer bullying, "He noted the learning disabilities experienced by both Ashkan and Amanda. 'When kids have any kind of disability, they are an easy target,' Mr. Sultani said. 'They are vulnerable, often targeted by other kids with low self-esteem.'"[108] Like teenager Amanda Todd, who captured the world's attention with the tragic goodbye she posted on YouTube before committing suicide, Mr. Sultani's teenaged son also committed suicide. At my former school, the Head Coach who called the team "fucking retards," or Assistant Coach who stood by and listened to this being said and did nothing, were well aware that our son had a learning disability. They must then have known that the word "retard"

---

[107] http://espn.go.com/new-york/mens-college-basketball/story/_/id/10114698/former-rutgers-scarlet-knights-player-sues-coach-mike-rice-behavior
[108] Rod Mickleburgh, "Before Amanda Todd, the Sultani family suffered silently," *The Globe and Mail*, October 23, 2012: http://www.theglobeandmail.com/news/british-columbia/before-amanda-todd-the-sultani-family-suffered-silently/article4633468/

resonated with particular pain for him. Rutgers' player, Derrick Randall's lawsuit spoke volumes to us as parents. For our son's sake, we wanted to hold the Headmaster and Board Members accountable because they were informed a year before about "child abuse" on the basketball teams and did nothing effective to stop it. However, we had to drop the lawsuit since we could not afford to battle such a wealthy institution in court.

One student at my former school wrote an essay on the effects of teacher bullying and said that not only did it affect her grades, but it also made her physically ill. Another student in fact became so physically sick that she had to return home just before exams in first year university. Doctors who examined her believed based on blood work results that she might have lupus. Only in time, when she began to tell her doctor about the bullying she suffered at school from her Coach, now confirmed by multiple student testimonies, did her body begin to recover. Not long after, she was diagnosed with PTSD. Multiple studies show that, in adolescents, PTSD is a demonstrated result of emotional abuse:

> A 2003 study by Dr. Stephen Joseph at University of Warwick found that "verbal abuse can have more impact upon victims' self-worth than physical attacks, such as punching…stealing or the destruction of belongings." Verbal attacks such as name-calling and humiliation can negatively affect self-worth to a dramatic degree. Rather than helping them to "toughen up," 33 percent of verbally abused children suffer from significant levels of post-traumatic stress disorder (PTSD). This is the same disorder that haunts many war veterans and victims of violent assault.

> A 2005 UCLA study demonstrated that there is no such thing as "harmless name-calling." The study, by Jaana Juvonen, Ph.D. found that those 6th graders who had been victimized felt humiliated, anxious, angry and disliked school more. What's more, the students who merely observed another student being

bullied reported more anxiety and disliked school to a greater degree than those who did not witness any bullying.

The major lesson here is that the more a child is bullied, or observes bullying, in a particular environment, the more they dislike being in that environment. So any bullying done by coaches will virtually guarantee a victim's hasty exit from the sport.[109]

There is burgeoning neuroscientific research that helps explain the onset of PTSD, and the athlete's traumatized associations with the once loved sport, when we learn that the brain as the control center for the body is adversely affected by bullying. Surely the significant damage done to the brain as a result of bullying is as serious as a physical strike to the body, if not more so. And yet because unlike a bruise or a cut, the damage cannot be seen, we do not treat it in the same manner. This is such primitive thinking. As Barbara Coloroso explains:

> Using fMRIs, researchers have demonstrated that when a child is intentionally excluded from his or her peer group or verbally taunted, the brain's pain response is similar to the pain response to a physical assault [. . .] Targeted children who are shunned and isolated by their peers will often express the wish that the bully had just hit them – it would have been less painful.[110]

Law enforcement and those we entrust with the care of our children must be trained to see psychological, emotional and verbal abuse in the same way as physical or sexual abuse. The Criminal Code needs to change.

---

[109] John Schinnerer, Ph.D, "'Help, My Coach is a Bully!': The Consequences of Verbally Abusive Coaching": http://www.selfgrowth.com/articles/Help_My_Coach_is_a_Bully_The_Consequences_of_Verbally_Abusive_Coaching.html
[110] Barbara Coloroso, *The Bully, the Bullied, and the not-so-innocent Bystander*, updated edition, Harper Collins: 2015 (50).

College basketball reporter for ESPN, Dana O'Neill articulates the slamming force words have when delivered from a coach to a student-athlete:

> Words matter, and they carry weight with as much heft as a shove. Every time a university looks the other way or dishes out a dismissive punishment, it's like sending an abuser back into the home of a domestic violence victim.
>
> And the argument, as Pernetti made, that he "didn't have players lining up outside his office" to complain is as disingenuous as it is foolish. Ask people who work with people who are abused. They're afraid to speak out, especially if, as with Rice, the guy is still empowered.[111]

O'Neill is not deferring to neuroscience to make her case; however, as a sports reporter she does not have any problem distinguishing between motivation and harm. Moreover, she has no problem understanding why athletes maintain a conflicted code of silence. Her experienced assessment of the force of verbal abuse becomes even more powerful with the added documentation by neuroscientists of harm caused to the brain.

In the March 2007 issue of the *Journal of Neuroscience*, one study conducted by Drs. Rosanne M. Thomas, Gregory Hotsenpiller, and Daniel A. Peterson "demonstrated the impact of bullying by a dominant other" which "caused hippocampal damage."[112] Insert the term "teacher" or "coach" for "dominant other" and, rather than falling back on the "old style coaching" argument, understand that the victims' brains are being harmed. Serious steps need to be taken to provide student-athletes with

---

[111] Dana O'Neill, "With Mike Rice, We Must Draw A Line," *ESPN* April 2013: http://espn.go.com/mens-college-basketball/story/_/id/9126491/mike-rice-actions-rutgers-reprehensible-tolerated-college-basketball
[112] http://www.jneurosci.org/content/27/11/2734.short

protection from abusive coaches, just as students need protection from abusive teachers.

Another study has shown that chronic stress, such as that caused by bullying, causes "mid-brain structural changes" like "frontostriatal reorganization" and therefore affects decision-making.[113] We constantly worry about the impaired decision-making capacity of adolescents; imagine how much more at risk they are when they are the targets of teacher bullying and their brain is being harmed in exactly the area responsible for learning and decision-making. Another study, in the journal *Psychosomatic Medicine*, reveals that high cortisol levels are associated with feelings of shame and threats to one's self-image.[114] One of the most vulnerable aspects of an adolescent is his or her "self-image" and for a teacher to compromise it in any way, let alone by bullying, clearly causes significant harm.

Dr. Joseph Burgo examines a case of cyber-bullying that resulted in the young victim's suicide. A group of her peers were sending repeated messages saying she was "ugly" and should "drink bleach." Burgo comments on the particularly vulnerable time of adolescence:

> Middle-schoolers need badly to feel that they belong, that they have value and respect within this new social hierarchy. In order to establish their own power and importance, bullies identify and then harass their victims (the losers), thereby elevating themselves as social winners. Through physical and psychological persecution, the bully off-loads her own shame and fear of not belonging. In the process, she deprives her target of

---

[113] See E. Dias-Ferreira, et al. *Science* 325, 2009: 621-625.

[114] See T. Gruenewald et al., "Acute threat to the social self: Shame, social self-esteem, and cortisol activity," *Psychomatic Medicine* 66, 2004: 915-924.

social membership, making the victim feel that she has no standing within their world.[115]

The research shows that a teacher or coach who calls an adolescent boy a "fucking pussy" is quite possibly doing far more damage to him than a teacher who actually hit him. A coach who throws her clipboard down and walks out on her team saying they're an "embarrassment" is more likely to cause lasting harm to her students' memory and ability to learn than if she struck a player with her hand. A teacher or coach who yells in a boy's face "that is fucking soft" is quite likely going to harm the student's ability to concentrate in academic classes, not to mention his sense of self-esteem, and therefore also impact his success in school and his ability to make decisions. The inability to concentrate and do well in school will be reinforced in brutal ways if the teacher then calls the students "retards." All this conduct was recorded in the multiple student testimonies taken at my former school.

When one measures the harm done to a student's brain, verbal, emotional, and psychological bullying is as serious as physical abuse. Yet law enforcement and child protection agencies will step in and lay charges or remove a child from an unsafe environment for a physical strike, but until emotional abuse is in the Criminal Code, the police cannot do anything for the student who may well suffer brain damage as a result of teacher or coach bullying. In a 2015 article in *Maclean's Magazine* about the teenage brain, Tamsin McMahon turns to neurologists to debunk the myth that only the first three years of life are critical for brain development. McMahon looks at the significant neurological studies

---

[115] Joseph Burgo, "All Bullies Are Narcissists: Stories of bullying and hazing in the news break down to narcissism and insecurity," *The Atlantic*, November 2013: http://www.theatlantic.com/health/archive/2013/11/all-bullies-are-narcissists/281407/

being published over the last ten years or so that argue "an improved understanding of the developing brain carries a growing acknowledgement that teenagers are uniquely susceptible to great risks." According to Harvard neuroscientist, Frances Jensen, "the teenage years comprise one of the brain's most critical periods for development – likely every bit as crucial as early childhood."[116] It is incumbent on all teachers, administrators, Ministries of Education, Commissioners of Teacher Regulation and lawmakers, to be informed about what neuroscience knows and has documented about the vulnerable brains of teenagers. As McMahon notes, the impact of bullying "has also been linked to changes in the teen brain that can raise the risk of mood disorders or learning disabilities. Scientists are only starting to explore those vulnerabilities – and the extent to which they may be permanent." In the medical community, there is enough research done to create urgency around the vulnerability of teens. McMahon quotes Harvard psycho-biologist, Bertha Madras who told a Boston medical research conference in 2014, "The derailment of an adolescent may or may not be reversible and we have to understand it." Although more research is needed, the data already collected reveals the dangerous impact of bullying:

> The hormone THP, which is released by the body in response to stress, has a calming effect in adults, but actually seems to have the opposite effect in teens, increasing stress. It's one reason why teens are prone to anxiety and post-traumatic stress disorder. It's also a good reason, Jensen says, why parents and schools should be sensitive to the problem of bullying.[117]

---

[116] Tamsin McMahon, "Inside Your Teenager's Scary Brain," *Maclean's Magazine*, January 2015: 48-53.
[117] Ibid.

In grade twelve, our son was diagnosed with PTSD by Dr. Alan Goldberg who specifically stated the condition resulted from the teacher bullying combined with the "hostile" environment created at the School by the Headmaster's process. The Headmaster did not respond to the letter except to exempt our son from writing his grade twelve exams. While it is a common reaction to a highly stressful environment, withdrawal from academics is not at all healthy for the adolescent brain:

> It's for this reason that Jay Giedd, an expert in child and adolescent brain imaging at the U. S. National Institute of Mental Health, describes the teen years as a special period of "use it or lose it" for the brain. Brain cells grown in childhood that continue to get used in adolescence form new connections, while those that go unused wither away. It's also another reason why parents should be anxious about what happens during the teen years – adolescence now appears to be a period that can make or break a child's intelligence.[118]

The process undertaken at my former school to address multiple student testimonies about teacher-coach bullying resulted in the harm spreading even more intensely from the court into the classroom. When multiple students report that they are being bullied by coaches or teachers, and School Administrators either do nothing, or act as if the problem lies with the students, it is little wonder that students and parents find it hard to speak up. However, the consequences are so dire for the adolescent brain that we as a society must change how we handle student reports of abuse.

• • •

Although we have more and more information about the serious consequences of bullying among peers, let alone emotional abuse from

---

[118] Tamsin McMahon, "Inside Your Teenager's Scary Brain," *Maclean's Magazine*, January 2015: 48-53.

teachers and coaches, there continues to be a struggle to protect children and teenagers. Parents should be worried, and especially in situations where schools or universities are invested in protecting their teachers, coaches, and brand rather than students. A massive increase in reports of abuse in British independent schools, specifically boarding schools, signals that far too often children are *not* being protected according to child abuse solicitor Liz Dux:

> Independent schools, Joel Shaw points out, are, in the end, businesses. The recent apology made at the BSA [Boarding Schools Association] annual conference, he says, was at least in part about managing their brand reputation. Prospective parents may want a more cast iron guarantee than an apology and a promise to do better. Dux observes pointedly that nothing has changed in English and Welsh law to compel schools to react any differently to suspected or known abuse than they did in the past. "There have been cases even in the last four years where heads have had reports [of abuse] and have not actioned those reports and abuse has occurred subsequently," she says. "That's why there has to be mandatory reporting of abuse." Without it, she does not believe children are safe.[119]

The vast majority of abuse reports being presently dealt with in British schools are from incidents that happened twenty to thirty years ago. This suggests that children need far better protection during childhood. The very fact that they are children means they can't protect themselves or report that they are being abused, especially when the adult is in a caregiver position and has power over the child. We need to admit that our laws are failing them, our monitoring systems are failing them, our

---

[119] Louise Tickle, "Britain's Elite Boarding Schools Are Facing an Explosion of Abuse Allegations," *Newsweek*, September 2014: http://www.newsweek.com/britain-elite-boarding-schools-facing-explosion-abuse-allegations-267201

institutions that are supposed to protect children are failing them. As a group of seriously concerned parents, over the course of three years, we appealed to School Administrators, the Board of Governors, the Inspector of Independent Schools, the police, the Commissioner for Teacher Regulation, the Ministry of Education, the Auditor General, the Ombudsperson (still in process) and the Attorney General. Not one of these empowered offices actually held the teachers accountable for their conduct or redressed the wrongs done to multiple students. Half of them did not even reply to our concerns.

As a society, we tend to believe that sexual abuse is clearly understood and quickly acted upon; in contrast, emotional abuse is tricky to identify and so it's not acted upon, but if we return to Malcolm Gladwell's 2012 article in the *New Yorker* and the story of a teacher in a Canadian elementary school, we see once again the difficulty parents face in trying to protect their children from abuse. The parallels, with our struggle to protect our children at my former school, are striking. As Gladwell recounts:

> The families then learned that there had been a previous complaint by a child against Clay, and they took their case to the school superintendent. He, too, advised caution. "If allegations do not clearly indicate sexual abuse, a gray area exists," he wrote to them. "The very act of overt investigation carries with it a charge, a conviction, and a sentence, a situation which is repugnant to fair-minded people." He was responsible not just to the children but also to the professional integrity of his teachers. What did they have? Just the story of three young boys, and young boys do, after all, have wild imaginations.[120]

---

[120] Malcolm Gladwell, "In Plain View: How Child Molesters Get Away With It," *The New Yorker*, September 2012: http://www.newyorker.com/magazine/2012/09/24/in-plain-view

Cautioned by the School superintendent about the "gray area" and told the boys had made it up essentially, the families went to the police who asked the children to be more specific: "The three boys named other boys who they said had been subjected to Mr. Clay's advances. Those boys, however, denied everything."[121] At my former school, there was a comparable pattern. The lawyers hired by the Headmaster and Board said that they found a majority of students who denied the abuse, which allowed them to argue the minority were a whole variety of things: liars, misinterpreting, resentful of having to work hard, unable to transition into higher level sports, too sensitive. There was no discussion about how the Headmaster had breached confidentiality and three boys had been exposed to the school community and targeted by peer bullying which surely made many students even more fearful of reporting in supposedly "confidential" interviews set up once again by the Headmaster. The lawyers' assessments of students, that focus on never-seen-before flaws in their characters, rather than hold adults accountable, compare to Malcolm Gladwell's analysis of sexual abuse and how molesters get away with it: the children have "wild imaginations" or are "exaggerating" or don't know what tickling and wrestling is all about with teachers. In the fall of 2012, at my former school, even when one of the teachers, in view of multiple teachers and a great number of students, yelled at a student and physically shoved him due to a disagreement in a supposedly fun Dodge Ball tournament, still nothing was done. He behaved this way while under investigation by the Commissioner for Teacher Regulation and still his conduct was not seen as corroborating the description of his behavior in the student testimonies. In fact, he was given a promotion while under investigation. Malcolm Gladwell's title for his article speaks powerfully

---

[121] Ibid.

to our societal failure to address abuse even when we witness it: "In Plain View: How Child Molesters Get Away with It." Gladwell documents the way in which adults assume the abuser's innocence when there are clear indicators, namely the reporting by multiple children, that he or she is harmful:

> A new, more specific allegation against Clay surfaced. He resigned, and went to see a therapist. But still the prosecutor's office didn't feel that it had enough evidence to press charges. And within the school there were teachers who felt that Clay was innocent. "I was running into my colleagues who were saying, 'Did you know that some rotten parents trumped up these charges against this poor man?' one teacher told van Dam. The teacher added, not just one person. Many teachers said this."[122]

At my former school, the Headmaster did not say that fourteen students had come forward with corroborating testimonies that recorded homophobic slurs, berating, screaming, degrading, swearing, restraining, throwing objects, pushing students to play when they were sick or injured, grabbing jerseys or arms, shunning, favoritism. Instead he made an announcement to School faculty that some students had had "an unhappy experience" on the boys' Senior Basketball team. Given the obtuse way the situation was down-played, the story that then seemed to circulate through the school community was along the lines of 'several parents complained; the parents' issues are about playing time; they're trying to hijack the PE department, some rotten parents trumped up these charges against these poor teachers.'

Reversal is a powerful tool to use, especially against children who struggle and oftentimes fail to assert their rights to safe, fair, and healthy treatment from the adults in their world.

---

[122] Ibid.

Unlike emotional abuse, sexual abuse *is* in the Criminal Code, and therefore one can reasonably assume at least the police *could* have intervened and protected students from Mr. Clay. However, Malcolm Gladwell's article makes one pause. Gladwell's story made me realize that even now, even with sexual abuse being defined in the Criminal Code, the way in which children's complaints about abuse are approached and handled is *abuser-sensitive*, not *victim-sensitive*. Still, I can't help believe that if the police could have intervened at my former school and protected these students from what they concluded to be a "definite pattern in the complaints, all pointing to verbal and emotional abuse," then perhaps these athletes would have been able to finish high-school without an unfair black mark on their characters, without having to carry the insinuated label of liar stemming from the report released by the Headmaster and Board. They would not have been the targets for peer bullies who echoed the terms their coaches had used such as "pussy." They would have been able to play basketball free from the kind of teacher bullying they reported in their testimonies. Some could have used their skills as athletes on their university applications to try and play on university teams or apply for athletic scholarships. They could have written their exams and attended their graduation ceremonies without panic attacks and fear of further humiliation. They wouldn't have been threatened with being beaten up by peers for having spoken up against the coach. If the police had the legal backing to intervene then a great deal of suffering by students might have been avoided.

Gladwell's article, with its reference to the "grey area," whether it's sexual or emotional abuse, puts child protection in doubt and suggests that our abuser-sensitive society privileges adults over children regardless of the nature of the abuse. It is hard to protect children from sex abuse and seemingly impossible to protect them from emotional abuse even though,

129

according to multiple studies, bullying done by an adult to children can negatively impact them throughout their lives: "Emotional abuse has serious, long term effects on children and can often outlast the impact of neglect or physical injury."[123] Surely there is enough reputable neuroscience in place to change the laws and protect the highly vulnerable brains of children and teenagers from bullying especially by adults in positions of trust and power. Surely there is enough documentation of our present failures to change our legal system so that it protects child-victims rather than protects adult-abusers.

---

[123] http://haltnow.ca/what-is-abuse/child-emotional-abuse/emotional-child-abuse-definition

# Chapter Five

# The Headmaster Exposes Certain Students

I am wondering if you are contemplating next year having the coaches teach and lead outdoor leadership programs etc. I cannot tell you how opposed I am to this. There will be a "special group of sensitive children" created - the ones who cannot handle the tough guys - the real men. You must isolate the abusers not the abused.

– from an email a parent sent to the Headmaster, May 2012

Throughout April and May 2012, the Headmaster privately supported students who had come forward, but when he went before the faculty and school community in June for his first, long-awaited statement about the abuse allegations, he behaved in a very different way. In his public address, the Headmaster stated that the allegations were limited to a number of students who were 'complaining' on the boys' Senior Basketball team, when he was well informed that there were also coaching issues with the Junior boys' team, and with the girls' Senior team, not to mention players on teams from previous years. At this meeting, where the speech focused solely on the boys' Senior Basketball team, the Headmaster minimized the seriousness of the abuse allegations so it seemed to those in attendance as if the problem lay with the students

131

who had come forward rather than the coaches. Not counting the Assistant Coach's son or a player whose father was the Assistant Coach's friend, and not counting a number of boys who boarded in residence, and could *not* be asked if they wanted to speak up, there were a majority of boys on the Senior Team who gave testimonies about the coaches' bullying conduct. The Headmaster did not say this. Nor did he inform faculty or families that the police had concluded there was "a definite pattern in the complaints, all pointing to verbal and emotional abuse" on the boys' and the girls' team; instead, the Headmaster told faculty and families that the police established that there was "no abuse." He said some boys on the team had "unhappy experiences."

Rather than discuss the *abusive teacher* conduct as reported by so many students, the Headmaster kept the focus on the *students* and made it appear as if they were dissatisfied individuals. One faculty member spoke up and asked how the Headmaster was going to protect teachers from "whiny students." Not one teacher in the meeting asked for further details about the allegations or seemed to show much in the way of concern, nor did anyone ask what kind of support the students who spoke up might need. The faculty at my former school are a very caring group of educators; however, they were put into an untenable situation because the teachers were not suspended during the investigations. Despite serious allegations of emotional abuse from so many students, the teachers remained on campus, teaching their courses, coaching and even maintaining their position as house-parents in the residences. Parents were never informed that not one or two – but fourteen students had given detailed testimonies describing the bullying done to them by four teachers.

Hardly surprising with the four teachers in attendance at the meeting, no one asked why they were not being suspended or at least off campus so a proper and thorough investigation could be conducted in a judgment-free environment where other students or concerned parents could come forward. There was no material discussion of what constitutes emotional or psychological abuse. There was no outlining of the standards to which teachers must adhere in BC, governed by the relatively new and notably strict Teacher Regulation Branch that has disciplined teachers for swearing, or raising their voice or saying a derogatory term in a student's presence, even in an isolated incident. There was no discussion around zero tolerance for bullying and the way it would be disciplined especially if it was done by a teacher. There was no explanation of why emotional abuse was so harmful to adolescents in terms of their self-esteem or their brain development. And there was no reference to just how vulnerable those students now were who had spoken up about the abuse they had suffered.

The Ministry of Education's *BC Handbook for Action on Child Abuse and Neglect* states that personnel responding to child abuse allegations need to be aware that "Children who may have been abused or neglected are particularly vulnerable. It is critical that, in responding to their needs, we take every caution to avoid upsetting or traumatizing them any further."[124] However, no such cautions were taken at my former school. Likewise, there was no discussion of how the Headmaster would create a safe environment for other students to come forward without fear of repercussions. Yet as the *World Health Organization* and *International Society for the Prevention of Child Abuse and Neglect* advises:

> If a child discloses abuse or neglect, it is essential that the person to whom the disclosure is made should respond appropriately, to support the child. This will avoid undermining the subsequent investigation, which would put the child at further risk. It is common for children to give a small piece of information first to

---

[124] http://www.bced.gov.bc.ca/independentschools/is_resources/SOS_guide.pdf

see how adults react and later to divulge more when they feel safe.[125]

If school administrators receive reports of child abuse and want to encourage students to come forward and report on what happened, it is crucial that to create a safe environment, the teachers named must therefore be suspended, or at the very least be asked to work off campus. Now, if school administrators *don't* want children to feel safe, *don't* want them to divulge any more information, and *don't* want to encourage further children from coming forward, keeping the teachers in positions of power at school is an excellent way to establish an *unsafe* environment, thereby ensuring no other children report their experiences. Moreover, it is an extremely effective way to intimidate those who have already spoken up.

At my former school, the Headmaster allowed the teachers reported on to keep coaching, teaching, being house parents, and running leadership workshops. As one parent expresses the impact of the Headmaster's decision not to suspend the teachers in an email:

> You have said the first order of business is that [one teacher] and [the other] will not coach basketball, but [one of these teachers] can have access to young men on the rugby field? With the documentation you have of his conduct (perhaps dating back as far as 1984), this decision is very concerning as the message that is now being presented at the school is that basketball parents complained, so to satisfy them the administration needs to pull him from basketball, but [this teacher] is actually fine, and his conduct is fine, so it will be business as usual in his other work with other athletes in his care. The optics of this kind of decision

---

[125] Alexander Butchart and Tony Kahane, *Preventing Child Maltreatment: A Guide to Taking Action and Generating Evidence*, World Health Organization and the International Society for the Prevention of Child Abuse and Neglect, 2006: http://whqlibdoc.who.int/publications/2006/9241594365_eng.pdf?ua=1

are that specific parents are vocal and controlling and can affect teachers in negative ways.

The reference to 1984 is due to a teacher at the school who had been asked by the then Headmaster to speak to this same Assistant Coach because his student-athletes were far too often in tears. There appears to be no records kept of this. From behind the closed doors of his office and via email, the Headmaster kept saying student safety and wellbeing were paramount, but in the school community, he was very visibly supporting the teacher-coaches. It was confusing and worrisome for me as a teacher, and for the students and their parents. Knowing how much our son was suffering along with the other students, it was also very upsetting and incredibly stressful. It frustrated the parents, as we felt we were failing to protect our children.

Without ever fully informing faculty of the allegations contained in the student testimonies – which did not require attaching any names as the students complained about the same conduct over and over again, year after year – the Headmaster announced he wanted to hear from students who had "happy experiences" playing on the basketball teams. He appeared to turn the reporting of emotional abuse into a distracting dispute that set teacher against teacher, student against student, and parent against parent. Instead of supporting the students who reported being bullied by teachers, he began what appeared to be a popularity contest.

● ● ●

By May 2012, the Headmaster had heard from at least thirty parents, read at least thirteen written testimonies from students, interviewed at least eight students directly, received an eleven-page document and a statement from the police outlining a pattern of verbal and emotional abuse occurring within the Basketball programs. However, despite his prior commitment to assign different coaches to several of the

135

following year's teams, take steps to heal the "emotional bruises" of the students involved, and honor his offer that the school would pay for psychological counseling for all students subjected to the teacher-coaches' actions, the Headmaster reversed his position and said he could not make a decision about what to do.

The Headmaster retained a lawyer who was brought in ostensibly to resolve the "dispute." When I met with this lawyer at the Headmaster's request, he patted a binder and told me that "prestigious" families had written in to support the teachers under investigation. I was at a loss to understand, as a parent and as a teacher, how that was relevant. I asked him how it was possible that Alumni had even been informed of what I understood were confidential student matters. He said "someone" from within the School must have contacted them. I found it difficult to wrap my mind around the idea that this lawyer was focused on the teachers' reputations and that he was seemingly hired to protect them, and therefore the school, rather than to ensure the matter was fully investigated and appropriate action taken to protect future students. This was my introduction to the sad irony of how bullies are often treated when they are called to account for their actions: the authorities in charge act as if *the bullies* have reason to be defended and protected. I learned in that moment, and have since confirmed through extensive research, that bullying communities at schools, universities, or workplaces flourish by means of reversal: the victims are blamed and the perpetrators are protected.

In this context, it is worthwhile to return to Rod Mickleburgh's *Globe and Mail* article, written after Amanda Todd's suicide as a result of bullying. He consulted with another family whose son, Ashkan Sultani, also committed suicide after being bullied. Ashkan's father pointed out that both his son and Amanda were vulnerable because they had learning disabilities. Rather than be accorded special care, as the Ministry of

Education documents state educators and administrators must use, Ashkan's father found that there was a reversal: bullies were exonerated and victims were held accountable: "Too often, [Ashkan's father] said, school officials become defensive when approached by parents with concerns their child is being bullied. 'They don't want to admit there's a problem. Or, the first thing they do is try to find out what is wrong with the person getting bullied. How come he doesn't fit in?'"[126] This man's son was at a public school and the bullies were children; imagine how much more intense this dynamic is if the bullying takes place in an independent school (whose reputation is at risk) and students have reported that the bullies are teachers or coaches. Rather than adult abusers being investigated, held accountable and potentially losing their jobs for their harmful conduct and breach of trust, it appears all too often that child victims and their parents are held accountable for putting in jeopardy the reputations of teachers and coaches and therefore the school itself.

Likewise, whistleblowers are suddenly seen as problem employees when they stand up and speak out about the abuse they witness. At Rutgers University, Assistant Coach Eric Murdock, whose video showed Mike Rice emotionally and physically abusing his players, did not have his contract renewed, and I ultimately resigned from my job due to the defamation of my character and the toxic atmosphere around me. I attempted to hold the Headmaster and Board to account for what I believe to be unfair treatment as a whistleblower. However, even with a lawyer working pro bono, filing in court is costly and I could not afford to

---

[126] Rod Mickleburgh, "Before Amanda Todd, the Sultani family suffered silently," *The Globe and Mail*, October 23, 2012: http://www.theglobeandmail.com/news/british-columbia/before-amanda-todd-the-sultani-family-suffered-silently/article4633468

fight such a wealthy institution. People who can draw on an institution's funds are able to afford extensive legal resources and processes, but someone on a teacher's salary will struggle to afford justice. In my eight years at the School, I never had a complaint, produced excellent results on externally marked exams, and spent far beyond the required time in extracurricular projects for students. The fact that the Board Member had me collect parental information for him, the fact that the Headmaster had me collect student testimonies for him and attend one of the student interviews surely speaks to my trustworthy reputation. All of this changed however when I refused to participate in the reversal whereby the students would be positioned as at fault and the teachers would be praised for their professionalism.

The lawyer hired by the School, the one armed with a binder full of self-selected letters praising the coaches, acted as though the students' testimonies were neutralized by letters of support from School Alumni. As if the situation called for a negotiated solution, the lawyer represented himself as an expert in dispute resolution rather than focusing on the facts: a Lawyer/ parent's eleven-page document detailing "child abuse"; concerns expressed by upwards of thirty parents; thirteen students giving detailed testimonies providing corroborating evidence of serious bullying; and finally, the police report establishing that indeed there was a "definite pattern in the complaints, all pointing to verbal and emotional abuse." He acted as though it was a popularity contest and planned to argue that the bullying teachers were more popular than the students asking for protection.

• • •

As whistleblower, misrepresented by the Headmaster's process, I had grown accustomed to the glares of a number of my colleagues over the past two months, the uncomfortable silence when I went into the staff lounge, the lack of response if I asked certain other teachers a question. It

138

was understandable, stressful, and sad. People will naturally draw their own conclusions in the absence of facts, but when his peers and even some teachers started to direct misplaced anger and threats at my son and other students who spoke up, my anxiety and misery grew exponentially. Our son started asking to stay home from school and having extreme headaches. He began to suffer panic attacks. One of his concerned teachers even wrote me the following email in June 2012:

> I have noticed that [your son] appears despondent and not his usual self. It is not my intent to pry but I just wanted you to know that I am here to support him especially as he prepares for the upcoming Economics exam. He is doing so well in this course and I so want him to excel in the exam as he has proven himself a fine student of economics.

Our son told us that two boys had started bullying him in that class in response to the Headmaster's process. We informed the Headmaster. He spoke to the boys and informed us that they denied bullying directed at our son. Although they admitted that they said "pussy," they added that they hadn't meant our son to hear it. The boys went on to win Athletic Awards from the Coaches that evening. Our son didn't write his Economics exam, or any of his other exams. He did not attend his grade eleven graduation ceremonies that year or the following year.

The Headmaster's process isolated a group of teenagers characterized, so it appeared to the School community, as particularly whiny or sensitive students who couldn't handle competitive sports. In June 2012, as recorded in an email to another parent, the Headmaster told the Assistant Coach, identified in student testimonies as a bully, which boys had come forward. He writes, "Just to clarify: the boys [the Coach] was asked not to engage with were the boys on the Senior Basketball team who had come forward. He has abided by this step." The Headmaster promised confidentiality to students when he asked them to

139

give testimonies and be interviewed in-person and yet he himself informed the Assistant Coach against whom so many players had lodged complaints.

Not all the students who spoke up were subsequently bullied by their peers, and so it seemed as if the Headmaster and the Assistant Coach only chose three students to expose to the school community. This made it appear as though there were only a few students who spoke up. Since it was only three boys and none of the girls who were bullied by peers, it didn't raise any problematic questions in the community. Perhaps the response from school faculty, parents, Alumni and students would have been different if it was openly communicated that fourteen written testimonies from students past and present, both boys and girls had been received.

The Headmaster's breach of confidentiality and decision not to suspend the teachers may well have caused fear in the students who had spoken up, but had not yet been exposed to the community. They now knew that they could become exposed at any time. The Headmaster's process compared to a strategy of divide and conquer: pit faculty against faculty, family against family, student against student and thereby distract everyone's attention from the facts of the matter, which were that students gave corroborating testimonies that detailed emotional, verbal, and some physical abuse. Exposing certain students sent a powerful message to anyone else who was planning to lodge a complaint: if you complain about a bullying teacher, or refuse to be a bystander and instead speak up, you will not receive support from the Headmaster, Board or select Alumni. In fact, they may reveal your name and expose you to further bullying.

Originally, the Headmaster had offered the students confidentiality, and also his assurance to students and parents that the teachers involved would *not* be coaching the team the next year, and thus

140

he secured the students' testimonies. As recorded in an email the Headmaster sent to my husband and me in April 2012, "The first thing I do want to reassure you about is that things will change for next year, and we will do our best to make sure that the boys' basketball experience is as positive as possible, with different coaching." He began negotiations with a fantastic coach in Vancouver and included us in the recruitment process. Based on his commitment, we were led to believe, and I promised the students, that they were safe to play basketball the following year and that they could tell the truth about what they experienced. However, the Headmaster never hired another coach, and once again, boys were put in the impossible position of playing for the coaches they reported on or quitting the sport they loved. Six senior boys chose not to even try out for the team and gave up their beloved game. For our son, it meant sacrificing his dream to try out for university teams and maybe even get a scholarship, but he decided that playing under the same conditions for another year was too unhealthy and harmful.

After giving their in-person statements to the Headmaster and Chaplain in what we all believed to be the confidential space of the Headmaster's office, three students found themselves being called names by their peers, and our son and another student were threatened with being beaten up. The police visited the homes of the boys who were threatening our son and the other player, to let them know how serious the consequences would be if they acted on their threats. Still, our son no longer wanted to attend school. He stopped going to parties where a fight could start. He didn't go to his graduation ceremony in grade eleven or twelve. The risk of being beaten up or called "pussy" made him fear for his social and physical safety. He became depressed and then started having panic attacks. His marks plummeted. Not playing basketball took away what was for him his greatest passion, and the school life he was left with was miserable. His depression and panic attacks are classic

141

reactions to bullying and abuse. I am aware of many other students involved who went through comparable decline and some who had even more serious reactions.

•　•　•

As we learn more about the harm caused by peer-to-peer bullying, society must establish laws that protect children and teenagers from adults in caregiver positions such as coaches and teachers. We cannot have zero tolerance for peer bullying at the same time as endless excuses for adult bullying. The failure to hold teachers to account surfaces in an article by Beth Morrissey that addresses teacher bullying in the UK. The article offers advice, and yet each step of the way, it in fact reveals the significant problems students face when being bullied by a teacher. It begins by suggesting the student may be fearful that no one will believe them when they report a teacher. The student is expected to speak directly to the teacher, which is a difficult and potentially risky thing to do if a student is already dealing with an adult who targets with harmful conduct and words. The student could then take the complaint up the administrative chain and ultimately transfer out of the class. There is nothing in the article that outlines what is an appropriate response by the teacher or administrator. In other words, the advice is all geared toward all the actions the child is expected to do to solve the problem, while it is apparent there are no formal processes in place for the teacher or administration.[127] It does not seem healthy or fair to expect children to solve the problem of bullying or emotional abuse directed at them by a teacher or coach. If the teacher hit or sexually molested the student, we would never find an advice column outlining a series of steps for the

---

[127] Beth Morrissey, "Being Bullied by a Teacher, *Teen Issues* February 10, 2013: http://www.teenissues.co.uk/beingbulliedbyateacher.html

student to follow to establish a safe and healthy environment for learning. It's highly likely that upon such allegations having been made, the school would immediately bring in the authorities and have an investigation conducted. One would hope the focus would be on protecting children, but factoring in Malcolm Gladwell's article on the way in which we tend to protect molesters not children, it is debatable.

The Chaplain at my former school also heard first hand from students reporting on teacher bullying; yet, like the Headmaster, he also allowed the suffering to continue and intensify. After the Headmaster published a report that positioned the students who spoke up as liars, the Chaplain wrote emails to me and the Lawyer/ parent saying he did not think the students lied, but he also would not stand up and share this publicly from his powerful moral position at the School. He explains:

> 1.  I believe the complainant students showed courage in coming forward with their concerns and I believe that they related their experiences honestly.
>
> 2.  In my own mind, I have concluded that these experiences led to harm, in some cases, significantly so. That being said, I am aware that harm can arise from a single factor or a combination of factors. Having listened to largely the complainant experiences rather than properly investigating the entire situation, I am not in a position to reasonably assess degrees of responsibility for the harm experienced by the students.

This may give an insight into what the atmosphere and ethos were like at my former school. Perhaps teachers and Administrators took the bystander position because they felt that their jobs were at risk or they could not draw any firm or clear lines about teacher conduct, because the Headmaster had not set clear standards.

When the Chaplain received the eleven-page document in 2011 from the Lawyer/ parent who believed that "child abuse" was occurring, and then a year later read multiple student testimonies confirming the

143

abusive conduct, and then heard first hand in the Headmaster's office at least eight students' experiences that indicated significant harm was being done, he remained in the role of bystander. The Chaplain let those same students be publicly labeled liars in the school community even when he communicated privately by email that he believed "that these experiences led to harm, in some cases, significantly so." He let the students be positioned publicly as being weak, yet in the email he stated, "students showed courage in coming forward." Perhaps those who administer Independent Schools should *not* be the ones making unilateral decisions as to child safety and wellbeing in their institutions; there would seem to be an inherent conflict of interest. Abusive coaching reported by fourteen students, thirty parents up in arms, law enforcement concluding abusive actions by teachers might not be good for "business."

The present crisis in Britain's education system, due to rising numbers of former students reporting the abuse they suffered as children, revolves predominantly around private schools.[128] The conflict of interest that arises in schools that are also businesses could be monitored if at the very least there were independent figures on the Board of Governors.[129] This

---

[128] "At Slater and Gordon, child abuse solicitor Liz Dux says she has seen 'a huge increase in claims against schools, the vast majority of which are independent.'" Louise Tickle, "Britain's Elite Boarding Schools Are Facing an Explosion of Abuse Allegations," *Newsweek*, September 2014: http://www.newsweek.com/britain-elite-boarding-schools-facing-explosion-abuse-allegations-267201

[129] Matt Spencer's study, Exploiting Children: School Board Members Who Cross The Line speaks powerfully to a potential problem with my former school's Board of Governors. While Spencer has concerns about the negative influence of a single member of a board, one wonders what can be done when the board appears to collude in silencing students and parents who strive to have their children attend a school free from teacher bullying. While Spencer focuses on the structure of American schools' governance, in Canada, one can agree certainly that private schools lack of an independent or two on their Boards means there are absolutely zero checks and balances on how these schools are run.

conflict of interest that exists in BC, and I would venture elsewhere, could be mitigated if there existed a means by which the Inspector of Independent Schools could hear directly from students about their experiences in a safe, trustworthy environment. This conflict of interest could be remedied if emotional abuse was in the Criminal Code; law enforcement would then have the grounds to lay charges rather than see a pattern of emotional and verbal abuse be investigated by those with a vested interest in the reputation and ongoing financial wellbeing of an independent school. An investigation should never be undertaken by individuals who were previously informed about the abuse and who had failed to protect students. That takes conflict of interest to a whole other level.

In Edmonton in 2003, a bylaw was passed that makes harassment or bullying illegal in schools; however, it only applies to children. Constable Dan Williams who proposed the legislation stated that, "he hopes the new bylaw will enable them to quash bullying before it goes too far." Councilor Jane Batty, chair of the community services board that put forth the issue, explains that they have "had lots of interest from all across the country, from other municipalities, from other police agencies and school boards asking for information about our proposal to city council." Ironically, the "bylaw is geared toward students and affects anyone under the age of 18 who is threatened. Bullying is defined as a person who communicates with someone in a way that makes the person feel harassed; the comment, threat or action is made in a public place and the threats are repeated." This is an exact description of what happened to students at my former school according to their testimonies. I believe we need more bylaws that hold bullies accountable when they are students and especially if they are teachers. In the workplace, we have anti-harassment rules, but when it was teacher to student, at my former school, there were multiple excuses made for the bullying behavior ranging from the students are *sensitive* to the intention was to *motivate*.

What inspired the police and government officials in Edmonton to make peer-bullying illegal were the "suicides" such harmful conduct could encourage as well as the statistics that connect bullying to "further criminal activity" when bullies become adults.[130] Therefore, whether it is studies by neuroscientists that show brain damage, or our knowledge that bullying encourages suicides or criminal activity, it is clear that bullying among peers, let alone from teacher or coach to student is harmful in the extreme.

It appears that bullying is a learned behavior, and like racism, anti-Semitism, homophobia and misogyny, it might be actually *learned* in schools if the child's role model is a bullying teacher, coach or administrator. A teacher in Britain, Alan Newland, writes a revealing article about how he believed fundamentally in his effective and applauded techniques of classroom management, until he was confronted by a student who told him that *he* was in fact the bully. He describes his treatment of the student as follows:

> I bore down on him in my well-rehearsed, iron-hard domineering way that had served me effectively with boys like him many times before. I towered over him, imposing my presence and physicality to emphasize his vulnerability. I fixed his gaze with an icy stare then embarked on a chastening tirade that began slowly with a tone of calculated menace and gradually rose to a crescendo of unfettered, ominous and voluble threat.

---

[130] Isabel Teotonio, "Edmonton passes anti-bullying bylaw," Toronto Star, Canadian Press, various newspapers across Canada, Mar. 11, 2003: http://www.canadiancrc. com/Newspaper_Articles/Tor_Star_Edmonton_passes_anti-bullying_bylaw_ 11MAR03.aspx

I watched as he visibly quailed and cowered, then he began to cry. To be honest I looked down at him and thought: "Good. That's given you a taste of your own medicine. It might even teach you a lesson."

Alan Newland was seen as a role model of classroom control and yet when the child was found later, still in tears, the head teacher did not minimize his suffering or deny what had happened. He listened to the child and had the teacher come in and listen to him. The boy labeled the teacher as a "bully" and rather than reverse the situation and accuse the boy of being sensitive or soft or problematic, the teacher realized he had in fact been modeling for his students how to become bullies. That was the real lesson he was teaching in his class:

> He looked up straight at me, and said: "You. You're just a bully." It was the most shocking moment I was ever to experience as a teacher and looking back, I think I learned more about myself in relation to children from that single incident than any other that I can think of more than 20 years of teaching.

> I realised I had been a role model in more ways than I imagined. [131]

Newland's epiphany is that bullying is a learned behavior. We cannot have zero tolerance for student bullying unless we also have it for teacher bullying. As educators and administrators at schools, we must be the ones who teach that bullying is harmful, not use it as a technique to run our classes or our teams.

Newland's story also applies to coaches who learn that bullying methods are wrong. As two coaches of elite athletes explain, "Going in and kicking over the Gatorade jug, there's no integrity in that. I think as a

---

[131] http://www.theguardian.com/teacher-network/teacher-blog/2013/may/02/behaviour-management-teaching-regrets-bullying

younger coach, I probably did a lot more of that, and now I've developed into the coach I think I want to be." Similarly, another coach stated, "I hope I'm not the same coach I was when I started. . . I definitely used to yell more."[132] More attention given to coach and teacher bullying, I am hopeful, will allow adults in positions of power over children to recognize just how much harm they can do to teenagers in particular, even if their school administrators and community condone bullying practices.

In an article about teacher-to-student bullying for WebMD, entitled "Teachers Who Bully," Katherine Kam notes that in "recent years, a slew of books have offered parents ample insight into the minds of young bullies." And then she asks a vital question: "But what if it's the teacher who screams, threatens, or uses biting sarcasm to humiliate a child in front of the class?" Kam poses this question to a psychiatrist:

> "Teacher bullying gets little attention," says Stuart Twemlow, MD, a psychiatrist who directs the Peaceful Schools and Communities Project at the Menninger Clinic in Houston. But his new study, published in *The International Journal of Social Psychiatry*, hints that the problem may be more common than people believe. Dr. Twemlow addresses the code of silence around teachers who emotionally abuse students and looks at why parents do not come forward. His study concludes that parents "worry that speaking up could cause a teacher to take revenge on their child -- and there's little escape. It really is on a different level than kid-to-kid bullying, the kid has no power."[133]

This is an apt description of the code of parental silence at my former school, especially since the Administrative response to parents was to position teachers, described as bullies by multiple students, as the victims.

---

[132] Ashley E. Stirling, "Understanding the Use of Emotionally Abusive Coaching Practices," *International Journal of Sports Science & Coaching* 8.4, 2013: 625-638.
[133] http://www.webmd.com/parenting/features/teachers-who-bully

The teachers were not publicly disciplined; instead, they were pitied and commended for their conduct by the Headmaster in a number of public documents.

In an article that focuses on abusive coaching of adolescents and addresses why it is so difficult for them or their parents to speak up, Dr. Carl Pickhardt writes:

> The student player can avoid speaking up for fear of being seen as a complainer or a troublemaker, injuring their opportunity to play. The player's parents can fear speaking up for fear of making a bad situation worse for their son or daughter, or invite censure from other parents who support the program. In both cases the coach is not confronted. The painful truth for players and their parents is that there are no self-made bullies. Bullies are partly made by the consent of those who allow themselves to be shut up and pushed around.[134]

In a 2009 study of coach abuse by Ashley Stirling and Gretchen Kerr, one elite athlete recounts exactly why parents do not speak up to protect their children: "Every parent tried at one time or another to talk to her [the coach] about her anger and name-calling, but it never made a difference. I think she scared them too. . . And then after the parent talked to her that athlete would get teased or chastised by the coach. She'd make the athlete pay for the parent's actions. . . so usually parents only tried this once."[135] Ironically, rather than complain, students and parents are more likely to write notes of gratitude and praise to teachers who bully in the hopes of insulating their child from being targeted.

---

[134] Carl Pickhardt, Ph.D., "Adolescents and Bullying Coaches: When secondary school coaches bully players, parents must step in," *Psychology Today*, January 2012. http://www.psychologytoday.com/blog/surviving-your-childs-adolescence/201201/adolescents-and-bullying-coaches

[135] Ashley E. Stirling and Gretchen A. Kerr, "Abused Athletes' Perceptions of the Coach-Athlete Relationship," *Sport in Society* Vol.12.2, March 2009: 227-239.

Before he secured the students' testimonies, it is relevant to examine how the Headmaster handled the parental concerns that were piling up on his desk. What the parents at my former school discovered was that this treatment of students was actually seen as acceptable, perhaps a little out of date, but essentially well established by tradition. When we first met with the Headmaster in April 2012, he said he had played for the Chicago Black Hawks feeder team back in the day and what we were dealing with was "old style coaching." In the 2012 fall, he gave a Chapel talk to the students about how he had met NHL legend, Darryl Sittler. He told another family that he'd played football at a high level and once again what our children were experiencing was "old style coaching." When emotional abuse occurs, the context is irrelevant. Parents should be instantly worried if an administrator or educational authority begins speaking about sports rather than abuse. The Headmaster could not do the usual routine, which would be to highlight team success since the basketball program, girls and boys, had not secured a provincial high-school Championship in over twenty years, but he attempted to keep our attention on *his* athletic credentials rather than address our concerns about our son and many students being harmed.

After his discussion with us about "old-style coaching," the Headmaster brought in the two teachers who had coached our son to discuss the complaints. On email, the Headmaster told us the following: "Of all the reports I have heard in this most recent series of complaints, the ones directed at [your son] are the ones that offend me the most, and they are in fact the most serious ones. I have spoken with both [the Head Coach] and [the Assistant Coach] and have additional meetings planned." He then assured us that "I definitely want you and [your son], to feel supported as the School resolves these issues. I have spoken with both the Assistant Coach and the Head Coach and they have committed to addressing all the issues I have put on the table, and all the issues I have put on the table are the ones you have mentioned."

It was very reassuring, but then a few days later the Headmaster sent another email saying he had to proceed on the basis that the teachers were "innocent." This was odd, as they had just acknowledged to him that they were going to address everything serious done to our son. Then the Headmaster alerted us that he was calling in the police school liaison to inform him of the situation. The mixed messages were very confusing – not just for our son, but also for other students awaiting decisive action. One parent wrote the Headmaster an email outlining how mixed the messages actually were and how potentially harmful to the now vulnerable students whose parents had come forward:

> Furthermore, while the coaches should be showing signs of remorse for what they have done, they instead are acting with the abused boys as if they, the coaches, are the victims of interfering parents. This is a clear sign that they will not change, but given the chance, will continue the abusive behavior (most recently shunning). They appear offended by what has happened because they do not believe they have done anything wrong. I cannot put into words how disturbing this is to us.

According to the government issued document, *Supporting Our Students: A Guide for Independent School Personnel Responding to Child Abuse*, the Headmaster had a series of duties he had to undertake as the "Appointed School Official" who responds to child abuse in an independent school. This role is clarified in the government guide:

> While reviewing and referring to the BC Handbook, independent school authorities and administrators should know the BC Handbook was written primarily for the public school system. It refers to superintendents, school districts, and boards of education. The critical difference between the public and independent systems is the requirement that independent school authorities nominate at least two 'Appointed School Officials', a

151

primary and an alternate, who are responsible for working with child care workers to determine whether a child has been harmed by someone who works or volunteers at the school, or works on contract for the school.[136]

Clearly as the "Appointed School Official," the Headmaster had certain responsibilities when abuse allegations were brought forward. We did not ever hear about who the alternate official was at the school who dealt with student reports of abuse. The parents' descriptions alone gave ample evidence to the Headmaster that students were suffering from conduct that would result in suspension and ultimately expulsion if done by a student or if done by a teacher at a public school. *The Guide for Independent School Personnel* defines what parents were witnessing and hearing from their children as "a pattern of destructive behavior or verbal attacks by an adult on a child. Typical behaviors may include rejecting, terrorizing, ignoring, isolating, humiliating, insulting, scapegoating."[137] Considering parental concerns revolved around every single one of the outlined destructive behaviors, the Headmaster had certain required duties, and while it's apparent he fulfilled some, he seems to have avoided others. The Ministry of Education's *Guide* directs the Headmaster to report to "child care workers" *not* lawyers and it lists his duties as follows:

- investigate where appropriate on behalf of the school authority;
- ensure a safe school environment during investigations;
- consult with the child welfare worker and/or police;
- ensure that no school employee interferes with any investigations;
- communicate with parents with respect to actions taken by the school authority;

---

[136] http://www.bced.gov.bc.ca/independentschools/is_resources/SOS_guide.pdf
[137] Ibid.

- report to the Commissioner for Teacher Regulation, Teacher Regulation Branch, Ministry of Education, when the School Authority dismisses, suspends or otherwise disciplines a certified teacher or school principal (*Independent School Act* section 7 and 7.2); and, refer student(s) for counseling according to the school's policies.[138]

The Headmaster investigated by meeting with parents, speaking with teacher-coaches about the allegations, having testimonies gathered from students, and interviewing students. However, he did *not* ensure a safe school environment during investigations. The teachers were never suspended or even off-campus. He consulted with police, but he *failed* to ensure that no School employee interfered with any investigation as he informed one of the teachers under investigation which boys had come forward. Also, Alumni were being contacted at this time and, therefore, he must have informed school employees about the students coming forward. He did *not* communicate with parents with respect to actions taken by the School authority. *No* actions were taken and the only parents informed were the ones who came forward with concerns. Other parents were left in the dark, even those whose children were in residence cared for by three teachers who were under investigation. The Headmaster did *not* report to the Commissioner and perhaps he did not have to since he never suspended the teachers under investigation. He referred students for counseling, but did *not* support them beyond a session or two.

There are four standards that govern the conduct of those invested with teaching licenses in BC; one of them is that license holders must communicate with parents:

**Educators value the involvement and support of parents, guardians, families and communities in schools.** Educators

---

[138] Ibid.

> understand, respect and support the role of parents and the
> community in the education of students. Educators communicate
> effectively and in a timely manner with parents and consider their
> advice on matters pertaining to their children.[139]

At my former school, parents were not informed about the serious allegations of verbal, emotional, and some physical abuse. Imagine the atmosphere for students who had spoken up and some whose names had been handed over to one of the bullying teachers identified in the student testimonies. Some of the students were either glared at by teachers, or approached by phone or in person, apparently to see if the teachers could encourage the students to change what they said. Hence, one day our son came home very stressed out because the Head Coach had asked him to go out for coffee and talk about the crisis. Our son said he would have liked to have told the coach straight out what he thought of him, but because he was a student and in a vulnerable position, he didn't dare.

In the spring 2012, after the Headmaster promised "different coaching," he brought in the prospective coach he was negotiating a contract with to do a six-week training session with the student-athletes to try to compensate for such a destructive year. While the boys were training, the Head Coach and Assistant Coach stood at the windows and watched them. The boys felt their displeasure. In the fall of 2012, when the two coaches had been reinstated by the Headmaster and the students positioned as liars, another teacher who was not involved in the coaching, but well aware of the crisis, asked our son if he was going to "play basketball" that year. He mumbled a reply and dropped that class. Another teacher, also not involved, used our son as an example to the class of what it would be like to score poorly on a future Advanced Placement exam. He dropped that class too. One day playing soccer, the

---

[139] http://www.bcteacherregulation.ca/Standards/StandardsDevelopment.aspx

Assistant Coach stood and watched him play with his friends; when our son went to retrieve the ball, he looked up to see him a few feet away glaring down. Already under extreme pressure from the peer bullying, followed by the Headmaster's exposure, our son felt extremely anxious and exposed.

We informed the Director of the Senior School, but our concerns were dismissed despite the fact that what our son and the other students were experiencing were well-documented techniques used by bullies and especially effective when the bully is a teacher in a position of influence and power.[140] In the fall of 2012, outside my classroom on two occasions, the Head Coach got up close and right into the face of a student who had given a testimony. The student was so distraught he could not concentrate in class or focus on his schoolwork. This overtly aggressive behavior was so distressing the parents contacted the police liaison officer who had identified the abuse pattern and was aware students had described the Head Coach's conduct as "vicious." Other families reported to School Administrators other comparable incidents only to receive dismissive responses. Dr. Alan Goldberg describes the conditions under which our son had to attend school after speaking up, not only as unsafe, but as outright "hostile." This is the letter he wrote to exempt our son from exams in May 2013:

To Whom It May Concern,

> I am writing on behalf of [the student], who has been in treatment with me weekly for approximately one year. I understand that he had advanced placement exams scheduled and I fully supported the decision to excuse him from these tests.

---

[140] "Veteran verbal abusers (a.k.a. adult bullies) often cultivate tiny "looks" and behaviors, known only to them and their victim, so they don't need to say a word to get what they want." http://www.healthyplace.com/abuse/verbal-abuse/what-is-verbal-abuse/

I have been treating [the student] for PTSD, (Post Traumatic Stress Disorder) as a result of a two year, on-going abusive situation that he experienced as a member of the [school] basketball team. He has had to tolerate an administrative and academic environment that has been hostile since he was one of a number of courageous children to speak up about their abusive experiences. Currently [the school] is undergoing a child abuse investigation being completed by the Ministry of Education. Their findings will be disclosed shortly. As a result [he] has experienced excessive anxiety and a loss of self-confidence whenever he is in a pressured performance situation. He suffers from an inability to concentrate on task and can also become physically ill.

[He] has a strong academic record and has also been accepted to college for next year. I believe it is in his best interest to be finished at [my former school].

Sincerely,

Dr. Alan Goldberg

PTSD is an expected reaction to teacher or coach abuse, especially in an adolescent, and neurologists now believe the brain is left permanently scarred as a result. Our son's diagnosis, while heartbreaking, is not atypical.

Having first been alerted in 2011 that teacher bullying was harming students at the school, followed by a great deal of corroborating evidence in 2012, the Headmaster's exemption of our son from exams for two years, according to abuse experts, could be considered part of a series of "educationally neglectful behaviors (e.g., failure to consider a child's educational needs)."[141] However, the Commissioner for Teacher

---

[141] Ashley E. Stirling and Gretchen A. Kerr, "Sport Psychology Consultants as Agents of Child Protection," *Journal of Applied Sport Psychology* 22, 2010: 305-319.

Regulation did not find the Headmaster's neglect worthy of any kind of public alert or discipline. Psychiatrist, Dr. Roland C. Summit, examines how serious the damage is when perpetrators are not held accountable and abuse victims are not believed. He refers specifically to sex abuse victims; however, his conclusions apply equally well to physical or emotional abuse:

> If a respectable, reasonable adult is accused of perverse, assaultive behavior by an uncertain, emotionally distraught child, most adults who hear the accusation will fault the child. Disbelief and rejection by potential adult caretakers increase the helplessness, hopelessness, isolation and self-blame that make up the most damaging aspects of child sexual victimization. Victims looking back are usually more embittered toward those who rejected their pleas than toward the one who initiated the sexual experiences. When no adult intervenes to acknowledge the reality of the abusive experience or to fix responsibility on the offending adult, there is a reinforcement of the child's tendency to deal with the trauma as an intrapsychic event and to incorporate a monstrous apparition of guilt, self-blame, pain and rage.[142]

This is an apt summary of how the students who came forward were treated at my former school. As the second lawyer brought in by the school to write a second report states, "there is a need to review and reconsider behavior and conduct that has been misinterpreted and misunderstood by several of the male students and I suspect, by a number of the parents." This is a confusing conclusion, because teachers and school Administrators should not need to review and reconsider teacher conduct if, in fact, the fault lay with students and parents who could not interpret or understand properly what was happening. If a schoolyard

---

[142] Dr. Roland C. Summit, "The Child Abuse Accommodation Syndrome," *This article appeared in Child Abuse & Neglect Vol 7, pp. 177 - 193, 1983*: http://www.secasa.com.au/sections/for-students/the-child-abuse-accommodation-syndrome/

bully called another kid "pussy" or "retard," and it was reported by many other students, do we argue the victim and his parents did not interpret or understand properly what was happening? It seems the lawyer is using circular logic to confuse the issue.

The student testimonies offer in straightforward language what occurred and how being treated in this derogatory manner felt for each student involved. The testimonies reinforced one another in clear, corroborating ways: similar terms, situations and behaviors were described across all fourteen. The sheer number and similarity of the accounts offers evidence that differs from that of a single student reporting on abuse and still, these students' testimonies were dismissed. Because their teachers' behavior while coaching was minimized and the adults were not held responsible, the students have been left to deal with the trauma as an *intrapyschic* event that Dr. Summit describes as a "monstrous apparition of guilt, self-blame, pain and rage" that shadows the victim.[143]

The Headmaster and the first lawyer hired by him were quick to speak of due process for the teachers, but never did they discuss with parents concerns about the impact on the children of multiple interviews or questioning. Even though the *BC Handbook on Child Abuse and Neglect* is clear that the goal should be to "avoid the stress of multiple interviews."[144] The Canadian Bar Association is in full agreement: "The investigation and prosecution of abuse cases is sensitive to the feelings of children. Whenever possible, the Ministry of Children and Family Development and the police conduct a joint investigation to reduce the

---

[143] Ibid.
[144] http://www.mcf.gov.bc.ca/child_protection/pdf/handbook_action_child_abuse.pdf

number of interviews and the anxiety felt by a child involved in the process."[145]

One cannot begin to imagine students' stress and anxiety in having to give multiple interviews: first with a lawyer or teacher, next with the Headmaster and Chaplain. This should have provided more than enough information to discipline teachers and ensure a safe and healthy environment for all students. However, the Headmaster brought in the first lawyer and parents said "no" to another interview; then the Board of Governors, ostensibly working with parents, brought in a second lawyer and parents were made to feel that the only way forward was to allow another interview. Finally, the students had to be interviewed in the Commissioner's process by the former Head of Commercial Crime for the RCMP who informed several parents and Dr. Alan Goldberg that he wasn't sure how to interview abuse victims because he didn't have experience with it. What should have been a safe environment for investigating child abuse became a hostile environment where any real examination of what had happened was fundamentally flawed. It seemed that what the Headmaster, Chaplain and Board Members needed was a reason to *disbelieve* the students or reject their testimonies. To date, there has been no credibility issue raised for any of the students and not a single student has retracted their testimony regardless of the pressure they have been put under.

When the Lawyer/ parent who had written the document in 2011 outlining "child abuse" took testimonies at the request of the Headmaster, she used the "Voice of the Child Protocol," an approach used by courts when dealing with children. And guided by the rules in the Ministry of Education's *Supporting Our Students: A Guide for Independent School*

---

[145] http://cbabc.org/For-the-Public/Dial-A-Law/Scripts/Family-Law/156

*Personnel Responding to Child Abuse*, I also took student testimonies. The independent school guide begins by stating the following:

> Child abuse is a serious problem. Its impacts can last a lifetime and even extend to future generations. Understanding child abuse and neglect and knowing how to respond are critical. School personnel are responsible both for reporting suspected child abuse and neglect and also for cooperating with resulting investigations. Identifying and supporting students who have experienced child abuse and neglect is important in meeting these responsibilities. Independent school authorities must have policies and procedures in place to respond promptly and effectively to incidents of child abuse and neglect.[146]

We were already a year late in identifying or supporting students, as it appeared nothing effective had been done when the Lawyer/ Board Member and the Chaplain received the document informing them of "child abuse" in 2011 which was then relayed verbally to the Headmaster. Hence, there was no chance for prompt or effective response to incidents of what appeared to be abuse. We later learned that at least five sets of parents had reiterated the message about coach bullying; still, nothing effective was done.

In the spring of 2012, an entire year after the first report of abuse, there was the promise of decisive and swift action from the Lawyer/ Board Member we initially contacted. We were hopeful as we began taking student testimonies. Whether "Voice of the Child" or the Ministry of Education's *Supporting Our Students Guide*, the process is to let the student talk while taking notes. The note-taker should ask clarifying questions such as "how did that make you feel?" or to receive more specific information such as "what words were said?" And when the

---

[146] http://www.bced.gov.bc.ca/independentschools/is_resources/SOS_guide.pdf

student is done, the note-taker tells him or her that the information is wholly theirs to control, but if he or she wants it to go forward to the Headmaster, with the promise of complete confidentiality, then it could be sent.

The Ministry of Education's *Supporting Our Students Guide* advises that the teacher or administrator should identify and reach out to vulnerable students.[147] When I spoke with students I asked them if there were particular students they thought I should speak with and if they suggested names, I followed up. Sometimes students were keen to share their experience and sometimes they weren't. Only those students whose parents gave permission and who wanted to speak were recorded as part of the written testimonies. Thirteen of the fourteen students who came forward agreed their respective testimonies could be sent to the Headmaster with the hope of putting an end to the teacher bullying (one student would only allow his to be read to the police). The other parent (as lawyer) and I (as teacher) typed up the students' testimonies, returned them to the students and asked if what their testimony said was accurate, or if not, if they could please make changes. Each student signed off on the accuracy and then gave permission for the testimony to go to the Headmaster. Therefore, he received at least thirteen detailed testimonies. It is shocking that with this information, the Headmaster did not suspend the teachers. In public schools, all it takes is a student and a witness for a teacher to be suspended for far less egregious conduct. For thirteen students to have articulated a pattern of harmful behavior and have to continue attending school with these teachers, in continuing positions of power, indicates a profound ignorance about child development and emotional abuse. When informed in 2011 about the Head Coach's abuse,

---

[147] Ibid.

the Headmaster stressed his "popularity." A year later, it appears that this quality continued to outweigh student testimonies that reported on his bullying.

In Malcolm Gladwell's article on sexual abusers and how they manage to get away with their conduct, as Penn State football Coach Jerry Sandusky did for years, he stresses their charisma:

> When monsters roam free, we assume that people in positions of authority ought to be able to catch them if only they did their jobs. But that might be wishful thinking. A pedophile, van Dam's story of Mr. Clay reminds us, is someone adept not just at preying on children but at confusing, deceiving, and charming the adults responsible for those children—which is something to keep in mind in the case of the scandal at Penn State and the conviction, earlier this year, of the former assistant football coach Jerry Sandusky on child-molestation charges.[148]

Former Rutgers, Scarlet Knights Coach Mike Rice has been called an "animal"; he has been referred to as "deranged." Here, Gladwell uses the term "monster." Yet these university coaches were so popular that children or student-athletes were handed over to them regardless of the concerning reports about their conduct.

As a teacher, I believe it is important to have a caring and supportive administration that treats one as a professional and defends one against unfair attacks of any kind. However, for a Headmaster to have interviewed students about how they have suffered at the hands of teachers, while behind their backs, he is aware that school insiders were contacting Alumni to make these students seem like a minority appears expressive of a "striking lack of empathy for child abuse victims." The

---

[148] Malcolm Gladwell, "In Plain View: How Child Molesters Get Away With It," *The New Yorker*, September 2012: http://www.newyorker.com/magazine/2012/09/24/in-plain-view

Alumni praise was being gathered to give to a lawyer, who instead of writing a report on child abuse made it clear he was there to do "dispute resolution," as if there was some kind of a disagreement between faculty or families. When the lawyer met with me in June he said that I had "vetted" the student testimonies. I asked him what "vetted" meant and he explained that it meant I had altered student testimonies. I was surprised. Over the course of eight years working at the School, I had never had a complaint against me from a student, parent, colleague or Administrator, but suddenly my credibility was not merely being questioned, it was being compromised. Apparently the lawyer, when he was handed the binder full of Alumni testimonies, was also informed that I could not be trusted.

I had taken eight formal, detailed complaints each one taking close to two hours to record. I knew of five others at that time and was asked to take another testimony in the fall 2012 which I then relayed directly to the police. Yet the lawyer the Headmaster hired, when it should have been a "child care worker," was acting as if it was par for the course to have thirteen students reporting in depth on the suffering they were experiencing due to their teachers. Then he reversed the situation so that instead of focusing on the teachers with serious abuse allegations against them, I was the one in doubt, my character was under discussion. The Headmaster recently sent a communication to parents where he denies asking me to take testimonies. Yet he received them from me and followed up with interviews. He even had me attend one of the interviews. The lawyer he hired did not explain why he thought I would want anything bad to happen to my colleagues. The situation for me was already extremely stressful and sad, let alone having him suggest I had altered what students had said. Now I was seen as a problem employee who had committed the serious crime of falsifying student information.

If the Headmaster had informed this lawyer that I was not trustworthy and was not acting in good faith, I should have faced a ten

163

thousand dollar fine and six months in jail according to the *BC Handbook on Child Abuse and Neglect*.[149] However, throughout this entire process, I was not once subject to any kind of discipline. The Headmaster told my colleagues at the meeting he called in June 2012 that he thought it was fair and effective to have me taking student testimonies. He could have clarified that I, along with every other teacher in the room, had a legal duty as a teacher to take testimonies and report child abuse when I hear about it directly or even indirectly from students. I had a duty to report even if it was merely a suspicion, let alone taking detailed testimonies from eight students. The Teacher Regulation Branch outlines Duty to Report as follows:

> The concept of "public interest" as it relates to regulatory discipline has two main elements:
>
> > 1. Students must be protected from certificate holders who inflict physical, emotional or sexual harm on them (intentionally or otherwise).
> > 2. Certificate holders cannot conduct themselves on or off duty in a way that breaches the Standards for the Education, Competence and Professional Conduct.
>
> If a certificate holder's conduct meets either of the following criteria, a regulatory response is required even if employment discipline has already been imposed:
>
> The conduct alleged involves emotional, physical or sexual harm, abuse or exploitation of a student by a certificate holder.
>
> The alleged conduct calls into question the integrity of the teaching profession or the school system, and/or conflicts with a

---

[149] http://www.mcf.gov.bc.ca/child_protection/pdf/handbook_action_child_abuse.pdf

fundamental value of the school system even if there is no direct harm to a student.

Simple rule:

When in doubt, err on the side of caution and report.
Let the Commissioner decide if it is truly a regulatory matter.[150]

The Commissioner contracted an outside investigator and conducted a six month investigation. He deliberated for a year and a half afterwards. He decided that his assessment of the conduct of four teachers, the Headmaster and the Chaplain would not be made public. Even though the only public reprimand the Commissioner issued was to the Head Coach for lying, I still had to err on the side of caution and report. And I still would report today because after hearing directly from many students, I believed that it was in the public interest for them to be protected and all students to be protected. I believed, after hearing and reading their testimonies that it was clear emotional and some physical harm was occurring regularly. I believed that the teachers and Administrators' conduct called into question the integrity of the teaching profession and was in conflict with the fundamental value of the school system which is that *all* students have a right to a fair, safe, and healthy education.

Now that I look back, being told by this lawyer that he believed I had "vetted" the student testimonies was the start of not only discrediting me, without anyone ever being able to say what my motivation or benefit would have been, it was also the start of discrediting the students who had spoken up. None of this defamatory insinuation was ever done in an upfront manner. Furthermore, if true, it should have resulted in serious

---

[150] https://www.bcteacherregulation.ca/documents/FormsandPublications/ProfConduct/duty_to_report_COQ.pdf

165

consequences, which it never did. After I took the testimonies, I was treated throughout the following processes as if I was an abusive person who was harming my colleagues, and these adults needed to be protected. This reversal would have been laughable except that it hurt so many students.

# CHAPTER SIX

## RE-VICTIMIZATION OF THE STUDENTS

> Just because something isn't a lie does not mean that it
> isn't deceptive. A liar knows that he is a liar, but one
> who speaks mere portions of truth in order to deceive
> is a craftsman of destruction.

> – Author, Criss Jami

In June 2012, my husband and I wrote again to the Lawyer/ Board
Member, whom we had previously sent the original package of parent
emails back in March, to describe how upset we were about the peer
bullying that was suddenly directed at our son. At the time, we did not
know the Headmaster had exposed him and other players to the Assistant
Coach identified in student testimonies as a bully. The Lawyer/ Board
Member agreed that the peer bullying was unacceptable. He and the Chair
of the Board approached the group of parents who were trying to protect
their children from the teacher-coaches' bullying and suggested that the
lawyer, who had earlier treated the situation like a dispute and also
suggested I had "vetted" the testimonies, had not done a thorough job or
established the proper conditions under which students could learn
without teacher or peer bullying. They would not let us read his report.

 Parents had not wanted this lawyer to interview their children as
they had already spent as long as two hours having their testimonies
transcribed, and they had already given interviews to the Headmaster and
Chaplain. It is well established in research that, each interview an abuse
victim gives forces him or her to relive the trauma, and thus repeating the

process any more times than absolutely necessary is to be avoided at all costs according to the government-issued *BC Handbook on Child Abuse and Neglect* and the Canadian Bar Association.[151] However, the parents of the students who came forward were getting anxious about the Headmaster's lack of action. The Chair of the Board and the Lawyer/ Board Member we initially contacted said that the first lawyer's report was flawed, because the parents would not allow their children to be interviewed again. Although they would not allow the parents to see this report, the Board Members appeared to be bypassing the Headmaster's process and were instead working directly with parents to protect students. The parents whose children had come forward and Board members worked together to select a second lawyer who appeared to be more "independent" than the first. This individual presented himself as a "fact-finder" and said he would interview the students to properly deal with the impasse of the first lawyer's report– that questioned student complaints because there were so many Alumni praising the teacher-coaches. However, certain aspects in the second lawyer's terms of reference seemed dubious and suggested that perhaps the lawyer was being brought in to protect the teachers and School, rather than get to the bottom of the situation and to then set the grounds for establishing a safe and healthy environment for students.

The most worrisome requirement in the lawyer's term of reference was the restriction that those students who had previously graduated – safely away from the School – and therefore likely to be more forthcoming about what they had experienced, were not allowed to be interviewed. Likewise, students who had quit the basketball teams were also not allowed to be interviewed even though the ultimate measuring

---

[151] http://www.mcf.gov.bc.ca/child_protection/pdf/handbook_action_child_abuse.pdf; and http://www.cba.org/bc/public_media/family/156.aspx

168

stick of an abusive coach is that student-athletes give up the sport they love. Parents worried that the investigation had bias built in before it even began. If the Board and Headmaster were secure in their beliefs that the coaches were non-abusive, then there should not have been any concerns about allowing *all* students a chance to speak about what they experienced.

An excellent indicator of coaching abuse is, in fact, when students quit a sport that they love and have played for years. It doesn't make sense that an athlete who has played most of their life, excels at a sport, and loves a sport would suddenly quit the team or give up their scholarship without good reason. A July 2012 article carried in the *IndyStar* discusses players who quit due to IUPUI Coach Shann Hart's emotional abuse:

> The interviews with players revealed respect for Hart's basketball knowledge but also a pattern of fear, favoritism and humiliation.
>
> But might this just be a case of players unable to play for a demanding coach?
>
> "If that was the case, all these players wouldn't have left," said one player who quit. "We were tough enough. . . . But the way she treated people was way over the line."[152]

Coach Hart was fired in September 2010 by University Chancellor Charles Bantz over allegations of abusing her players and a number of NCAA violations.[153] It's wrong that often, when a teacher or coach

---

[152] Mark Alesia, Heather Gillers and Tim Evans, "'Emotional Abuse': 28 have left women's basketball program," *IndyStar.com*, July 2010: http://archive.indystar.com/article/20100727/NEWS14/307270003/-Emotional-abuse-IUPUI-

[153] Mark Alesia, Tim Evans, Heather Gillers, "IUPUI Fires Basketball Coach Shann Hart," IndyStar.com, September 2012: http://www.indystar.com/article/20100924/NEWS14/9240354/

bullies a student-athlete, the student's only recourse is to quit the team. This indicates a significant problem with athletes reporting abuse and being protected from it. Comparably, when a student is being bullied, the first question a lawyer will ask is "well then why didn't you transfer to another school?" It's hard to imagine this question being posed in any other situation where someone is being harmed. If a person robs your house, the police do not ask you why you didn't move. If a person sexually harasses you at work, the Human Resources person does not ask you why you didn't get another job. However, this is the question that is posed when children report on bullying or emotional abuse.

In BC, when an athlete transfers to a similarly competitive school athletic program, the office that governs such transfers, BC School Sports won't allow the student to compete until a year has passed. For an aspiring grade eleven student-athlete, that means not being able to apply to universities in their graduation year or apply for athletic scholarships. BC School Sports penalizes students by not allowing them to play if they move schools. They have a strict code of conduct for coaches as well as for teachers who coach; yet there appears to be no monitoring, or repercussions, or allowances given to athletes who are being mistreated and want to transfer.[154] There have been newspaper articles and courtroom battles, stories of students' struggles to play when they are blocked by BC School Sports from transferring to a team that is healthy

---

[154] These are the old standards of BC School Sports which were saved on a school district's website: http://www.sd6.bc.ca/sss-ath/pdfs/ Coach Code of Conduct.pdf; and these are the new ones: http://www.bcschoolsports.ca/sites/ default/files/Section%20III%20B.pdf; note there are some interesting omissions such as "with moral and legislative obligations required of the coach at all times."

and safe.[155] To transfer to another school team, there must be "unusual" circumstances, such as one might assume coach abuse occasions.[156] I spent a great deal of time on the phone with people at BC School Sports trying to figure out a way for our son to be allowed to play in a non-abusive school environment in his grade twelve year. When I detailed the abuse alleged by so many students, I was advised to only speak to the Executive Director and no one else. When it was determined that it was simply not possible to transfer our son and maintain his eligibility to play, we hoped that he could at least play on a "B-Team" at my former school away from the coaches identified in the player-testimonies.

I copied the BC School Sports Executive Director on emails to the Director of the Senior School pleading for the creation of a B-Team to at least allow for those boys, who refused to play for the teachers from whom they asked to be protected, an opportunity to play in their senior year. The Director of the Senior School would not allow a B-Team to be created. Despite being fully informed of how not playing in grade twelve would impact our son's future as a student-athlete; we did not receive even a response, let alone support, from the Executive Director at BC School Sports. It could be argued that *reversal* is once again at work and the adults charged with protecting students' interests, instead appeared to take steps to protect the adults involved; even if it meant sacrificing the wellbeing of children. It should not be coaches but instead student-athletes who receive protection in circumstances like those at my former school. It is difficult to understand the concern over an adult's reputation

---

[155] Jesse Johnston, "Basketball teen challenges B. C. School Sports in Supreme Court," *CBC News*, February 2014: http://www.cbc.ca/news/canada/british-columbia/basketball-teen-challenges-b-c-school-sports-in-supreme-court-1.2553177
[156] Mona Mattel, "Student pursues legal angle to get the right to play," *Rossland Telegraph*, November: 2011: http://rosslandtelegraph.com/news/student-pursues-legal-angle-get-right-play-volleyball-15343#.U8_p8F67kZ4

when the real worry should be over the lifelong damage that may occur to students when coaches bully.

If we want to truly address bullying and the harm it does, the bullies must be held accountable, not the victims; however, all too often, students being abused by their coaches simply quit in a silent act of desperation. The students who came forward at my former school, after they gave testimonies, not only lost opportunities to play the sport they loved, but also to participate in leadership opportunities, attend certain classes without a teacher drawing attention to them through belittling comments or questions, walk around the campus or the city without fear of being bullied by their peers, write exams with confidence, or attend graduation ceremonies. By speaking up and supplying the Headmaster with the testimonies he requested, the students ended up extending the abusive conditions from the basketball court to the whole campus and even beyond.

It would appear that coming up against an educational administration that protects bullying teachers, rather than student victims, is not an isolated incident. In the summer of 1999, an article published by Caroline Willcocks in Britain, offers several anecdotal stories of parents failing to protect their children in the British school system. What's interesting is that the Board of Governors and the Head Teacher indicate in no uncertain terms that bullying by their teachers is essentially fine unless the teacher is caught hitting the student or stealing.[157] Proof of this same approach has been recently discussed in terms of American

---

[157] Caroline Willcocks, "Education: When the bully making your child's life hell is his teacher." *Independent.* August 1999. "It is rare, but it can turn lives upside-down. Children who find themselves victims of adults who should be guiding them are often not believed, and parents find complaints met by closed ranks." http://www.independent.co.uk/arts-entertainment/education-when-the-bully-making-your-childs-life-hell-is-his-teacher-1110773.html

Speedskating coaches who were known to be emotionally abusive, but did not lose their positions until caught stealing.[158]

There is a general sense that emotional abuse is not serious or permanently damaging despite the great body of research that documents that it is. Physically hitting a student and stealing money result in discipline; however, scarring a victim's brain and robbing them of their self-esteem, their sport, their scholarship, or in some cases their desire to live, far too often does not result in proper protection for student-athletes.

• • •

Our son asked us not to go to his graduation dinner dance, because as parents who had spoken up against the abuse reported in the student testimonies, we were no longer welcome in the school community and would make him more of a target. After the last three years, I understand intimately why teachers and parents don't speak up and why students don't report abuse. Even for adults, there is a huge amount on the line: one's relationship to colleagues, one's position in the community, one's job, not to mention the extreme anxiety around what might be done to one's child. In an article for the *GreatSchools* organization, Jessica Kelmon discovers many have "painful" stories of teacher bullying and how reporting is complicated:

> …but none had a clear way to redress the situation. When children bully other children, experts offer viable theories on how to deal with the problem: Fight back, walk away, ignore the bully and he'll move on, tell a teacher, tell your parents, ask any adult for help. But when the bully is the grown-up in charge, how

---

[158] Kelly Whiteside, "Document Details Alleged Abuse by Speedskating Coach," *USA Today Sports*, September 2012: http://usatoday30.usatoday.com/sports/olympics/story/2012/09/28/document-details-alleged-abuse-by-speedskating-coach/57849402/1

should a child respond? With a bully teacher, fighting back, walking out of the class, or ignoring the teacher are hardly viable solutions, and ones that will most likely get kids in even more trouble. Even telling another teacher or the principal gets tricky.[159]

While reporting peer bullying is difficult, this problem becomes much more difficult when a student reports that a coach or a teacher is the bully. Moreover, it is well documented that speaking up as an abuse victim is equally challenging, if not wholly impossible. The more one has been influenced by abusive terms, such as the ones described in the student testimonies at my former school – *pussy, retard, soft, pathetic, loser, embarrassment, hopeless, waste of player* – the less likely one is to have the necessary self-respect or self-esteem to speak up, and therefore one suffers in silence. Dr. Alan Goldberg discusses the psychology of abuse that encourages victims to remain silent:

> When you're in an abusive situation you end up feeling scared a lot of the time. This fear is usually related to what the coach may say or do if you mess up or fail. The fear that you feel also compels you to want to keep things to yourself. Abusive coaches use this fear to manipulate athletes and prevent them from talking about the coaching situation with other adults who might be able to help.[160]

Moreover, as the school police liaison officer explained, especially for adolescent boys who have been humiliated, their fear is that speaking up, not being able to tolerate the abuse, means in fact, in their own minds,

---

[159] http://www.greatschools.org/parenting/bullying/5063-when-the-teacher-is-the-bully.gs
[160] Dr. Alan Goldberg, ""Coaching ABUSE: The dirty, not-so-little secret in sports." http://gazette.teachers.net/gazette/wordpress/dr-alan-goldberg/coaching-abuse-the-dirty-not-so-little-secret-in-sports-by-dr-alan-goldberg/

they are weak. Therefore, when the Headmaster and the Board published the second lawyer's report, it acted as an amazingly powerful gesture to silence students who had asked for protection. The technique it used was exactly what the students most feared and most wanted to be safe from: humiliation.

The terms of reference set out by the Board had blocked certain students from speaking up or being interviewed. The lawyer did not ask to speak to parents of students who gave testimonies; however, one father went in to listen to the interview with his son. He reported that the second lawyer asked leading questions: "Do you think it's harder to move from sports at a junior level to a senior level?" Our son left his interview disgusted saying that he was asked nothing about the abusive conduct, only questions such as "so in a day at school, you don't see one of the teachers very often do you?" There are significant flaws with the lawyer's ten-page report; the most disappointing was that it did not provide any findings; it only gave conclusions that read more like uninformed opinions.

In comparable investigations done at universities, such as the one done by lawyer Christy Fargnoli in reference to basketball coach, Doug Wojcik's conduct, the detailed complaints are attached.[161] In the lawyer's report done at my former school, it makes it difficult for anyone to understand the conclusions when they cannot see the findings upon which they were based. Moreover, there appear to be many problems with the conclusions. For instance, two whole pages out of ten are dedicated to making a rationale for teacher conduct that is so obviously biased that it puts the rest of the report in doubt. Also, the lawyer used a very narrow

---

[161] Christy R. Fargnoli, "Investigative Summary and Report, Re: Doug Wojcik Investigation," June 2014: http://www.postandcourier.com/assets/pdf/Investigative%20Report%20-%20Wojcik%202014%2006%2026.pdf

scope of whom he spoke to and so the report is therefore fundamentally flawed. Equally problematic, the report is drafted in such a way as to perpetuate the themes which were running through the school's first process which was designed to create an us-versus-them mentality, pit Alumni against students, and in this case, distinguish the minority from the majority; it isolated student complainants inferring they are the ones with the problem; and it blamed those that had complained for not being tough enough to transition into higher-level competition. The stated goal of this second report was to achieve "reconciliation and...benefit...the School community." If this was the goal, the report was likely never going to recommend that the teachers be disciplined. This was another flaw in the terms of reference. The goal should have been to ensure that all students could play their sport in a safe and healthy environment.

Although I was away on summer holidays and out of the country, when asked to comment on terms of reference, I sent the following email saying that "reconciliation" must *not* be the stated goal of the report:

> In terms of the paragraph with the goal being reconciliation and benefits to all...I believe we want to stress the first priority is to protect all students, especially abused students, especially considering that the process to date has exposed three students to peer bullying that echoes and thus reinforces exactly teacher bullying.

My concerns about the terms of reference did not lead to any changes. The goal of the report should have been to ensure that students were able to attend school safe from bullying from either teachers or peers in light of very worrisome, corroborating testimonies detailing teacher bullying. The goal of the report should have been to assess just how much harm had been done to multiple adolescents, but this kind of report is more likely written by a "child care worker," the one who should be doing the report according to the Ministry of Education, not a lawyer.

176

The lawyer stated on page two of his report that the "test" he was undertaking was to "determine if there were any behaviors that were abusive or demeaning, or if viewed by a reasonable person, would be considered interference with a person's enjoyment of a school activity." However, he changes these terms when he provides the results. On page ten, the question he answers instead is whether or not there were behaviors "that were *deliberately* abusive or demeaning and constituted *inappropriate* interference with a person's enjoyment of a school activity" (emphasis mine). He no longer uses the "reasonable person" as his measuring stick. Moreover, he inserts the terms "deliberately" and "inappropriate": the first insertion ultimately leads to excusing the four coaches' behavior by saying it wasn't intentional, and the second insertion then suggests the coaches' behavior was justified: students deserved the treatment they got.

When thirty parents and fourteen students come forward with allegations of abuse, it is utterly irrelevant whether or not the teacher or coach was purposeful or deliberate. Intention is not the measuring stick used to determine abuse. The Ministry of Education's Teacher Regulation Branch has set out very clear policies that indicate the question of whether harmful actions by teachers are deliberate or not is irrelevant: "students must be protected from certificate holders who inflict physical, emotional or sexual harm on them (intentionally or otherwise)."[162] Ashley Stirling and Gretchen Kerr explain in no uncertain terms that intention is irrelevant when dealing with emotional abuse:

> Although the commission of an act must be deliberate, the intent to inflict harm is not required for a coach's behavior to be classified as emotional abuse. As described above, many athletes

---

[162] http://www.bcteacherregulation.ca/documents/FormsandPublications/ ProfConduct/duty_to_report_COQ.pdf

177

suggested that emotional abuse was inflicted by their coaches in the name of performance and winning, outcomes that benefit both the coach and the athlete, and are highly valued in sport. Although these behaviors were not intended to bring harm to the athlete, the long-term detrimental effects of the abuse were still endured.[163]

Abuse is not measured by whether or not the perpetrator deliberately set out to harm; it is measured by the damage done.

Further problems with the lawyer's report result from its failure to establish a standard of comparison for what constitutes appropriate coaching. The lawyer does not draw on BC School Sports' guidelines for coaches, let alone teachers. He does not compare to coaching conduct at other schools. There is no discussion around the distinction between intense coaching that teaches self-responsibility and intense coaching focused on blame or bullying. The report's on-going self-referencing to the development of intense, disciplined athletes, versus players not being able to handle it, is a gross oversimplification: coaches can be tough, but respectful; they can push players and push personal accountability, but that does not mean they must repeatedly scream at, blame, humiliate, and shun certain targeted players.

As Dr. Laurence Steinberg explains, "Organized sports, when overseen by coaches who understand and genuinely care about their players' mental as well as physical health, can also contribute to the development of self-control, grit, and the ability to function as a member of a team" (210).[164] The key to Steinberg's opinion, based on forty years of work with adolescents, extensive research, and contributing to the field

---

[163] Ashley E. Stirling and Gretchen A. Kerr, "Defining and categorizing emotional abuse in sport," *European Journal of Sport Science*, July 2008: 8 (4): 173-181.
[164] Laurence Steinberg, *Age of Opportunity: Lessons from the New Science of Adolescence*, Boston and New York: Houghton, Mifflin, Harcourt, 2014.

by means of his five book-length studies is the inclusive idea of "players." Not some players, while others pay a price. Not one player at the expense of another. The care extends to all and the coach is an individual who is defined by understanding and overseeing adolescent health.

In the report done at my former school, in the lawyer's conclusions, he does not address the fact that the terms of reference drafted by the Board of Governors for the investigation excluded certain students from reporting their experiences to him. At least one student who wanted to tell him her experience appealed to him to do so and he refused because the terms of reference only covered students who had played during the 2012 season. With this in mind, the lawyer could have at least acknowledged in the report the weaknesses of self-selected interviewees. While he hinges his decisions on majority versus minority, he does not acknowledge in the report that students had been exposed by the Headmaster, then bullied by peers, and therefore some players may have been afraid to speak up. He does not address the fact that students in residence had some of the coaches as "house-parents" and one of the coaches was a player's father. These ties make speaking up exceedingly difficult. In an argument that is based on majority versus minority, it is surely relevant that some students could not risk speaking up because if they were exposed, as happened previously in a process where confidentiality was breached by the Headmaster, they could lose the opportunity for letters of reference or scholarships. Highly motivated students at a university prep-school have applications and hoped-for acceptances as a significant pressure throughout grade eleven and twelve.

In the lawyer's report, the terms of reference "whether human rights principles" had been violated suggests that the complaints included allegations of racist, homophobic or sexist remarks or remarks averse to those with disabilities. Surely in today's society, it is no longer acceptable to refer to anyone as a "retard" or "pussy," or refer to a First Nations player as "lazy" or say in an email that the team needs to sharpen its knives to go out "scalp-hunting," all of which students reported in their testimonies or are recorded on email. Three players on the team had learning disabilities, which makes the use of "retard" a discriminatory insult. All the boys on the team were slammed with homophobic terms according to the students' testimonies, but the lawyer never mentions human rights principles in his report despite it being one of his terms of reference. Recently, the Court of Appeal in BC has recognized that a person does not need to be gay or appear gay to have their Human Rights violated in this way:

> The B.C. Human Rights Tribunal accepted that Mr. Jubran was not homosexual, and that the students who engaged in homophobic taunting did not necessarily believe that he was. Nonetheless, the Tribunal found that the conduct was harassment on the basis of sexual orientation. Whether his fellow students believed Mr. Jubran was homosexual or not, they used homophobic epithets to ridicule and belittle him.[165]

At my former school, the boys state clearly in their testimonies that when called "pussy" and "soft" or told to "grow some balls," it in no way assisted them in improving at basketball. Instead, they felt ridiculed and belittled. However, the lawyer does not include the students' testimonies or even an abridged version or even a few quotations; therefore, it is difficult for people reading it to know if the second lawyer's characterizations or conclusions are valid. The Headmaster had told the faculty that students had "unhappy experiences." That was the extent of their knowledge of what students had experienced. Likewise, parents had not been informed.

---

[165] http://www.cdn-hr-reporter.ca/hr_topics/sexual-orientation/homophobic-harassment-student-breaches-code

In his report, the lawyer included "interfering parents," "nasty lies," "hijacked," "awesome," "caring and committed," "manufacturing evidence of abuse" and an entire email justifying the behavior of the coaches. Only one quote from one of the players who has concerns is included. From the perspective of both the credibility of the report, and even for the skewed goal of "reconciliation," this is a serious weakness. The insulting comments made by anonymous students in the lawyer's report appear to be an effective way for the lawyer to side-step responsibility for defaming those who had come forward, as well as to reverse the whole issue so that somehow the student-athletes seemed to be the problem while the teachers were suddenly the ones with complaints.

According to experts, reversal also occurs in the workplace when narcissists and bullies run the show, as discussed by Jean Ritala, author of *Narcissism in the Workplace*:

> In the workplace, says Ritala, narcissists tend to be successful and goal-oriented, with no concern for others who get in their way. They feel a need to control co-workers, projects and situations around them, and they can be manipulative, spinning situations
>
> and facts to make it appear that others around them are the problem, not them.[166]

At my former school, the attention shifted from the abusive teachers, as reported by the students, and instead focused on those very same students and their parents as if they were troublemakers.

Finally, in a number of places, the lawyer's report falls back on cagey drafting that is essentially confusing; for instance, it states that the

---

[166] Thomas Hoffman, "Narcissists at work: How to deal with arrogant, controlling, manipulative bullies," *Computer World*, June 2008: http://www.computerworld.com/article/2535227/it-management/narcissists-at-work--how-to-deal-with-arrogant--controlling--manipulative-bullies.html

181

players who had concerns "did not say that the coach was consciously swearing at any individuals." Does the lawyer mean that he never asked those players that question? Does he mean it didn't come up? Or did those players say that they did not think the coach was swearing at anyone? The second lawyer's conclusion may not be that compelling in light of the transcripts. Every single testimony details that irate or disgusted swearing at the team or at individuals happened all the time.

While the police reported a "definite pattern in the complaints, all pointing to verbal and emotional abuse," the lawyer's report stated that the students do not use the word "abuse" to describe their experience. However, the fact that the players with concerns did not use the word "abuse" is immaterial, particularly without reviewing the testimonies and factoring in the age of the interviewees and the culture. It would make far more sense for the testimonies to be sent to an expert in the use of emotional abuse in coaching or a "child care worker" to ascertain whether or not the behavior was abusive. Most importantly, the lawyer seems to forget that investigating multiple students' reports of bullying by teachers is not about majority rule. All it takes is one student to be abused and that is abuse, let alone fourteen. He seems to miss that point.

In Dr. Laurence Steinberg's 2014 study of adolescence, he discusses how a teenager can be easily manipulated by an adult investigator even into confessing to a crime he did not do: "Adolescents are especially susceptible" to the techniques of interrogators "not only because they are less savvy than adults, but because the methods exploit adolescents' cognitive immaturity."[167] When the Lawyer/ parent and I took testimonies, they were handed back to the students to ensure accuracy and to ensure no misunderstanding, let alone manipulation, had

---

[167] Laurence Steinberg, *Age of Opportunity: Lessons from the New Science of Adolescence*, Boston and New York: Houghton, Mifflin, Harcourt, 2014 (195).

occurred. Dr. Steinberg's research raises a serious issue with regard to students being exposed to investigators, like the ones hired by the Headmaster and Board, who are well versed in labor and employment law, but are unaccustomed to interviewing adolescents. It is hard to understand why a Headmaster and a Board of Governors would respond to student reports of abuse by hiring two lawyers – both specializing in dispute resolution and neither with expertise, or experience as far as I can tell, with child or teen abuse victims. It is even more difficult to understand why the Commissioner for Teacher Regulation by-passed his in-house, experienced investigators and contracted out to a lawyer and a former police interrogator to conduct his investigation. If lawyers and interrogators can manipulate children and teens into giving them the answers they want, then the legal system does not appear to operate like an equal playing field when it comes to abuse victims, especially when these victims are children or teens. This must change.

In August 2012, just before students were to return for their second to last or final year at the school, the Headmaster and the Board of Governors published the second lawyer's report to Administrators, faculty and staff at school, and to at least sixty families. They published the report fully aware that the students, who had already been exposed, by the Headmaster himself, had already suffered terribly as targets of peer bullying for having spoken up. The Headmaster and Board's wide distribution of this report appeared to silence anyone else from reporting on teacher bullying at the school. The report successfully re-established a code of silence among students and parents.

In his report, the lawyer makes the argument that if you find the courage to speak up about teacher bullying, it means you're not a disciplined athlete, your ego is not well developed and you lack confidence. He states that, "Basketball is an intense game that demands discipline." The implication seems to be that the players who report on the coach's bullying can't handle the sport's intensity and they lack discipline. The second lawyer effectively shifts the focus from emotional abuse inflicted by teachers, to the weakness and sensitivity of students. He clarifies further by saying, "My point is to remind us of the obvious: for some players, what was a fun game in which they could fully compete with their teammates and others, has become an increasingly demanding burden on their ego and self-confidence." One wonders how this lawyer reached this conclusion and why he spoke about students' psychological make-up rather than addressing the issue at hand: teacher misconduct and attendant harm. He could have just said more straightforwardly that some students did not want to be called "pussies" or "fucking soft'" or "embarrassments" by their teachers, but instead, he explains why in his opinion multiple students and their parents want the teacher bullying to stop. The lawyer implies that students who report on abusive conduct by a teacher can't handle the "increasingly demanding burden on their ego" of basketball because they are weak and insecure; or to use the teachers' terms, they're soft or pussies. This is the equivalent of saying a woman was sexually harassed because she dressed in a particular way or a woman was raped because she went to the wrong part of town. Instead of addressing the conduct of the harasser or the rapist, a lawyer holds the victim accountable for what has happened. The lawyer writing the report apparently believed bullying from teacher to student has a place in a coach's repertoire of teaching practices that can be used to assist ego-development. However, it is interesting to put this assessment side by side with the student testimonies. The teenagers are very clear that the yelling and degrading does not contribute positively to their ego development. In the words of one female basketball player,

> I was so worried about making a mistake that I would make a mistake because of the yelling which made me worse because I was so worried all the time. It hurts to see her yell at Nadine and Andrea all the time. It was bad because their confidence got shot.

*They didn't live up to their potential. She singles them out and yells only bad stuff. There's no recognition of doing anything right. "Keep up the fucking pace."*

*"Was that a shot? That was nothing."*

*She would say fuck all the time. "Fucking pathetic."*

This testimony, like the others, reads like the ones university students gave about Mike Rice or Shann Hart: the student-athlete is riddled with anxiety, fear, and humiliation. Some of these student-athletes became suicidal. These reactions do not gel with the lawyer's report at my former school as he implies that greater levels of competition – namely transitioning from high school to university – requires student athletes to develop in abusive conditions. If the lawyer is right and students should be faulted as athletes who aren't committed, disciplined and dedicated, then how does he explain the university level coaches who are fired for the kind of coaching conduct he praises. The lawyer's argument seems completely out of touch with university athletes who have repeatedly reported experiencing similar, if not identical, behavior on the part of their coaches. Every university coach discussed in the news, even one with four students reporting on the coach's emotionally abusive conduct and thirty athletes defending her, has been fired.

As Charles M. Blow writes in the *New York Times* in response to Mike Rice's firing by Rutgers Administration, "The good coach must not only be the model, but must teach our child athletes that there is a line between demanding and demeaning that no one who truly cares for others would cross."[168] Notably, he is focused on the coach's demeaning conduct that should also have been the issue at hand in the lawyer's report made

---

[168] Charles M. Blow, "Calm Down, Coaches," *New York Times*, April 2013: http://www.nytimes.com/2013/04/04/opinion/blow-is-coach-rices-behavior-typical.html?_r=1&

widely available at my former school. I wonder how readers of the *New York Times* would respond if Charles Blow argued that Mike Rice's use of homophobic terms, his ranting and raving, his shoving and swearing indicated that the student-athletes on the basketball team at Rutgers wanted to play recreational basketball and were lacking in "commitment" to their sport. It would seem to me that being subjected to this horrific bullying, practice after practice, game after game, season after season shows in fact a strong "commitment" to basketball.

Imagine this scenario on the playground: one kid calls the other a pussy and a retard. A number of children are interviewed independently and they confirm the incident. One assumes at this juncture, the principal would act, but instead, he brings in a lawyer to write a report. The lawyer re-interviews the students and again they confirm this was said. The lawyer then concludes that the kid who was called a pussy and a retard wasn't fully committed to playground activities and, while it wasn't very nice, bottom line is the victim was not transitioning fully into grade one and thus had it coming to him.

> On our son's 2012 report card, the Head Coach wrote the following comment:
>
> [Your son] is on the cusp of becoming one of the best ever of [of the school's] performers. At times, I think the only one who may not realize this is him! He looks he might grow to be as tall as 6'6, and possesses an ever-developing array of offensive moves. He does need to be physically tougher on a more consistent basis, but, in saying that, he has also more than shown an ability to guard multiple positions and rebound effectively. In my opinion, he should be a much sought after CIS [Canadian Interuniversity Sport] player upon graduation [. . .] in 2013 – with the caveat of course that he wants to invest the necessary blood, sweat and tears to reach this standard.

This report card comment predicts athletic greatness, but there is the underlying refrain about toughness. In grade seven, our son was asked to play up with the School's grade eight rugby team. He played soccer and basketball in grade eight as well as rowed on the school's gold medal winning quad. He won Athlete of the Year in Middle School. On top of his other sports, he also played competitive ice-hockey outside of school. He'd played since grade four and only stopped to concentrate on basketball. On his grade nine report, before his growth spurt, our son was commended by his coaches specifically for being "tough" and for going up against much larger opponents. As a junior player in grade ten, he was brought along by the Senior Basketball coaches to play in the Senior boys' Provincial Championships such was his commitment and skill. Almost every single basketball camp he attended, and there were many in Victoria, Vancouver, even Santa Barbara, every chance he got he went to training camps, he was repeatedly given awards for his hard work and skill, but he hadn't yet encountered coaches who repeatedly made student-athletes cower and cry. He committed to giving them his blood and sweat, but he set his mind to never giving them his "tears."

The humiliating diatribe that he was "soft," not tough enough, a "retard" and a "pussy" was muttered in grade ten and yelled in his face in grade eleven. Still, he never shed a tear. He set as his goal not to let the teachers break him. The lawyer's report does not refer to any of these facts when he says that our son lacked commitment, discipline, and ego-development. We could have supplied the lawyer with the information, but he did not ask to meet with us or any other parents with concerns. In his report, he refers to parents that were pleased with the students' treatment, but there is no reference in the report to parents who came to the Administration with serious concerns about emotional abuse. We were not part of his investigation. We were not consulted about our children's concerns and interviews being published by the Headmaster.

In the staff lounge one day, in the fall of 2011, the Head Coach, who wrote the report card comment about our son becoming one of the School's best ever performers, asked me how he could better reach our son, how he could galvanize him. I thought about it and sent him an email saying that our son had been bullied in grade one and in grade three and that was why we had moved him to an independent school and that he loved it. I advised the Head Coach to get him to play for the school. He thanked me for my insight. I could never have imagined that in the following spring, I would take testimonies hearing over and over again from boys on the team that this same coach targeted our son with vicious, relentless bullying.

In *Raising Cain: Protecting the Emotional Life of Boys*, two of America's leading child psychologists, Dan Kindlon and Michael Thompson expose the lie told to boys about toughness:

> Stereotypical notions of masculine toughness deny a boy his emotions and rob him of the chance to develop the full range of emotional resources. We call this process, in which a boy is steered away from his inner world, the emotional *mis*education of boys. It is a training away from healthful attachment and emotional understanding and expression, and it affects even the youngest boy, who learns quickly, for instance, that he must hide his feelings and silence his fears. A boy is left to manage conflict, adversity, and change in his life with a limited emotional repertoire. If your toolbox contains only a hammer, it's not a problem as long as all your equipment is running right or repairs call only for pounding. But as tasks grow more complex, the hammer's limitations become clear.[169]

---

[169] Dan Kindlon and Michael Thompson, *Raising Cain: Protecting the Emotional Life of Boys*, New York and Toronto: Random House, 1999: 4.

This description may well have applied to the Head Coach himself who was young and may well have suffered. In contrast, the fourteen students who came forward at my former school must have had such a deep sense of what constituted "healthful attachment" and "emotional understanding" that they could identify and speak up about what felt to them to be a violation of such relationships. Even while they were hammered by the authorities in their world – from the Coaches to the Headmaster and Board of Governors to the legal and educational authorities – they still refused to give up their "inner world" filled with a whole host of complex emotional and intellectual tools that made these authorities' hammers appear primitive and, although very painful, ultimately limited.

In the midst of the crisis, these insights are meaningful, but they can't protect children or teenagers. The catch twenty-two for parents and students when dealing with a bullying teacher is that speaking up could result in more punishment or loss of opportunity. We worried that if our son, or worse, we spoke up, his chances to play university ball would be ruined. He needed playing time; he needed the chance to win awards; he needed to be seen as an elite athlete; he needed letters of reference. Now that I look back, I can't believe that we were ever forced into that position at a high-school: how do you get to a place where you ultimately have to allow your child to be bullied by his teachers because his future hangs in the balance? The power that high-school teachers and administrators have over students and therefore their parents is enormous and needs to be examined and questioned.

We asked for letters of reference from the teachers; the Head Coach never replied despite his glowing report card comments in 2012, and the Assistant Coach sent a letter, but it couldn't be used as it contained incorrect statistics and damned him with faint praise. Ironically enough, our son wasn't able to get any proper statistics, or ever be considered for awards, because the coaches kept him on the bench while

189

constantly telling him and the team he was the best player. When he was put on the All-Star Team by other coaches at a tournament, he was pulled aside and privately told about his award by his own coaches as if it was something to keep quiet. The following year, when our son played a once a week pick-up game with the former Assistant Athletic Director at University of Victoria, we asked for a letter of reference, and in his letter, he predicts greatness, a "champion" in the making just like the report card comments made by the Head Coach – the one who did not reply to our request for a recommendation letter. As a teacher, I know professionally that my personal relationship with a student or his parents is irrelevant. It's not my job to ever act or speak from a personally invested place in terms of how I communicate with post-secondary institutions. My job requires me to assess pure and simple student achievement and potential. The fact that not even this professional duty could be completed by either teacher at my former school, in their role as coach, speaks volumes about how that institution operates.

We could not have imagined that the refusal to give an honest and fair assessment of our son's potential as a basketball player could go any lower in terms of failing him as a student. However, in August 2012, the Headmaster published the lawyer's report that positioned our son, along with the other students who came forward, as liars. Not only could he not apply to university as a student athlete, he now had the added worry that teachers and Administrators might jeopardize his university applications by foregrounding that their lawyer's report positioned him as undisciplined, frivolous, a manufacturer of evidence and a liar.

There was no opportunity for students or parents to read the lawyer's report and debate its conclusions or respond to them before the Headmaster published it to the community. The lawyer's ten-page report devoted a whole page to an email sent by an anonymous student, which the lawyer believed would explain why there were multiple students reporting abuse at the same time others were defending the teachers. The student's explanation was this: "I believe that at this level, the coaches are not here to babysit us, but are here to push us to reach our fullest potential."

Instead of turning to an email sent to him during his investigation, it might have made more sense for the lawyer to check in with authorities such as the RCMP in terms of understanding how to assess a situation where multiple students have reported abuse. As the RCMP advises,

- Child abuse usually reflects patterns of behavior rather than an isolated incident.
- The vast majority of child abusers are parents, relatives, or trusted adults, not strangers.
- Children rarely lie about abuse. They are more likely to deny abuse and take back truthful statements than to make false reports.[170]

More important advice from the RCMP on child abuse is "Believe in the child" because "lack of belief will discourage the abused from disclosing."[171] It would appear that unlike most investigations into alleged child abuse, the goal at my former school certainly seemed as if it was to "discourage the abused from disclosing." What with the Headmaster's breach of confidentiality, the humiliating and harmful report he published was an effective way to "discourage the abused from disclosing." Students who may have come forward, if supported and respected, were now far more likely to avoid reporting and even deny that anything had happened. Lack of belief is one thing, but having it publicly insinuated that students were lying and manufacturing evidence, and that they are

---

[170] http://www.rcmp-grc.gc.ca/pubs/ccaps-spcca/chi-enf-eng.htm#Emotional
[171] Ibid.

immature, uncommitted and babyish is a whole other level of discouraging students from reporting on abuse.

Rather than turning to a teenager to assess a serious situation in a randomly sent anonymous email, it might have been more reasonable for the lawyer to turn to more informed sources such as *Canada's Safety Council* so that he would not have been swayed so easily. The Council notes that bosses are almost always the bullies in the workplace, as one needs power over another in order to abuse, then adds the following: "And contrary to popular belief, bullies don't go after the weakest link, they tend to aim for the strongest." *The Safety Council's* report states that "bullies pick on capable, co-operative people they identify as a threat."[172] These don't sound like people who need a babysitter.

Likewise, a study of elite athletes in Britain revealed that athletes were greater targets of coach abuse when they were identified as being exceptional.[173] Perhaps the anonymous student quoted by the lawyer is wrong; perhaps the teachers were in fact targeting skilled, dedicated, hard-working athletes. These students might have posed a threat to the coaches' egos. If an athlete feels afraid of the coach, it does not mean that he or she is weak and lacks the competitive drive to excel, as the lawyer claims in his report. As discussed in the *Abused Athletes' Perceptions of the Coach-Athlete Relationship*, a 2009 study of elite athletes: "Participants recalled being intimidated both physically and mentally by

---

[172] http://www.canadianliving.com/life/work/dealing_with_workplace_bullies.php
[173] "Interviews with 12 former elite child athletes from the UK (Gervis & Dunn, 2004) indicated that athletes perceived their coach's behavior as more negative after the athlete was identified as an elite performer compared with pre-elite levels. Accordingly, compared with other levels of athletes, elite athletes may be most likely to have experienced a pattern of emotionally abusive behaviors in the coach–athlete relationship." Ashley E. Stirling and Gretchen A. Kerr, "The perceived effects of elite athletes' experiences of emotional abuse in the coach–athlete relationship." *The International Journal of Sport and Exercise Psychology* 11.1, 2013: 87-100.

the coach, and the fear of upsetting or disappointing the coach was expressed as a major concern for athletes."[174] Notably, the coach's conduct is investigated here, not the egos of players. Their fear, anxiety, and intimidation are discussed in terms of how the coach impacts them, not as some integral weakness in their characters.

In an article written for *CBC Sports* in 2012, Teddy Katz examines complaints lodged by elite Olympic rowers against legendary coach, Mike Spracklen. Katz records Olympic medalist Darren Barber's experience suffering coach abuse. When Barber returned to the team after taking some time off for his studies and was bringing in exceptional times, Spracklen held races to see who would earn their position in the boat at the Olympic Games. Barber showed repeatedly that he was the best with the best time, but still Spracklen blocked him:

> "He wasn't the guy that Mike [Spracklen] wanted in the eight. So Mike kept doing the seat race over and over again and Darren [Barber] kept winning but Mike was going to continue to do that seat race until his guy won."

> Brian Richardson, the head coach at the time, was dumfounded too.

> "I feel like I let Darren down a bit because I got a surprise, I didn't think it was an issue whether Darren was going to be in the boat or not, and suddenly he's out of the boat."

> He says even worse, Spracklen didn't give the news to Barber in person.

> "The tragic side of that I thought, was that he never even spoke to Darren. This was a guy that won a Gold Medal for him [in

---

[174] Ashley E. Stirling and Gretchen A. Kerr, "Abused Athletes' Perceptions of the Coach-Athlete Relationship," *Sport in Society* Vol.12.2, March 2009: 227-239.

1992] and rowed his heart out, a terrific competitor, incredibly tough, a guy I have enormous respect for and he just cut him out."

According to Teddy Katz's article, Spracklen not only appeared to be a coach who targeted, penalized, and then ignored some of his best athletes, but not surprisingly, he also falls into the category of charismatic bully: while he has staunch defenders and has won many Olympic medals for Canada, others "allege that Spracklen grinds down athletes, plays favorites, trains in dangerous conditions, and verbally picks on rowers." Elite athletes quit Spracklen's teams at great personal cost. Katz writes, "Tracy Cameron quit rowing and walked away from her Olympic spot just two months before these Games. It was an unusual move by an athlete who had worked hard to come back from injury to earn her Olympic spot on the lightweight women's double team." It would be hard to argue that this elite athlete lacked talent, didn't want to work hard, wasn't tough or any of the others excuses that people come up with to try and rationalize or normalize why a once passionate and committed athlete gives up a sport at which they excel. Instead, society must turn to the coach and wonder why, to use rower Tracy Cameron's words, the coach finds it necessary to "emotionally hurt" their athletes.[175]

Continuing his exploration of coach Mike Spracklen's conflicted approach, Teddy Katz consults Olympic rower, David Calder who describes scenes that sound near-identical to what was repeatedly done to our son as described in student testimonies. Calder was a target after he had a family and Spracklen thought he had lost focus and so tore into him with a "tirade that lasted a full five minutes in front of the whole team." None of the rowers spoke up and instead simply watched the coach

---

[175] Teddy Katz, "No Middle Ground with Mike Spracklen," *CBCSports*, August 2012: http://www.cbc.ca/sports-content/opinion/olympics2012/2012/08/there-is-no-middle-ground-with-rowing-coach-mike-spracklen.html

publicly humiliate Calder: "Nobody on that team said anything, everybody stuck their head down because there's that environment of fear – the culture of fear that if you stick your neck out then you're the next person on the chopping block."[176] If adult athletes being bullied by a coach experience this fear, imagine how intense it is for teenagers especially when the coach is also a teacher.

• • •

If a student harmed another student's character by emailing, posting or tweeting comments that anonymously called their target a liar and said he was in need of a babysitter, particularly humiliating for adolescent boys, it would fall into the category of cyber bullying. At my former school, however, these character-assassinating comments were written and published by adults in positions of authority and power. Cyber bullying lacks any kind of physical or sexual interaction and yet more and more laws are being written to regulate the harm people do via social media. This is ironic considering that emotional abuse continues to be outside of the Criminal Code even when it's done by caregivers in positions of power over children as opposed to unknown figures on the internet. According to the Canadian Bar Association:

> Cyber bullying is a type of harassment using new technology. Whether it is criminal harassment depends on the facts of a case. Cyber bullies use social media (such as *Facebook*, *Twitter*, and *YouTube*), blogs, texting, instant messaging, and other internet avenues to engage in deliberate, repeated, and hostile behavior intended to harm, embarrass, or slander someone. Although their work is public, cyber bullies are often anonymous and it is often harder to identify and stop them.

---

[176] Ibid.

Cyber bullying may also be defamation. The *Criminal Code* (section 300) outlaws publishing a defamatory libel – material published, without lawful justification or excuse, likely to injure the reputation of any person by exposing them to hatred, contempt or ridicule, or designed to insult the person. But criminal defamation is rare. More common is civil defamation – communication about a person that tends to hurt their reputation.[177]

Three boys had already been exposed by the Headmaster; those boys had already been targeted by peer bullies, and therefore, their names were essentially attached to the lawyer's report prepared for the Board and published widely by the Headmaster. The Headmaster and Board did not ask permission to publish the second lawyer's report and students and their families who had been working in good faith with school Administration were understandably shocked when it was emailed out to all staff, faculty, and Administrators as well as at least sixty families. The report was now in the hands of the very teachers that the students reported on and this report could now be sent anywhere: to schools that parents might have wanted to transfer their children to or to university admissions or to coaches if they wanted to try out as student-athletes. The Headmaster put a potentially effective weapon into the hands of teachers about whom students had explained in detail that they felt harmed by, did not trust and, more seriously, feared.

In the 2012 spring, even before the second lawyer's report was published, the boys, exposed by the Headmaster, were victims of further contempt and hatred in the school community and beyond. They could not defend themselves without support from the school Administrators. In my opinion as a teacher and as a parent, the Headmaster and Board did not

---

[177] http://www.cbabc.org/For-the-Public/Dial-A-Law/Scripts/Criminal-Law/206.aspx

have lawful justification or excuse for publishing the second lawyer's report: they did not ask permission of parents or students to share confidential information and the report was defamatory, especially to those students already exposed by the Headmaster and targeted by peers.

Parents know how much power and influence the Headmaster has that could even affect their ability to work. I know of at least five parents whose careers have been affected by their decision to stand up in the name of protecting their children and other students. In March 2012, I wrote in a letter to the Lawyer/ Board Member that we initially contacted that by speaking up, I was aware, I was putting my job and hence my livelihood on the line. He asked if he could share my letter with the Headmaster and I agreed. It would have been a lot easier to just remain quiet. There's a lot of safety in being a bystander and my former school was an emotionally and ethically unsafe place for me. As I anticipated, a poisonous work environment developed around me and I ultimately was forced to leave the school and find another job or sacrifice my health and sanity. This does not appear to be an isolated incident. What's profoundly disturbing is that this kind of conduct appears to go on elsewhere, perhaps in many places where there is a power imbalance of adult to child, coach to athlete, teacher to student. When I was educating myself about coaching abuse, the dynamics discussed in an article, "Coaching Abuse: The Dirty, Not-So-Little Secret in Sports" by Dr. Alan Goldberg was so painfully familiar. He discusses the response of an Athletic Director to a student-athlete who came forward about being emotionally abused by her coach:

> What the AD was very much interested in was maintaining the school and program's image as a wonderful place for student-athletes to learn and compete. Shamefully, she colluded with this out of control coach, making her equally as guilty of the abuse. (And the really comforting thing for parents of student-athletes at this fine institution to keep in mind is that this dangerously self-

197

centered, incompetent individual is still in charge of women's athletics!)[178]

In contrast, regardless of his staunch supporters, regardless of his many Olympic medals earned, Mike Spracklen's contract was not renewed by Rowing Canada. This gives me hope that we can all learn as a society that emotional abuse is so highly destructive it is not worth any medals, even Olympic ones.

---

[178] Dr. Alan Goldberg, ""Coaching ABUSE: The Dirty, Not-So-Little Secret In Sports." http://gazette.teachers.net/gazette/wordpress/dr-alan-goldberg/coaching-abuse-the-dirty-not-so-little-secret-in-sports-by-dr-alan-goldberg/

# CHAPTER SEVEN

# THE COURAGE TO SPEAK UP

> *If it was a kid yelling like that in the face of another kid, I would shove him away. We don't with the coaches because we are afraid. He'll bench us and we want to play.*

> – Student Testimony

Students who wanted to play their sport pleaded with their parents not to say anything, knowing that a complaint might result in lost playing time. Students who wanted to take their sport beyond high school couldn't afford to allow these teachers to target them even more. Still, some parents spoke to the Administrators, and were led to believe that they were expressing an isolated complaint and that no one else had a problem. Different families were told there were no records of abusive conduct. I subsequently learned that denying and minimizing bullying behaviors are considered abusive tactics in themselves. They create the necessary conditions for bullying to flourish.

Parents find it very difficult to speak up when a teacher is surrounded by a vocal group of supporters, not only students, but also their parents. When parents or students report a teacher or coach for bullying, there is often an equal or greater outcry from the teacher or coach's supporters. I have learned that this phenomenon is a fundamental component of bullying itself. As one of the students explains the dynamic, *"[the coaches] do want to win, desperately, but only with certain kids."* What emerged from fourteen student testimonies, noted by every single

199

student, was a two-tiered system: the favored students and the bullied students. If you're not on the list of chosen ones, your experience on the team may be extreme frustration, humiliation, and suffering. It shows up in testimony after testimony. This system ensures that some students and their parents will defend the teachers perhaps because they fear becoming the targets or perhaps because they receive other benefits. In their testimonies, all the students remark on how certain players can do no wrong; they are put on pedestals. As one student expressed it, "*The yelling wasn't constructive. I can't remember what was said, but it was a personal attack and it was always directed at me, Frank and Morris. He would never yell at Simon or the Johnsons. [The Assistant Coach] always worked with the Johnsons. They're friends.*"

Another student comments on how the coach would scream humiliating, harsh directives at certain students while pulling others aside, putting his arm around them, and quietly telling them what they needed to work on. Every single testimony spoke to the fact that the teams were not run as a meritocracy; they were about limiting some students and privileging others. As one student recounted,

> *I would get yelled at for something I couldn't fix because I was put in post and didn't have the height. I was yelled at over and over "fucking boxing out." [The coach] doesn't care that it's not possible. It's just a reason for him to get upset. Half the time it's not your fault, but he'd haul you off and yell at you. He would say: "that was useless of you." "You're fucking useless." "Fucking pathetic."*

Another pattern that shows up repeatedly in the testimonies was a student who was skilled enough to help the team win being benched for most of it, and then being lambasted for "*not trying*." As recorded in one student's testimony,

200

> *After the Brentwood game at the Cities we were losing and at half time we all went up [to meet as a team]. I had barely played. In the room [the Head Coach] said I was the reason that we were losing – I was an example of not playing hard. Since I had hardly played I did not feel this was fair. I felt I could never live up to their expectations.*

> *They were always telling me my mistakes. They would say, "You are the best player on the court. Play like it." [The Head Coach] would take me aside and say rhetorical questions in my face. "Do you deserve to be out there? "Do you want to play the next game?" I never felt like I could answer right because if I said yes he would yell at me to play harder or not be so soft. It's hard to take that because you don't know what to do differently.*

Another bullying strategy recorded in multiple testimonies was that certain players were only allowed to pass the ball and not allowed to shoot. Even if they forgot for a moment, shot and scored, they'd be pulled off and reamed out by the coach because the rule was that only the students chosen by the teachers were allowed to shoot baskets. According to one student,

> *...when our team was playing Mt. Doug in one of our final games. I had just shot and scored an open three-pointer and had been put on the bench right away. I was then told by [the coach] that the shot I took was "not one that I should have taken," even though it had gone in! My frustration and anger continued to escalate as one of the favorites on the court then turned it over three times in a row, but [the coach] didn't even bat an eye. That was probably the most frustrating experience I have endured playing basketball.*

Another player describes the same treatment: "*At the Police Tournament, I started hitting threes, they pulled me off and said my defense wasn't good. Everything I did was not good enough.*" This pattern illustrating specific players being favored over others appears again in the testimonies

201

that describe the team being close to winning and the teacher ensuring the game is lost because the stronger, and not favored, players sat on the bench while the favored and weaker players were overwhelmed by the other team. These losses were then typically followed by the teacher tearing into those same stronger players in the locker room for losing the game, or ignoring them, as if the team's loss rendered these teenagers unworthy of attention. As one student recounts,

> We were playing the game of our lives. Everyone was playing so well. We were so happy. There were four minutes left and we were down by two. But [the coach] didn't assign any plays. She said only Joan could take down the ball and try and score. Told us no offense, no defense plays. It doesn't make sense, because this is the kind of play we run when there's only five seconds left in the game and we're down. But we had four minutes.

> I wanted to scream at her. You're a coach. We're playing the best team in the Province (they won Provincials this year). And [the coach] wouldn't call a play. We couldn't do anything so we started to lose points and [the coach] got up and walked off to the far end of the bench and just ignored us. We lost by six when the win was well within our grasp.

If these accounts were one-offs, from perhaps a less skilled player or two, during a bad season, perhaps they could be caulked up to an isolated issue, but there was a definite pattern that emerged in the student testimonies of systemic favoring and targeting. When fourteen students ranging from grade ten to second-year university described in their testimonies the same bullying tactics, year after year, then it would suggest a pattern of psychological abuse. When parents whose children graduated two years earlier spoke to parents whose children were in grade ten and the coaches' behavior, even the phrases used were still the same, it became possible and worrisome that the coaches were playing out a bullying dynamic and not actually interacting with students as individuals.

202

It would be highly unlikely that each year these same coaches had players who could do no wrong side by side with a group who they characterized as "embarrassments." Surely over the course of five years, these coaches must have had one season when the students were a homogenous team, not divided into two clearly defined camps of those worthy to be built up, and those deserving to be torn down.

The favored students would get playing time, awards, pictures in the newspaper, frequent mention in the coach reviews, opportunities to work at the school in the fitness room, assistant coach and most important, immunity from verbal attacks, public humiliation, and shunning. And when complaints came forward from the bullied kids, some of these favored students and their parents came rushing to the coaches' defense. Throughout this experience, I've learned that bystanders – especially when they are beneficiaries – may well be a quiet group until their favoured position is questioned, then they appear to vociferously defend what they believe to be their entitled turf.

Bullying causes such anxiety that it's near impossible to get students to speak up and avoid the safe place of being a bystander. It is striking in the student testimonies that the students, bullied by their coaches, could make a distinction: they were aware that if it was only peer to peer, the players would have stepped in and put a stop to it. However, the student-athletes were paralyzed, because it was the coaches and they were also teachers. It's not appropriate for a student to tell a teacher what to do, let alone say that his or her conduct is wrong and harmful. Added into this dynamic, established since kindergarten, is that the teacher is invested with enormous power to impact the students' present and future; hence, parents teach their children to respect and "listen to your teacher." There are clear risks involved in speaking up to try to stop the bullying. The students who faced this intolerable situation leave a demoralizing record of what it was like to witness other students being bullied, and of how powerless they felt to do anything to stop it:

> *Sometimes I wanted to stop what was happening. There were a lot of times when [the coach] would grab Malcolm by the arm when he would try to get away and [the coach] would pull him back for more yelling. Malcolm would try to zone him out. I would have stepped in and stopped it if it was player to player, but you can't when it was a teacher. A lot of guys wanted to step in.*

This is a telling moment in which to recall the neuroscientific studies discussed previously. As noted, research shows that there are not just psychological reasons why so many students do not report on their abuse; there are also physical ones.

Dr. John Schinnerer wrote that the "2007 Penn State study found that the trauma endured by bullied children results in physical changes. The study, performed by JoLynn Carney, found that levels of cortisol, the stress hormone, were elevated in the saliva both of children who had been bullied recently and in those children who were anticipating being bullied in the near future."[179] In terms of why so many student-athletes don't report on coach-abuse the following is vital: "Ironically, when cortisol levels spike, our ability to think clearly, learn or remember goes right out the window." Dr. Schinnerer offers a compelling reason why bullied athletes may remain silent about their abuse, or are unable to recognize it for what it is. Due to spikes in cortisol levels, "those coaches who rely on fear and intimidation ensure their athletes won't recall any of what they said while they are ranting and raving."[180] As one of the students expresses this phenomenon, "*I can't remember a lot of the bad stuff. I*

---

[179] http://psychcentral.com/lib/the-consequences-of-verbally-abusive-athletic-coaches/0001152
[180] Ibid.

*blocked it out.* " This offers a plausible explanation for why it is that student-athletes will defend their coach's conduct when allegations of abuse are brought forward: it is possible that they don't remember being abused especially if the abuse was repetitive and relentless, and they were full of fear. It is possible that, coached by teachers who instilled fear, the Alumni at my former school who wrote in to praise the teachers might not have recalled the ranting and raving for this reason. When their letters of praise are put side by side with recent video footage capturing the Assistant Coach expressing apparent disgust while screaming, ranting, and raving in a wholly inarticulate way, pulling on his hair, putting his head in his hands and gesturing wildly, there appears to be a disconnect. None of the involved parents have seen the Alumni letters and it's possible they praise the Assistant Coach, described above, but not the Head Coach, who the players described in their testimonies as worse.

Although the Headmaster says there are no records in the Assistant Coach's file, there was a very public instance of complaints about his conduct with student-athletes. In fact, the present Headmaster found himself in his position at the school as a result of parental concerns about the Assistant Coach. In 1995, the Assistant Coach had multiple complaints by parents whose children were on the rugby team. Supposedly their complaints were about "playing time" which is what has been said repeatedly about the students who spoke up in 2012. This is a partial truth that effectively deflects concerns about humiliation, fear, and favoritism. In yet another textbook example of reversal, the Assistant Coach claimed that the former Headmaster was not protecting *him*. He called a vote of non-confidence with the faculty, and the former Headmaster lost his position. The present Headmaster likes to tell the story about how after this crisis, the School "came calling" and he was hired. The Assistant Coach has immense influence at the school so that when student and parent complaints about his treatment of children arise, year after year, he has many effective strategies to silence them.

Considering it is so rare for victims to speak up, when fourteen students come forward to ask for constructive change, as they did at my former school, one would assume that the Headmaster and Board of Governors would pay attention, especially when this is not the first time they'd heard complaints about these particular teachers. Even if we ignore red flags from the past and just restrict the available evidence to this particular instance, it is remarkable when a detailed document from a Lawyer/ parent, concerns from the police, phone calls from an educational psychologist, a letter from an expert in the psychology of coach abuse, video footage, complaints from many parents and testimonies by students and interviews with students, are dismissed by a Headmaster and a Board of Governors using two separate reports drafted by lawyers they hired which perhaps is meant to give their minimizing and dismissing an official stamp. Although repeatedly referring to it, they have suppressed one of these reports without explanation. More surprising, they have widely published the other report. These administrators of a school, vested with the safety and wellbeing of students, appear to have ignored the students and their families, as well as experts; even more harmful, they seem to have minimized the students' suffering and let it continue. The Headmaster and the Board never outright deny that there are concerns or issues or a need to review, but they minimize students' suffering. Experts recognize that this may well be an essential technique of emotional abuse itself:

- Minimizing is a less extreme form of denial. When minimizing, the abuser may not deny that a particular event occurred, but they question the recipient's emotional experience or reaction to an event. Statements such as "You're too sensitive," "You're exaggerating," or "You're blowing this out of proportion" all suggest that the recipient's emotions and perceptions are faulty and not to be trusted.

- Trivializing, which occurs when the abuser suggests that what you have done or communicated is inconsequential or unimportant, is a more subtle form of minimizing.
- Denying and minimizing can be particularly damaging. In addition to lowering self-esteem and creating conflict, the invalidation of reality, feelings, and experiences can eventually lead you to question and mistrust your own perceptions and emotional experience.[181]

Not only did the Headmaster and Board try to minimize the students' request to learn in a non-abusive environment, potentially as a way to dissuade them from going anywhere with their complaints, the Chaplain also went to my Head of Department and suggested that I might risk "defamation" if I addressed the faculty about my concerns.

When I expressed to the Headmaster and Chaplain in May of 2012 that I believed as a teacher I had a duty to report to the Teacher Regulation Branch, the Chaplain sent me a detailed message to dissuade me. The Teacher Regulation Branch clearly outlines that any certificate holder, whether a teacher or administrator, has a duty to report if they even have a *suspicion* that abuse is occurring. The rationale behind this strict policy is "students must be protected from certificate holders who inflict physical, emotional or sexual harm on them (intentionally or otherwise)." Furthermore, "certificate holders cannot conduct themselves – on or off duty – in a way that breaches the Standards."[182] Four standards refer to competency; they are not relevant as the teachers were very

---

[181] http://www.counselingcenter.illinois.edu/self-help-brochures/relationship-problems/emotional-abuse/

[182] http://www.bcteacherregulation.ca/documents/FormsandPublications/ProfConduct/duty_to_report_COQ.pdf

competent coaches. The other four standards refer to conduct and they are as follows:

> **One:** Educators value and care for all students and act in their best interests.

> **Two:** Educators are role models who act ethically and honestly.

> **Three:** Educators understand and apply knowledge of student growth and development.

> **Four:** Educators value the involvement and support of parents, guardians, families and communities in schools.[183]

According to student testimonies, while coaching, the teachers breached all these standards repeatedly and in extreme ways. When I communicated to the Headmaster that after having taken the student testimonies I believed I needed to report, the Chaplain wrote me an email to consider "some of the hurdles in reaching the outcome." First, the Chaplain warns that the:

> …respondents will have written praise from a variety of sources, including respected colleagues. Often, this will include past material from individuals who are amongst those now lodging the complaint. Although things seem transparent to the complainant, the evidence is weighed by others. To a neutral party, bound by due process, the truth of the matter is usually less than clear.

It is very likely in their positions that Jian Ghomeshi, Mike Rice, Shann Hart and Mike Spracklen all had many "respected colleagues" who praised them and they are likely to also have "written praise" from their victims. However, this does not erase the abusive conduct reported on by those asking for protection. Moreover, it was at this time that Alumni

---

[183] https://www.bcteacherregulation.ca/documents/AboutUs/Standards/edu_stds.pdf

were being contacted from within the School to write in and praise the teachers. So in fact the Chaplain was right, regardless of how inappropriate it was in terms of student confidentiality or protection, it was a way that the school Administration was responding to multiple student testimonies reporting on teacher bullying. Nowhere in the Ministry of Education's Guide for *Independent School Personnel Responding to Child Abuse* does it instruct school administrators to consult with Alumni or encourage them to defend teachers under investigation.[184]

It took me a long time to realize that the Chaplain was surprisingly well informed about the ways a legal process would unfold if I fulfilled my duty to report as a teacher and certificate holder. It appears as if he wanted to be sure that I knew before proceeding that a court process, which the Commissioner for Teacher Regulation may take, would favor adult abusers and not child-victims. Apparently, the Chaplain wanted to be sure that I knew how hard it would be on my son and the other students if I fulfilled my legal duty to report. Therefore, he lays out a process whereby students' testimonies will be weighed against letters from respected colleagues and ultimately Alumni. Furthermore, if students and parents have praised the teachers in the past, this will be held against them. One parent even donated significant funds to support the basketball program in the building of a new gym: does this somehow erase the fact that both his children were victims and he did not know until it was too late? With a bully in power, but especially a charismatic bully, it is *likely* that parents will write in to support since the teacher or coach has so much power over their children.

---

[184] https://www.bced.gov.bc.ca/independentschools/is_resources/SOS_guide.pdf; and http://www.mcf.gov.bc.ca/child_protection/pdf/handbook_action_child_abuse.pdf

The Chaplain continues in the email to explain how the Teacher Regulation Branch will proceed, and puts the whole situation into a courtroom setting:

> When the questioned behavior is public, as opposed to one on one, statements will likely need to be verified by third parties, who will be questioned in some detail. Usually, there will be other third parties for the respondent, who will have an alternative recollection of specific events (slight modifications that change meaning/severity). Of course, memory itself is a tricky thing and such hearings often demand a great deal of consistency and certainty — the kind that stands up to rigorous scrutiny.

This "hurdle" the Chaplain describes seems to suggest that traumatized kids trying to articulate the harm done to them will not make great witnesses. Moreover, as recorded in the testimonies, many students suffered abusive conduct for over a year, and it was constant and repeated; thus, when they are asked to verify dates and times and incidents, they won't be convincing or "stand up to rigorous scrutiny," simply because the bullying was not a one-off incident, but repeated over and over again. If the teacher had yelled a derogatory comment once or twice, it might be easier for a student to say when it happened and another to corroborate. This becomes much more difficult when the teacher's bullying is relentless and repeated, but that does not mean it didn't happen or that the teacher can't be held accountable for it.

According to the Chaplain, the next "hurdle" if I reported would be that the students' motives would be questioned. The Chaplain warns that:

> The motives of everyone will be questioned. In particular, complainants will be asked why, if the actions were terrible or long standing, they stayed in the situation. Alternative motives for complaint, real and imagined, will be explored. Usually, every aspect of due process will be afforded the respondent.

The Chaplain clarified that the system is geared toward "due process" for the alleged abuser, while it treats the complainants (children in this case) as if they have ulterior motives for their complaints. It appears that the legal system lays responsibility for proper conduct at the feet of the victims: it requires the victim to quit the team or leave school if bullied or abused and holds them to account if they "stayed in the situation." This does not acknowledge the impossible scenario for student-athletes: play and be abused or quit and lose the chance to play the sport you love. For serious athletes hoping to play the next level the choice is this: play and be abused or quit and give up the dream and plan you have for your future. It is inane in all bullying situations that we repeat this refrain to children: if you are bullied, you should leave, if you don't, then you are complicit in your abuse and you will be doubted. If children are bullied, especially when it is by adults in caregiver positions, the adult bullies are the ones who should leave.

It is well researched and documented that abuse victims, by the very fact they are abused, even as adults, stay in the situation because their confidence and self-esteem are badly damaged. This is why children are encouraged to report abuse to adults, exactly because they are not in a position to protect themselves. Moreover, factoring in neurological research, spikes in cortisol levels appear to make victims literally forget what was said and done, and their decision-making ability is also affected. The impacts abuse has on individuals put them in a position whereby it is extremely hard for them to stand up for themselves. This same phenomenon is well researched and documented among women who suffer domestic abuse as they too find it incredibly difficult, if not impossible, to escape an abusive situation, and they are adults. Still, we expect children to decide that the harm done by the abuse they are suffering is too serious to remain on the team playing the sport they love

211

or that leaving their friends and their school is the answer to their bullying crisis.

Often, emotionally abused students are ashamed to speak up, especially the boys, because it might mean that they are "pussies." Students don't speak up because they believe the bullying behavior they experienced was their fault, and that the adult they have been trained to respect all their lives must be *right* while they must be *wrong*. These same thoughts may well stop the reporting on abuse or removing oneself from an emotionally abusive situation.[185] A student must sacrifice a great deal when leaving a team and a school: friends, who are fundamental to an adolescent's sense of self and developing identity; teachers, with whom the student has a good relationship; and, programs, the student may only be partially done to achieve certification. Leaving a team or a school as a teenager is possibly worse than an adult being forced to leave a job. And yet, the legal system expects bullies' victims to leave, rather than the bullies.

The Chaplain's email continued on as he presented his reasoning as to why I should not fulfill my legal duty to report what I had learned to the Teacher Regulation Branch:

> Of the greatest concern to me in these formal processes is that those most vulnerable will be required to detail how they are victims. If the process follows the usual protocols (not sure in this case), [your son] will need to describe exactly what he faced, outlining the "abuse," and then he'll be questioned in precise detail, especially about anything that seems remotely hazy or contradictory. Again, given that these were largely public acts, any differing stories will lead to further questioning. The process

---

[185] Ashley E. Stirling and Gretchen A. Kerr, "Initiating and Sustaining Emotional Abuse in the Coach-Athlete Relationship: An Ecological Transactional Model of Vulnerability," *Journal of Aggression, Maltreatment & Trauma*, vol. 23, 2014: 116-135.

can be awful, but the complainant usually has to portray themselves as "victim" (emphasizing their weakness /vulnerability/ lack of control, rather than their strength/ courage/ resilience).

The Chaplain appeared to worry that our son and the other students would be portrayed as weak, which once again reveals a flaw in the system. Students asking for a teacher to stop bullying them do not *portray* themselves as victims; they simply *are* victims. By the very fact that students are children under the adult / teacher's care, they are inherently vulnerable. The teacher has a great deal more power and therefore the students are de facto "weak." Hence, students *must* find the courage to report to authorities, as they are not in an equal position to the teacher and unable to protect themselves.

The Chaplain sums up his email by saying that reporting to the Teacher Regulation Branch will be worse for the students:

> If the governing body's verdict points to insufficient evidence of abuse, the complainant can feel demoralized; the respondent, vindicated; and the legitimacy of any other consequence, undermined. Such a verdict, though not necessarily true, carries the perception of truth. Until the verdict is reached, everything might stand still, perhaps for years in some systems.

First of all, if one correctly assumes the "governing body" is the Teacher Regulation Branch, their job is not to establish "abuse" in disciplining teacher conduct; their job is merely to decide if the teacher at any time breached any of the eight standards of conduct and competency. Past disciplinary actions by the Teacher Regulation Branch show that even if in one instance a standard was breached, then the teacher is disciplined accordingly and the Commissioner's decision made public.

In August 2012, after the Headmaster published the lawyer's report that positioned the students who came forward as liars, I filed complaints with the Teacher Regulation Branch as required by law. Many

213

parents wanted to file complaints but the Intake Officer advised the many families to file one complaint via me as teacher. If we had all filed, it would have bogged down the process and taken more time to address. I had a legal duty to report, so it was decided that I should file. The Intake Officer informed me that all that was needed was one student report of abuse and one witness for the Commissioner to realize what was happening at the School and how students were being affected. In fact, she stressed that I did not need to supply more. At this time, the Intake Officer had four testimonies and there were fourteen. Normally, in the public school system, the Board of Education, Superintendent, or School District have already suspended and disciplined the teacher before the file goes to the Commissioner. The Commissioner then makes the decision whether or not the teacher receives a further reprimand, a suspension or his or her certificate is revoked. His decisions are public and recorded in detail on the Teacher Regulation Branch website.

Although in his email to me the Chaplain warned that, in his estimation, years could pass before anything would be done, the parents whose children came forward assumed the Commissioner would prioritize this case knowing that students had been re-victimized in seriously harmful ways, the teachers had not been suspended while the investigation into their conduct was held, and they were currently fulfilling their coaching, teaching, and in some cases "house-parent" duties. However, it seemed the Chaplain was correct; we waited over two years for the Commissioner to make his decisions: one teacher received a reprimand for lying about an award, the other three did not receive reprimands nor did the Headmaster or Chaplain, and the Commissioner's rationale for his decisions was not shared with the public. The Teacher Regulation Branch had advised me to file the complaints as a representative figure for the other families, but now they would not let me share the Commissioner's reports. Families were very upset. I informed the Ombudsperson's Office and while they often used this process of a representative figure filing for a number of others, they said they could not do anything about it. The Commissioner's decision to keep the reports confidential even from families who supplied him with their personal information is surprising because transparency is a key principle of the Teacher Regulation Branch's mandate.

> The *Teachers Act* is based on two foundational principles: the paramount nature of the public interest and transparency. As set out in the Act, the Commissioner for Teacher Regulation, an independent statutory decision maker, oversees all discipline processes and addresses concerns about the competence and conduct of certificate holders.
>
> The Teacher Regulation Branch provides operational and administrative support to the Commissioner and publishes the discipline outcomes on its website. The purpose of publishing discipline outcomes is to provide the public with the confidence that educators who fail to meet the Standards are held accountable.[186]

While the Commissioner found that standards were breached, he decided to keep that information from the public. The Ombudsperson's office has recently contacted me to say that they are keeping the file open and are continuing to investigate the Commissioner's decisions. They have had the file since August 2014.

Teachers may well feel conflicted about fulfilling their Duty to Report if they are made aware that the Teacher Regulation Branch process is very hard on students. This is ironic considering the whole point of the process is to protect students and to have transparency for parents who send their children into the school system. The Ministry of Education's guide on responding to reports of child abuse stresses that

---

[186] https://www.bcteacherregulation.ca/ProfessionalConduct/DisciplineDecisions.aspx

children who speak up are extremely vulnerable and thus adults must minimize the number of interviews, move quickly to resolve the situation, and offer support and safety, so that children will continue to feel they may tell the truth.[187] However, for the students at my former school, the Commissioner required a fourth interview, moved incredibly slowly, and did not offer support or safety. It is hard to imagine that other children felt safe to come forward, or for those who had already spoken up, that they continued to feel that it was safe to tell the truth.

In May 2012, according to the Chaplain, the Headmaster was prepared to discipline one teacher and monitor the other three teachers identified in the testimonies – but only if I did not report to the Teacher Regulation Branch. The Chaplain said in the email to me, "Mostly, I'm concerned for [your son]. At this point, without him having to do anything more, he can have his Head of School confirm that he was treated wrongly, that the school wants to extend help (physical and otherwise), that the teacher is being punished and that the whole program is going to be changed."

Moreover, all four teachers will be "mentored and monitored." The Chaplain's email stressed that *my* son would be protected: "without him having to do anything more." However, my duty was not only as a parent to my son; I also had a professional duty and legal obligation as a teacher to inform the Teacher Regulation Branch on behalf of the other thirteen students. The Teacher Regulation Branch website is very clear about a certificate holder's legal Duty to Report when abuse is suspected.

> All certificate holders have a duty under section 38 of the *Teachers Act* to report – in the form of a written and signed report to the Teacher Regulation Branch for the Commissioner's review

---

[187] http://www.mcf.gov.bc.ca/child_protection/pdf/handbook_action_child_abuse.pdf

– any conduct involving physical harm, sexual abuse or exploitation, or significant emotional harm to a student or students, when they have reason to believe that another certificate holder has engaged in such conduct.[188]

The Headmaster and Chaplain, as certificate holders, also had a Duty to Report.

In this context, it is important to understand the Teacher Regulation Branch's Duty to Report because it is in the "public interest." There are two key components. First, "Students must be protected from certificate holders who inflict physical, emotional or sexual harm on them (intentionally or otherwise)." The Headmaster, Chaplain, and I had all heard directly from students that teachers were inflicting emotional and some physical harm on them or others. And second, "Certificate holders cannot conduct themselves on or off duty in a way that breaches the Standards for the Education, Competence and Professional Conduct."[189] Students would be at the very least suspended, if not expelled, for the kind of conduct they reported being done by their teachers. Even off duty, teachers cannot breach the standards that govern professional conduct let alone be on duty, doing an extracurricular activity such as coaching. I would be breaking the law if I did not report. The Teacher Regulation Branch penalizes teachers with reprimands and suspensions for failing to report. In addition, I could not shirk my duty to the other students, even if it meant losing the chance to have my son protected.

I had listened to students tell me how terrible their suffering had been. I watched some of them cry while they spoke. I watched them feel guilty for speaking up about teachers they thought had so much potential and knowledge and just needed to fix this one aspect of their coaching.

---

[188] https://www.bcteacherregulation.ca/ProfessionalConduct/DutyToReport.aspx
[189] Ibid.

217

Therefore, I could not participate in the Chaplain's plan not to report what had happened to students even if it bought my son a year of protection and allowed him to pursue his dream to try out for university level basketball.

I did not sign on to the deal offered to me. Instead, I suffered the shunning and disdain of certain ill-informed colleagues. And far worse, I watched my son suffer over and over again as Administrators failed to protect him from bullying by peers and the teachers identified in student testimonies. I also watched him draw on his sense of integrity and his courage, and that of his friends, and the many supportive teachers and all the students who spoke up and all the ones who quietly offered support despite being in positions where it was too risky for them to give testimonies. I have never admired a group of students more than the ones who spoke up.

The School's contradictory response to teacher bullying, "we will discipline the teachers if you keep quiet," juxtaposed with "students will suffer if you report to the Teacher Regulation Branch," demonstrates that something is not quite right in the system that regulates teacher conduct and is ostensibly in place to protect students. If the four teachers had done no wrong, why would the Chaplain, apparently taking some kind of Human Resources role, say that they would be disciplined and monitored? If they had been disciplined and monitored in 2011 when Board Members, the Chaplain and Headmaster were informed that "child abuse" was occurring, my son and so many other students would not have suffered. Why would the Chaplain encourage me to ignore future students as long as my own son was protected in grade twelve? I started to wonder if other teachers at the School had been encouraged to make deals like this one in the past.

The Lawyer/ parent who had also taken testimonies at the Headmaster's request was much more experienced than I was in legal

218

processes. In May 2012, she also cautioned that reporting to the Teacher Regulation Branch might make the students suffer more. At that time, she had faith that the Headmaster, who was working closely with her, would protect all students and ensure they healed from the bullying they had suffered. She believed him when he said he would ensure teachers were removed from their positions, would remain on salary, and have the opportunity to seek treatment before returning to the School. So I gave the Headmaster time to set things right, not just for my son, but for all students. However, in August 2012, when the Headmaster published the second lawyer's report that used the anonymous words of other students to say those who came forward told "nasty lies" and "manufactured evidence," I fulfilled my legal duty and filed complaints with the Teacher Regulation Branch naming the four teachers, as well as the Headmaster and the School Chaplain. Bullying students under the auspices of coaching was one thing, but defaming students' characters by publicly insinuating that they are liars was a whole other level of bullying.

The Lawyer/parent with whom I had taken student testimonies fully supported my decision, as did the other families who asked me to represent their children in the complaint. I handed over the student testimonies, the many emails, video footage of the Assistant Coach screaming at students and slamming his hands down in an apparent rage inches from the faces of scorekeepers, the police statement that there was "a definite pattern in the complaints, all pointing to verbal and emotional abuse," and the lawyer's report, widely published by the Headmaster that positioned the students who came forward as liars. After a six-month investigation and a year and a half of deliberation, the Commissioner for Teacher Regulation concluded that the teachers would not receive a reprimand for breaching the standards that govern teachers. As the complainant, I alone was permitted read the reasoning behind his decisions, as apparently he did not feel the issue was in the public interest.

219

# CHAPTER EIGHT

# THE COMMISSIONER

> I swore never to be silent whenever and wherever
> human beings endure suffering and humiliation. We
> must always take sides. Neutrality helps the oppressor,
> never the victim. Silence encourages the tormentor,
> never the tormented.
>
> – Elie Wiesel, *Nobel-Prize winning
> writer, teacher and activist*

The definition of a teacher in my mind is a professional who puts the
needs of students before any kind of personal need or agenda. That is
what defines our profession. In my role as teacher, I filed my concerns
about the Commissioner's decisions with the Office of the Ombudsperson
and the Minister of Education. To date, neither of these offices has taken
any action. To my mind, lack of action, when abuse reports are made by
parents, students, and corroborated by law enforcement and coaching
abuse experts, would suggest a much larger issue is at hand.

    While one of the teachers was under investigation by the
Commissioner for Teacher Regulation for the emotional abuse recorded
in student testimonies, a local TV cameraman zoomed in on him during a
Senior Boys' basketball game and his frenzied and furious conduct was
captured on video for all to see. The news footage that showed him
literally pulling at his hair and screaming incoherently at players was
more mesmerizing than the game itself. Normally during games, this

Assistant Coach moves up and down the sidelines trying to get as close to students as possible while he yells in what looks to be apparent disgust and frustration; however, in the TV segment broadcast in December, 2013, he couldn't get close to the students he was yelling at, because he'd had ankle surgery and so remained in his chair. The sports commentators describe the screaming Assistant Coach as "frenetic as always," and they comment that he's "clearly distressed" as he screams at the students.

Dr. Laurence Steinberg comments on the atmosphere created by such a coach and how it could harm adolescents. He addresses the behavior in the context of a home environment. Regardless, his informed insight applies equally well to a basketball court. As is often discussed, teenagers spend more time with teachers and coaches than they do with parents at this stage in their lives and thus this "frenetic" behavior has the potential to do harm. Steinberg's research shows that teenagers "are harmed by [being in an environment] that is conflict-ridden, tense, unpredictable, or frenetic."[190] It is concerning that the Assistant Coach conducts himself this way even while under supposed investigation and in public. According to student testimonies, he was far worse behind closed doors of practices and the Head Coach was even more frenetic and "vicious" than the Assistant.

Even though it is only the start of the season, the sports commentators remark that the Assistant Coach is in "midseason form." One can only surmise what his form would be like by the actual midseason. The sportscasters comment that this teacher should drink "Sanka" to calm down. They say he should "relax" and "celebrate the moments of [his] life."[191] The Assistant Coach featured on TV appears to

---

[190] Laurence Steinberg, *Age of Opportunity: Lessons from the New Science of Adolescence*, Boston and New York: Houghton, Mifflin, Harcourt, 2014 (211).
[191] http://vancouverisland.ctvnews.ca/video?clipId=215622

be having what, to the untrained eye, amounts to a temper tantrum, which is potentially problematic conduct when he is in charge of his players' health, wellbeing and skills development. One wonders if he had these clearly frenetic outbursts in public, while under investigation by the Teacher Regulation Branch, what his conduct was like behind the closed doors of practices *before* he knew he was under investigation.

Emil Coccaro, Professor of Psychiatry at the University of Chicago, in an article on "intermittent explosive disorder," says this kind of behavior comes on rapidly and with little or no provocation.[192] The teacher-coach's rages are described in detail in student testimonies. One student reported, *"I've never seen him so mad though as when he was grabbing his chair, not subtly, but rocking it."* Another states, *"[The Assistant Coach] gets so mad and he bunches up his fists and he is a big guy and he is unpredictable. I have never seen him get physically angry with a player, but it feels like he might."* And as another recorded, *"[The Assistant Coach] went into the passageway between the gyms and he isolated himself. He looked like an animal in a cage."* When video of Rutgers Coach Mike Rice, described by journalists, as a "hot-headed basketball coach angrily ranting at his team," aired on ESPN, and his homophobic slurs were heard, he was fired the next day.[193] In contrast, even though he was under investigation by the Teacher Regulation Branch, the teacher at my former school did not cover up his rage in public as it appeared to be "normalized" in this particular community's

---

[192] http://www.currentpsychiatry.com/the-publication/past-issue-single-view/intermittent-explosive-disorder-taming-temper-tantrums-in-the-volatile-impulsive-adult/8bf5dc9f015f0601c6eb7764000a9073.html
[193] Ted Sherman and Kelly Heyboer, "Rutgers coaching scandal goes into overtime, as focus settles on Pernetti," *The Star-Ledger*, April 2013: http://www.nj.com/news/index.ssf/2013/04/rutgers_coaching_scandal_goes.html

sports culture; however, according to student testimonies, the rage at practices was layered with homophobic, derogatory, humiliating language like that used by Mike Rice. After a bullied gay student committed suicide, Rutgers had become a community where harassment and bullying were no longer acceptable in their culture. I hope it does not take a suicide at my former school for this kind of change to occur.

I find it concerning that there are three students I am personally aware of who, according to their testimonies, were bullied by teachers at my former school, and in the last three years have been put on suicide watch. In early 2013, a young coaching intern attempted suicide in the school's dorm rooms, which he felt was partially in response to bullying by the basketball coaches and the Director of Athletics. They wouldn't allow him to watch practices, coach a Basketball B-Team of Senior Boys, made fun of his appearance and ultimately ostracized him. The Director of the Senior School spent forty minutes telling him he was out of line in requesting to coach a B-Team of Senior Boys. He was so insulting and humiliating that the coaching intern had to fight back tears on a number of occasions. Shortly thereafter, the police found the coaching intern in his room in School residence, intoxicated and suicidal with his belt around his neck. They took him to a psychiatric facility. It is difficult to point a finger and say that suicide attempts are "caused" by bullying, but there is such a documented correlation between the two that to ignore the power bullying has over people would be irresponsible and ignorant.

Barbara Coloroso discusses in detail adolescents who commit suicide in response to peer bullying. In October 2009, seventeen-year-old Tyler, who suffered from autism, was called "gay" and "faggot" by other kids who bullied him for years. Even after he hanged himself by his belt and was found by his dad in his room, "some of the bullies wore leather belts on their necks to mock" his suicide. Our son and another student who spoke up publicly about what was done to them have received

224

countless bullying messages from former and current students at the school that echo the coaches' homophobic language and bullying approach. The students use social media as a way to continue delivering the hateful messaging they would appear to have learned on the court from their teachers as documented in student testimonies. Barbara Coloroso writes about Tyler, "Had the first acts of cruelty been dealt with swiftly and effectively," in an echo of his parents' description of his decline, "Tyler would not have changed from a fun-loving child to 'just a shell of the boy we once knew.'"[194] Bullying by peers must be dealt with swiftly and effectively, because it has the potential to literally destroy peoples' lives. When it's an adult, in a position of power over children, who is the bully, we need to act even more swiftly and effectively. Moreover, we need to take a hard look, an honest look at the fact that suicide is the second leading cause of death in adolescence. In 2010, in the US there were approximately one hundred and five youths who committed suicide *per day*. For each of those suicides, there were one to two hundred attempted suicides. And suicide is on the increase.[195]

A suicide risk linked back to the actions of basketball coach Kelly Greenberg at Boston University led to the coach being fired. In April 2014, four students quit the Boston University women's basketball team due to emotional abuse by Coach Greenberg. One student quoted in *The Boston Globe* said, "'Giving up a $60,000-a-year scholarship is the hardest thing I've ever done. I hate that I'm not in school, but it had to be done. My spirit was broken.'" This student subsequently became suicidal. Thirty players rallied to Coach Greenberg's defense against the claims by the four players; however, Greenberg and Boston University "parted

---

[194] Barbara Coloroso, *The Bully, the Bullied, and the not-so-innocent Bystander*, updated edition, Harper Collins: 2015 (51).
[195] http://www.cdc.gov/ViolencePrevention/pdf/Suicide_DataSheet-a.pdf

ways" in late April following the Review Panel's findings.[196] Todd Klipp, senior counsel at the University, was quoted by *BU Today* as saying that many of the complaints could not be substantiated, but that "a compelling case was made, based on interviews with the team as a whole, that the manner in which Coach Greenberg interacted with many of her players was incompatible with the expectations and standards for university employees, including our coaches."[197]

While there was significant support for Coach Greenberg, it did not mean the four students were somehow exaggerating what had happened or were found to be overly sensitive. During the review panel's investigation, two former players from the 2001–2002 and 2004 season under Greenberg came forward claiming they too had been bullied and emotionally abused by the coach. This parallels what happened at my former school: three university students came forward saying they too had been bullied, and they gave written testimonies. Greenberg had also been investigated based on similar allegations from two other student-athletes in 2008; at that time, she apologized and promised to change. Breaking the spirits of athletes to the point where they were suicidal is not coaching basketball, it is bullying. A comparable pattern was established at my former school. Over the course of five years, students had come forward with detailed testimonies. Moreover, I informed the Teacher Regulation Branch each time there was a further development such as the coaching intern attempting suicide and students being put on suicide watch.

---

[196] Bob Hohler, "Bully Accusations Continue Against BU coach," *The Boston Globe*, April 2014: http://www.bostonglobe.com/sports/2014/03/08/women-basketball-coach-accused-bullying/TtKz57Gs9qXbvk1SBtIpuM/story.html
[197] http://www.bostonglobe.com/sports/2014/04/22/boston-university-women-basketball-coach-leaving-after-allegations-emotional-abuse/2z7A50mrw7Rx0yNIVsVRKJ/story.html

It is worrisome that students so often rally in an abusive coach's defense.[198] Research says these students may well become the new bullies. Despite our knowledge, guidelines, government documents, and programs, like suicide, bullying is on the rise and it not only impacts school children, it is rampant in the workforce. We must ask difficult questions about where it comes from. The students who defended Coach Greenberg may well have absorbed and normalized a teaching practice that decimates certain targets under the guise of motivation or passionate coaching. They may enter the workforce, and bully others, because they think that is how to compete, win, and succeed. The workforce is overwhelmed with bullying issues; it's not a stretch to suggest that during a student's formative years in high-school and college certain teachers and coaches teach them how to bully, and considering their developmental state and the power these mentors have, they develop the belief that this conduct is connected to success.

T. F. Charlton examines this phenomenon in her 2013 *Salon.com* article looking at why Mike Rice's players did not understand that they were being abused and therefore did not speak up:

> A culture that accepts, expects and encourages adults in positions of power to use a certain level of abuse to 'motivate' players enables coaches whose abuses go far beyond what's considered 'normal.' It also makes it much harder for young players — and the adults who are supposed to protect them — to recognize and speak out against the most egregious abuses when they occur.[199]

---

[198] http://espn.go.com/womens-college-basketball/story/_/id/10825264/boston-university-terriers-part-ways-coach-kelly-greenberg

[199] T. F. Charlton: "Why do athletes tolerate abusive coaches? In locker rooms, insubordination is a worse crime than abuse of authority. Unless that changes, nothing else will." *Salon.com*: http://www.salon.com/2013/04/05/why_do_athletes_tolerate_abusive_coaches/

It is remarkable that at an independent school over a hundred years old, apparently steeped in a normalizing culture of 'motivating' through bullying, fourteen students actually recognized that lines were being crossed and spoke out against four coaches.

In a concerning editorial, published in the *Toronto Star* in April 2012, Charles Pascal, professor of human development at the Ontario Institute of Studies in Education and a former Ontario Deputy Minister, exposes how the ability to bypass, or serve a different set of rules, appears to be an issue at independent schools. His article speaks to a need for more monitoring of independent schools, as well as a need to become far more aware of the way in which *reversals* occur so frequently in bullying situations. He recounts the story of a child who was bullied by a peer. The parents reported the bullying to the school; however, the bully was from a powerful family and the child who was the bully's target was asked to leave. Pascal concludes:

> And while I am certain that a majority of private elementary schools know how to do the right things, just like their publicly funded counterparts, they all need legislation, oversight and professional development to ensure the health and safety of our children. No elementary school in Ontario should be able to fly under the radar of responsible and informed educational leadership. It is way past the time that all elementary schools in Ontario have some measure of public oversight.[200]

Among all the decisions published by the Commissioner for Teacher Regulation, I have been unable to find anywhere a teacher at an independent school was disciplined. This could mean that teachers at independent schools never breach the standards *or* it may suggest that

---

[200] http://www.thestar.com/opinion/editorialopinion/2012/04/21/ ontario_ private_schools_free_to_ignore_bullying.html

when complaints come before the school administrators and the boards of these schools, the issues are dealt with internally and not reported. Perhaps it suggests that when the Commissioner receives complaints from independent schools, they may be handled differently from public school complaints. Comparably, the Inspector of Independent Schools does not appear to intervene, monitor, or keep records of teacher or administrative conduct.

In the Commissioner's 2013–2014 *Annual Report*, it was surprising to see that in 2013, when there were approximately 546, 219 students in the public school system, there were fifty-five complaints against public school teachers. These statistics suggest that lodging a formal complaint is extremely rare and that teachers in BC do not breach conduct standards very often. In this same year, independent school teachers received twenty-eight complaints although they were only teaching approximately 71, 615 students.[201] Independent schools only teach about seven and a half percent of the student population; however, they account for more than half of the complaints being lodged with the Commissioner. While public school teachers are disciplined and it is posted on the Teacher Regulation Branch website and in their biannual *Learn Magazine*, independent school teachers do not appear to have disciplinary action taken in response to these complaints as there is no public record.

Although taxpayers contribute a third to a half of the cost of students' education at independent schools in BC, these schools do not report to the School Board or District, nor do they appear to have independent watchdogs on their private Boards. Surely they should have

---

[201] http://www.bctf.ca/uploadedfiles/public/publications/2012edfacts.pdf; and https://www.bcteacherregulation.ca/documents/FormsandPublications/AnnualMe etings/CTR_annual_rpt_2013_2014.pdf

some greater measure of public oversight to ensure the health, safety, and wellbeing of students, especially when some of them are boarding schools. I have read the vast majority of the available archived and contemporary decisions by the Commissioner for Teacher Regulation that reprimand, suspend or even withdraw for an extended period of time the teaching certificates of teachers whose conduct is far less serious than that described by students at my former school. However, the Commissioner did not find the fourteen student testimonies, or the eleven-page letter the year before from the lawyer/ parent, or the interviews, or the videos, or the emails promising different coaching and that the teachers would address everything they'd done, or the School paying for counseling, or even the Chaplain's email offering to protect my son if I didn't report to the Teacher Regulation Branch, or the publication of a defamatory report that re-victimized vulnerable students, or the breach of confidentiality on the part of the Headmaster, or the behind-the-scenes contacting of Alumni asking for support for the teachers, none of this was worthy of the mildest form of discipline. The Administrators and teachers were not held publicly accountable for anything except for one teacher who received a reprimand for lying.

The Commissioner's decisions not to hold teachers and Administrators accountable for breaching the standards that govern conduct with even the mildest of disciplinary acts are concerning when put side by side with the documentation compiled over the years this situation has gone on. The students clearly, and with great detail, express that they felt emotionally, psychologically, and in some cases physically harmed. A brief glimpse at the last twenty or so years of research should be enough to worry any parent or educator about the impact of emotional abuse, even though the studies are from parent to child rather than teacher to student.

Other reported implications of emotional abuse in parent–child relationship include, **low mood** (Ney, Fung, & Wickett, 1994), **low self-esteem** (Gross & Keller, 1992; Mullen, Martin, Anderson, Romans, & Herbison, 1996), **emotional instability** (Braver, Bumberry, Green, & Rawson, 1992; Crittenden, Claussen, & Sugarman, 1994), **anger** (Engels & Moisan, 1994), **physical self-abuse** (Engels & Moisan, 1994), **eating disorders** (Mullen et al., 1996; Rorty, Yager, & Rosotto, 1994), **substance abuse** (Mullen et al., 1996), **attachment problems** (Mullen et al., 1996), **delinquency** (Vissing, Straus, Gelles, & Harrop, 1991), **impairments to learning** (Claussen & Crittenden, 1991; Crittenden et al., 1994), **and low school performance** (Hart & Brassard, 1991), as some examples. Detailed reviews of the literature on the effects of the psychological forms of maltreatment have been previously published (Binggeli, Hart, & Brassard, 2001; Iwaniec, Larkin, & Higgins, 2006). [emphasis mine][202]

Recent research done at University of Toronto by Gretchen Kerr and Ashley Stirling into the harmful effect of coaches' emotional abuse of athletes parallels the results found in parent to child abuse:

Although this form of coaching may or may not be effective in producing athletic success, along with this coaching approach can come at a severe cost to the psychological wellbeing of the athlete, making it an unethical method for coaching athletes. The general child abuse literature indicates that the long-term sequealae of emotional abuse are significant and harmful (Miller-Perrin & Perrin, 2007). Athletes in this study also spoke about the

---

[202] Ashley E. Stirling and Gretchen A. Kerr, "The perceived effects of elite athletes' experiences of emotional abuse in the coach–athlete relationship." *The International Journal of Sport and Exercise Psychology* 11.1, 2013: 87-100.

lingering psychological consequences of their emotionally abusive experiences in sport.[203]

At my former School, I learned that staff and students' responses during this crisis included attempted suicide, being on suicide watch, depression, performance anxiety, self-medicating with drugs and alcohol, panic attacks, nervous breakdowns, and failing out of first year university programs. These are the immediate reactions; psychological and neurological research tells us that the harm may well last a lifetime and impact these victims in a whole host of damaging ways in many areas of their lives.[204] As Dr. Alan Goldberg, explains,

> The damage that abusive coaches can do to preadolescent and adolescent athletes oftentimes haunts them well into adulthood, negatively shaping their future performance experiences and relationships both in and out of competitive sports. Depression, anxiety, low self-esteem, identity issues and recurring performance problems are often the result of this kind of negative coaching.[205]

Dr. Alan Goldberg, has listed behaviors that a coach might exhibit that would categorize him or her as abusive:

- Regularly uses public embarrassment and humiliation on his/her athletes
- Is disinterested in the feelings and sensitivities of his/her players
- Rarely uses praise or positive feedback

---

[203] See Stirling and Kerr (97).
[204] http://www.slate.com/blogs/xx_factor/2013/02/20/new_duke_study_on_bullying_childhood_victims_bullies_and_bully_victims_all.html
[205] Dr. Alan Goldberg, "Coaching ABUSE: The dirty, not-so-little secret in sports." http://gazette.teachers.net/gazette/wordpress/dr-alan-goldberg/coaching-abuse-the-dirty-not-so-little-secret-in-sports-by-dr-alan-goldberg/

- Is a yeller
- Demeans his/her players
- Plays "head games" with his/her athletes
- Is personally dishonest and untrustworthy
- Creates a team environment based on fear and devoid of safety
- Is never satisfied with what his/her athletes do
- Is overly negative and a pro at catching athletes doing things wrong
- Is more interested in his/her needs then those of his/her players
- Over-emphasizes the importance of winning
- Tends to be rigid and over-controlling, defensive and angry
- Is not open to constructive feedback from players or other parents
- Uses excessive conditioning as punishment
- Can be physically abusive
- Ignores his/her athletes when angry or displeased
- Is a bully (and therefore a real coward)
- Coaches through fear and intimidation
- Is a "know-it-all"
- Is a poor communicator
- Only cares about his/her athletes as performers, not as individuals
- Consistently leaves his/her athletes feeling bad about themselves
- Kills his/her athletes' joy and enthusiasm for the sport
- Is a bad role model
- Is emotionally unstable and insecure
- Earns contempt from players and parents
- Coaches through guilt
- Is a master of DENIAL!!!!!

Every single behavior on Dr. Goldberg's list was documented multiple times in the student testimonies provided to the Headmaster. Dr. Goldberg goes on to explain the following:

> A coach doesn't have to be guilty of all of these behaviors to be an abusive coach. In fact, regularly engaging in a select two or three of these is enough to qualify a coach for abuser status. Unfortunately, most coaches who engage in abuse also refuse to take an honest look at themselves. Because of a well-honed sense of denial, they would never admit to themselves or others that they might be doing something wrong. In fact, the abusive coach sees him/herself as a very good coach![206]

An abusive coach's or teacher's inability to recognize that they are doing harm is probably why colleagues, parents, and students are *not* encouraged to address their conduct with them directly according to the *BC Handbook for Action on Child Abuse and Neglect: For Service Providers.*[207] In this context, it also makes sense that the Teacher Regulation Branch's Duty to Report document specifies that whether or not teachers *intend* to do harm is irrelevant. Moreover, even if teachers are *not* on duty, hence they may well forget that their actions impact students, they are still held to account.[208] If teachers' intentions are not the measuring stick, what might be some of the signs that students are at risk?

The measuring stick for abuse should *not* be based on majority and minority because, based on research, we know very few if any will ever speak up. The measuring stick for abuse should be based on the harm being done. As soon as students who previously loved their sport begin to

---

[206] Ibid.

[207] http://www.mcf.gov.bc.ca/child_protection/pdf/handbook_action_child_abuse.pdf

[208] https://www.bcteacherregulation.ca/documents/FormsandPublications/ProfConduct/duty_to_report_COQ.pdf

quit, it should raise the alarm that abusive coaching may be at work. When athletes on scholarship quit the sport that got them into an independent school or university, it may be that abusive coaching is to blame. When students stand up and report abusive behavior they must be heard, valued, protected and the bully forced to leave – not the victim. One emotionally damaged, psychologically or verbally abused student is one too many.

A concerned father in New Jersey, Stuart Chaifetz, sent his ten-year-old son to school wearing a hidden recording device to hear if the school employees caring for him were in fact bullying him. He found out that his concerns were well founded. He released on YouTube the recording of the caretakers' verbal abuse, which included the boy being told to "shut up" and referred to as a "bastard." Millions of people tuned in to watch the video. In a *USA Today* article about this father's refusal to let his son be bullied at school, Jim Walsh and Phil Dunn speak to the irony that New Jersey passed "one of the toughest anti-bullying laws in the country aimed at stopping kids from bullying one another" while at the same time there are multiple instances of teacher or staff bullying of students.[209] Abusive coaching conduct in New Jersey appears to be equally problematic, as author Harlan Coben exclaims, "New Jersey has just adopted some of the toughest anti-bullying legislation to which our own children are accountable. Shouldn't we demand the same from our coaches? Could you ever imagine a schoolteacher or debate coach behaving in such a manner?"[210] At my former school, it appears that the teachers were excused conduct such as yelling or using obscenities

---

[209] http://usatoday30.usatoday.com/news/education/story/2012-04-29/autism-education-abuse-reform/54616582/1
[210] Harlan Coben, "That's Not Coaching. It's Child Abuse," *BloombergView*, May 2013: http://www.bloombergview.com/articles/2013-05-30/that-s-not-coaching-it-s-child-abuse

because it occurred while they were "coaching" even though the Teacher Regulation Branch specifies that it is irrelevant if a teacher is off-duty when abusive conduct occurs. And in fact, I would argue that "coaching" like any extra-curricular activity a teacher does falls firmly into the category of being on-duty as it's part of our jobs. The other argument was that not all the students spoke up about the coaches' bullying conduct and so the administrators and Commissioner excused it.

In a recent article in the *Guardian* on teacher bullying in Britain's boarding schools, Alex Renton recalls his childhood abuse experience and explains that the ultimate sin is speaking up and therefore students are trained from early on to keep quiet: "One of us new boys – I still don't know who – had complained about the regime in Dormitory V to his parents. This was the cardinal sin. What happened in school, stayed in school. [The Headmaster] punished us all. We didn't tell tales again."[211] At my former school, as documented powerfully by the second lawyer's report, speaking up resulted in public humiliation. Insinuating that students who speak up are liars and weak certainly seems like humiliation meted out to ensure all students realize that what happened at practices and games, should stay at practices and games. At my former school, like the school in the Britain, reporting on abuse was penalized. As a teacher whistleblower, I was made to suffer so greatly by the toxic atmosphere around me at the School that I resigned.

● ● ●

Regardless of the risks associated with speaking up in educational institutions like my former school, certain parents over the last three years

---

[211] Alex Renton, "Abuse in Britain's Boarding Schools: Why I decided to confront my demons," May 4, 2014 in the *Observer* / *Guardian*: http://www.theguardian.com/society/2014/may/04/abuse-britain-private-schools-personal-memoir

expressed their distress directly to the coaches and the Assistant Coach in particular argued that his bullying approach was to "toughen students up"; when another parent spoke with the Head Coach and another one of his Assistants, he offered an apology and a promise to be more positive; the son of the concerned mother was given an award that should have gone to another student. It seems the award was to placate a distressed parent. The Assistant Coach said he should "go on probation," but the former Director of the Senior School, who was present at the meeting, never followed through. Had here been some demonstrable actions in this case or in response to previous complaints by parents perhaps those involved would have been removed and could have attended workshops or other professional development opportunities to address their bullying behavior. Reports of bullying should be dealt with swiftly and effectively especially when they are about teachers and coaches.

Although the Headmaster continues to publicly state that the School's processes "made no findings of bullying, verbal abuse or unfair playing against the coaches," he follows this erroneous statement by outlining a significant array of changes made at the school in response to "no findings." The Headmaster conducted an Athletic Review; there were new Codes of Conduct written, not just for teachers, but for parents and students although no complaints were lodged about them as far as I know. The Headmaster brought in a sports expert who acted as a "coaches' coach" observing and training the teachers. Even the Commissioner wrote and published new guidelines for teachers who coach and has recently announced that he will be working with BC School Sports.[212] Both public statements are surprising, because there are already clear guidelines

---

[212] http://www.news1130.com/2013/10/16/commissioner-wants-guidelines-for-teachers-who-coach-in-bc/; and https://www.bcteacherregulation.ca/documents/Learn/LearnMagazine_Current.pdf#page=26

237

published by the Teacher Regulation Branch, as well as BC School Sports, that govern teacher conduct.

"No findings" caused a great deal of upheaval at the School and some explanation was needed to account for this apparent discrepancy. After the police stated there was a "definite pattern in the complaints, all pointing to verbal and emotional abuse," the lawyers brought in by the Headmaster and Board needed to provide explanations as to why the teachers did *not* need to be held accountable for their conduct while at the same time making many recommendations. The lawyers offered excuses such as the teacher didn't intend the harm; the gym was noisy and the teacher had to yell; Alumni like the teachers; the teachers are passionate and intense; swearwords are commonplace these days; the teacher muttered the harmful insults; the teacher was motivating; the students are too sensitive; the students can't transition into higher-level competitive sports; the majority like the coaches and so on.

When the question was raised about why Coach Rice's student-athletes submitted to ongoing verbal, emotional, psychological and physical abuse without speaking up, Matthew Davidson, president of the *Institute for Excellence and Ethics,* which conducts research and creates programming on character development in sport, explained that student-athletes in high-school programs are trained to submit to abusive conduct all too often. Davidson notes that student-athletes at the high-school level are "conditioned to think that the coach controls everything. They get you into prep schools, help you get scholarships to college. Once you're there, if you want to transfer because he throws a ball at your head, he can tell another school that you have character issues."[213] Mike Rice's players

---

[213] Joe Drape and Nate Taylor, "Question Arises as Scandal Unfolds: Where's the Line?" April 2013: http://natetaylorsports.wordpress.com/2014/07/10/question-arises-as-scandal-unfolds-wheres-the-line/

may well have been trained by high-school coaches to submit to emotional abuse due to the widely held view that it was *motivational*, layered upon the reality that if you speak up about a coach, he can penalize you in terrible ways if you love your sport. The expectation that a child will speak up about abusive teacher conduct is as psychologically out to lunch as expecting a child to transfer schools when being bullied as if *they* are the problem. However, it is a constant refrain from adults in the system that seem to lack knowledge about child development or the insidious damage abuse causes that ensures the victims feel as if the harm is deserved and will intensify if they ask for support or protection. The way the system is at present, children appear to be right: in an abuser-sensitive process, victims will pay a heavy price for speaking up and reporting on abuse. So let's stop telling them "zero tolerance for bullying" and let's stop encouraging them *not* to be bystanders. The hypocrisy is damaging.

In December 2013, in another case of teacher bullying in Britain, as recorded in the *Telegraph*, the panel that investigated the incidents did not suggest a series of solutions like workshops or teacher-monitoring, codes of conduct, new reviews or updated guidelines. Instead, the panel examined the teacher's deep-seated attitudes and repeated bullying behavior that was found to be harmful to his students. The panel listened to the student reports of the teacher's conduct – conduct much less egregious than what the students reported having experienced at my former school. Notably, it was the repeated complaints coupled with the continued behavior that resulted in the teacher's certification being suspended for three years: "Mr. Green's behavior was a serious departure from the Teachers' Standards and impacted upon the wellbeing of pupils." Moreover, the "panel have found evidence of a deep-seated attitude that leads to harmful behavior and insufficient evidence that Mr. Green recognises this."[214]

In yet another teacher abuse case in Britain, as reported by the BBC in 2010, a teacher in Wales who poked students with a stick and grabbed them by their collar, referring to them as "dumbo" and "twit" had been seen as dangerous enough to have had his teaching certificate revoked indefinitely.[215] In contrast, the teachers at my former school did not even receive a reprimand for bullying. In the few sections of the first lawyer's report, parts that had not been redacted, he concludes that the teachers could not be held accountable for their conduct because they did not have "due process." He argued that the Headmaster's timeline of two months was unreasonable because it was too long; moreover, he thought that the Headmaster had not properly informed the teachers of the allegations. This was surprising because the Headmaster had sent my husband and me an email saying he had informed at least two of the teachers about the allegations and the teachers had said they would address them. Even more perplexing, the lawyer wrote his report on letterhead for his job as the Ombudsman of the Independent Schools Association, a surprising decision because the Headmaster had insisted on email that he was *not* acting in his capacity as Ombudsman. When we asked to see the lawyer's report, he specified that it was not an independent report; it had been commissioned by the Headmaster and belonged to the school and therefore, we were not permitted to read it. We ordered a copy under the *Freedom of Information and Protection of Privacy Act*, but it was hard to assess because so much of it had been redacted. The Headmaster repeatedly has issued public statements that

---

[214] http://www.telegraph.co.uk/news/uknews/law-and-order/10508486/Bullying-teacher-labelled-overweight-pupil-JCB-and-others-ugly-and-big-ears.html
[215] http://www.bbc.co.uk/news/uk-wales-11848069

this lawyer's report was written in his capacity as Ombudsman and was an "independent report."

Teenagers don't have a chance when they are pitted against adults that use the power of their offices to control the public narrative.

The second report commissioned and paid for by the Board of Governors was the one that characterized the four teachers as if they were victims of fourteen students telling "nasty lies." He used quotes from other students to suggest that the players who came forward were babyish and lacking in commitment. The Commissioner for Teacher Regulation Branch found that the teachers' conduct *did* breach the established standards of conduct, but that he would not take their files forward to a panel hearing accessible to the public. In fact, he wouldn't even share his decisions with the involved students and parents or put his decisions into the court of public opinion.

• • •

At my former school, students who may have found the courage to report that they are the targets of teacher bullying ultimately graduate. Typically and understandably, their families do not want to have anything more to do with battling the Headmaster and Board over what their children may have experienced at the hands of the coaches and the school administration. So what happens when the next group of students enters into the abusive coaching dynamic that students reported on and by all accounts has long been engrained in the School's culture? The answer — the cycle starts again. After assessing six testimonies, Dr. Alan Goldberg explains this in reference to the teachers at my former school: "In cases of abuse, lack of action appears to condone or collude with the abuse, leaving victims further abused. There have been complaints about these coaches for years and the school just waits for the 'complainers' to graduate or leave." His reasoning as to why the teachers were never held accountable was essentially that the Headmaster and Board used the sin of

241

omission to deal with the situation: lack of action, in terms of holding teachers accountable, combined with a great show of activity (the band aid solutions– that one could argue in light of recent video footage showing the Assistant Coach in a raging courtside display of apparently inarticulate anger and disgust – do not actually address deep-seated attitudes). Just as we were, concerned parents appear to be fed the same platitudes: the parental complaint is isolated; everyone else is happy; the teacher is toning it down; the teacher has apologized; the student has issues or is sensitive or is misperceiving what's happening; the Athletic Department is hiring a specialist; the teacher is taking a workshop; the Athletic Department is being reviewed; the students are being toughened up for a harsh world; a new coaching philosophy is being written, a new code of conduct has been established, new guidelines are being drawn up, and so on and so on. But all these gestures, which may be meant to address the problem, only serve to cloud the issue which is that the offending teachers, according to student testimonies, were not held publicly accountable or disciplined, their deep-seated attitudes never addressed. It is possible that the bullying might have stopped after so many investigations, so much scrutiny, so many workshops and specialized "coaching" clinics, but that still does not address the fact that students, according to their own testimonies, were bullied and harmed in at least 2011 and 2012. When bullied students leave the school, the abuse they described in their testimonies doesn't simply vanish. Based on clinical research, the damaging effects may well last a lifetime.

In a 2010 article in *The Toronto Star*, award-winning investigative journalist Robert Cribb discussed the failure to hold coaches to account despite the documented damage resulting from abusive coaches:

242

> Amateur sport coaches routinely commit psychological abuses against young athletes that trigger a "toxic tornado" with long-lasting effects on their development, say researchers.
>
> About 40 per cent of youth hockey, baseball and football games contain either direct or indirect abuse, according to striking new data collected by JustPlay, a national sport research firm that logs critical incidents in youth sports leagues.
>
> "No one has been monitoring it," says JustPlay president Elaine Raakman. "There's been no accountability. There has to be a framework in place to protect children."
>
> Direct abuses include coaches berating or threatening players, inciting violent play and demoralizing young players.[216]

This article was written five years ago and there is still not enough accountability and not nearly enough frameworks that protect student-athletes. Our experience was that there is no accountability and no framework. In fact, if the teacher is coaching then it appears the Commissioner for Teacher Regulation excuses conduct that would otherwise be considered harmful.

The administrative response of surprise and failure to act regarding Canadian teachers is particularly surprising, because in the eyes of the law, teachers are held to an extremely high standard of conduct. In BC's Court of Appeal and in the Supreme Court of Canada, teachers – both on and off duty – must conduct themselves as role models. In 1987, the BC Court of Appeal ruled that:

> Teachers must maintain the confidence and respect of their superiors, their peers, and in particular, the students, and those who send their children to our public schools. Teachers must not

---

[216] Robert Cribb, "Out of Control Amateur Coaches Mentally Abuse Players," *The Toronto Star*, July 2010: http://www.thestar.com/sports/hockey/2010/07/08/outofcontrol_amateur_coaches_mentally_abuse_players.html

only be competent but they are expected to lead by example. Any loss of confidence or respect will impair the system, and have an adverse effect upon those who maintain a standard of behavior, which most other citizens need not observe because they do not have such public responsibilities to fulfill. [217]

Perhaps with the defining term "public," private schools do not have to adhere to such high standards; if so, this needs to change. In 1996, high standards for teacher conduct were endorsed by the Supreme Court of Canada with their ruling:

> By their conduct, teachers as 'medium' must be perceived to uphold the values, beliefs, and knowledge sought to be transmitted by the school system. The conduct of a teacher is evaluated on the basis of his or her position, rather than whether the conduct occurs within the classroom or beyond. Teachers are seen by the community to be the medium for the educational message and, because of the community position they occupy, they are not able to 'choose which hat they will wear on what occasion'... teachers do not necessarily check their teaching hats at the school yard gate and may be perceived to be wearing their teaching hats even off duty. [218]

---

[217] In the USA, according to legal counsel, John M. Drye, for Educator Resources: "the duty a teacher owes to students is a foregone conclusion that is summarized in the legal doctrine of "In Loco Parentis." Literally defined as 'in the place of parents' [...] this theory accounts for a heightened degree of responsibility for the care and well being of students under the control of a teacher, just as if the teacher were acting in the capacity of a parent. The student teacher relationship by definition is a special relationship." http://wintersoliverinsurance.com/active/WebDoc.asp?s=1200415103&P=2002140415

[218] Jack Berryman is an education officer in the School Governance Branch of the Ontario Ministry has for the past twelve years managed the process relating to suspending, cancelling and reinstating teachers' certificates. http://professionallyspeaking.oct.ca/june_1998/role.htm

However, in BC, as the fourteen students who came forward and their families have learned the hard way, certain teachers who bully students, according to their testimonies, do not appear to be held accountable. At the same time that the Commissioner for Teacher Regulation ruled no reprimand for bullying at my former school, he issued the following specific guidelines for teachers who coach students:

> I have received a number of complaints about the conduct of coaches in the school athletic environment. The most common complaints from parents are those in which a coach's comments – rather than being motivating – are seen as bullying in that they belittle and demean the student athletes. This type of behavior may take place in professional sports when a coach deals with mature, seasoned and professional athletes; however, it has no place when the recipient of the demeaning or belittling comments is a student of an age and at a stage of development when being singled out can have profound consequences. Students, whatever their age, are vulnerable to emotional injury when such behavior is directed at them from persons in positions of authority, such as coaches. The potential for damage is enhanced by the fact that these incidents often occur in front of others, including teammates and parents, and in an atmosphere of heightened emotion during competitive sporting events.[219]

It seems odd that the Commissioner does not mention *students'* complaints when he has fourteen from my former school. Instead, he puts the focus on parents. It's also interesting that he writes "rather than be motivating," comments that belittle and demean "are *seen* as bullying" [emphasis mine]. The Commissioner continues to seem unsure about what constitutes bullying as he lays accountability at the feet of the victim. In other words, he warns teachers that despite their belief that they will

---

[219] https://www.bcteacherregulation.ca/documents/Learn/LearnMagazine_Current.pdf#page=26

motivate students by repeated belittling and demeaning, it is possible that the child treated this way might actually *see* it as bullying. Psychiatrist and author, Dr. Daniel J. Siegel, in his recent book *Brainstorm: The Power and Purpose of the Teenage Brain* addresses how harmful demeaning comments are by teachers:

> Unfortunately, what others believe about us can shape how we see ourselves and how we behave. This is especially true when it comes to teens and how they "receive" commonly held negative attitudes that many adults project (whether directly or indirectly) – that teens are "out of control" or "lazy" or "unfocused." Studies show that when teachers were told that certain students had "limited intelligence," these students performed worse than other students whose teachers were not similarly informed. But when teachers were informed that these same students had exceptional abilities, the students showed marked improvement in their test scores. Adolescents who are absorbing negative messages about who they are and what is expected of them may sink to that level instead of realizing their true potential.[220]

The students at my former school spoke up about the negative attitudes with which they were being coached. As they recorded in their testimonies, the belittling and demeaning messages were relentless. Dr. Siegel's book celebrates the emotional intensity, creativity and rebellious qualities that define adolescence and the testimonies produced by these young people show they don't want to believe the hurtful words directed at them day in day out by teacher-coaches.

While the Commissioner's public statement seems partially in line with the B.C. Court of Appeal and the Supreme Court of Canada, it does not appear to align with his assessment of the teachers at my former

---

[220] Daniel J. Siegel, *Brainstorm: The Power and Purpose of the Teenage Brain*, New York: Penguin, 2013.

246

school, which cannot be shared with the families involved, let alone the public. The Commissioner had the option to bring the students' complaints forward to a hearing; however, with all six certificate holders, four teachers and the Headmaster and Chaplain, he decided not to bring the matter before a panel. His decision differs from a parallel situation in Ontario where a coach was bullying players on the school hockey team. One boy quit the team in protest. As he explains,

> "It made me not want to go to my games and practices because I was going to get yelled at. It demoralizes you." A complaint to the league triggered a hearing in which GTHL officials ruled the coach committed four instances of misconduct. The coach was suspended for four games and placed on probation for one year.[221]

In Ontario youth sports, one complaint triggered a hearing by the league, even when the coach was not a certified teacher, but just an amateur coach. In contrast, fourteen complaints were not enough for the Commissioner for Teacher Regulation in BC to think that a hearing was required when the coaches were also certified teachers.

The Commissioner's decision also forms a significant contrast with how basketball coach Mike Rice was dealt with at Rutgers University. The Athletic Director, Tim Pernetti, explained that he initially did not fire Coach Rice because his abusive conduct was a "first offense." Even though it was a first offense, Rice was dealing with university-age students, and he was not a certified teacher; Pernetti still suspended and fined Rice thousands of dollars. Pernetti also had Rice attend anger management courses. In comparison with my former school, Pernetti appears to have taken significant steps to hold the coach responsible and

---

[221] Robert Cribb; http://www.thestar.com/sports/hockey/2010/07/08/outofcontrol_amateur_coaches_mentally_abuse_players.html

discipline him; nonetheless, *ESPN's* Dana O'Neil castigates Pernetti for the way he dealt with Mike Rice:

> In fact, [the Athletic Director] repeated the words "first offense" at least a half-dozen times. So, just wondering, how many chances do you get to assault an athlete? Missed that information in the student-athlete handbook. Coaches, colleges, conferences and the NCAA love to prattle on about what's best for the student-athlete. Here's what's not best for them -- personal verbal attacks and physical abuse from the coaches charged with their care.[222]

Despite established guidelines by multiple government agencies including the Ministry of Education that clearly outline there is no place for personal verbal attacks and physical abuse from teachers, or coaches, the Commissioner decided not to hold teachers publicly accountable at my former school. The Teacher Regulation Branch usually disciplines certificate holders who breach student confidentiality, who do not fulfill their duty to report, who publicly expose students to contempt and ridicule. However, the Commissioner decided not to hold the Headmaster or Chaplain publicly accountable. Our son says the bullying by the coaches was terrible, but the being positioned as a liar by the Headmaster was worse.

One student-victim looks back as a young adult on the bullying she suffered at the hands of her coach at my former school. Impossible to articulate while immersed in the School environment, after a significant health breakdown and discussions with health practitioners about the abuse she survived, she is now an advocate for other student-athletes. She argues that student-athletes are at risk. While several regulatory bodies

---

[222] Dana O'Neil, "With Mike Rice, we must draw a line," *ESPN.com,* April 2013: http://espn.go.com/mens-college-basketball/story/_/id/9126491/mike-rice-actions-rutgers-reprehensible-tolerated-college-basketball

such as BC School Sports and Basketball B.C. who, like the Ministry of Education, have set out guidelines about coaching conduct they do not appear able to enforce them in a consistent or material fashion. In an opinion piece, published by the *Vancouver Sun* on May 21, 2013, the student from my former school outlined the ways in which student athletes are at risk in BC despite the many guidelines already in effect.

> The video of Rutgers University basketball coach Mike Rice abusing his student athletes verbally and physically shocked ESPN and YouTube viewers and resulted in his firing on April 3. Rice's anger and disgust triggered memories of my own experience.
>
> I was a reliable producer, always competing and regularly regarded as an MVP. I was scolded to "get up" after collapsing with a debilitating knee injury, then spent nearly half a year recovering. Had I accepted my coach's view that writhing in pain was a sign of weakness, the injury could have been much worse.[223]
>
> My environment was purely focused on results, and I was made to feel my best would never be good enough. Today, I better understand the risks of long-term ramifications of abusive coaching. It's not enough for the B.C. Liberals to promote a strong stance against bullying. It's time for them to take a serious look at policy gaps with regard to regulations and enforcement specific to youth athletics.

---

[223] Dr. Alan Goldberg discusses another abusive coach in exactly these terms (names changed for privacy): "She explained that she was in too much pain to play. However, in Mark's mind, you were never too injured to play and athletes who complained about being in pain were weak and fakers! In fact, "Mark hated injured athletes!" In other student testimonies, this teacher's equation of illness or injury with weakness is reported on as extremely harmful. "Coaching ABUSE: The dirty, not-so-little secret in sports." http://gazette.teachers.net/gazette/wordpress/dr-alan-goldberg/coaching-abuse-the-dirty-not-so-little-secret-in-sports-by-dr-alan-goldberg/

Clearly, society has rules and regulations regarding physical and sexual abuse, but the protection for youth athletes from psychological and emotional abuse is difficult to find. Abusive coaches lack self-control and are prone to sudden outbursts of anger, a toxic mix for those who rule over child athletes. Children can easily submit to abusive regimes and keep quiet to win their coach's approval. The stakes are high when one's hopes and dreams hang in the balance.

Should a child suffer abuse in silence to avoid losing opportunity in the sport they love?

After investigating current policy in B.C., I discovered an alarming lack of oversight when it comes to coaching abuse. Is there a requirement that high school basketball coaches, for instance, be certified? There are no post-game evaluations by referees of coaching conduct as there are in other provinces.

Coaching codes of conduct exist in the province, but there are no requirements for coaches to sign on to them. There are conduct guidelines set out for teachers within the Teaching Regulation Branch, but what if your coach isn't a teacher? Are background checks required? Are there rules for coaches when they are travelling with children? Seemingly not.

B.C. has a complicated and confusing process to file complaints against coaches. Representing myself as a concerned parent, I tried to find out how I would go about filing a complaint against my imaginary child's high-school basketball coach. Ultimately transferred to B.C. School Sports, I was told the agency only deals with complaints if the incident occurred at one of their own sponsored games. If the incident occurred during a practice, I had to first report it to the school's administration. The school would then report the complaint back to BCSS if it couldn't be worked out internally. This gives school administrators a lot of power.

What if your child's school, like Rutgers University or Penn State, chooses to do nothing? What if the school favors the coach over the victimized student?

Although B.C. has an anti-bullying mandate, there are clearly gaps to fill. If we want to protect kids in the hallways and the playgrounds, we should also want to protect them in gymnasiums and on the fields. Coaches need to have mandatory standards and families need an easily accessible avenue to pursue when breaches of conduct occur. This policy gap also extends beyond schools and into community-based sporting programs.

The B.C. government needs to establish a provincial regulatory board to protect children from the risks of abusive coaching. It is in a unique position since it can pass legislation that authorizes the new Teacher's Regulation Branch to simply extend its jurisdiction to cover school coaches. B.C. teacher-focused legislation could provide a template for all youth athletics for coaching conduct standards outside of schools.

Coaching abuse can inflict serious harm on a reliant and impressionable youth. Many studies link bullying to a vast array of serious subsequent psychological issues: addiction, depression and suicide, among others. Child athletes are especially vulnerable, since they are looking only to the next level in their sport and are unable to understand the long-term ramifications of their experience.

Let us all appreciate the inordinate trust that a youth athlete might place in the hands of what could be a bullying adult coach.

The lack of a standardized code of conduct for all school coaches that is enforced by an independent government agency represents a policy gap that must be closed. B.C. has an opportunity to ensure the protection of our child athletes.[224]

The issue in BC is not the lack of guidelines, but rather it's that the officials who produce them don't appear to systematically or equitably adhere to them or enforce them.

---

[224] http://blogs.vancouversun.com/2013/05/21/b-c-s-young-athletes-need-protection-from-abusive-coaches-opinion/

In his new guidelines for teachers who coach, the Commissioner stated that belittling and demeaning kinds of behaviors "may take place in professional sports when a coach deals with mature, seasoned and professional athletes," but it has no place in school athletics. Perhaps the Commissioner is unaware that the professional world of sports has expressed outrage at coaches' bullying conduct even when directed at adults, let alone teenagers or children. In April 2013, in response to the Mike Rice's exposé, veteran journalist for *Sports Illustrated*, Austin Murphy wrote "A Message to Coaches: Stop Screaming and Start Teaching." In his article, he details in a shift in sports culture whereby bullying methods are no longer acceptable:

> ...tolerance of coaches behaving like bullies is on the wane. Brecht was suspended a week after Wisconsin-Green Bay opened an investigation of basketball coach Brian Wardle, who's accused of verbally and emotionally abusing players. A high school basketball coach in Saratoga Springs, N.Y. was suspended last week for reportedly verbally abusing players. On Tuesday, Eastern Connecticut State University suspended longtime baseball coach Bill Holowaty for violations including 'alleged throwing of a helmet in the bleachers during a game' and 'complaints of alleged public cursing and abusive language,' according to the Hartford Courant.[225]

Conduct parallel to that described by Murphy was well documented by the student testimonies at my former school. The teacher-coaches had been ejected from games by referees because of their conduct; conduct that ranged from throwing objects in a rage onto the court, to yelling,

---

[225] Austin Murphy, "A Message to Coaches: Stop Screaming and Start Teaching," *Sports Illustrated*, April 2013: http://www.si.com/college-basketball/2013/04/24/college-coaches

swearing, gesticulating in anger or disgust from the sidelines. And these are only the public displays.

Students came forward to say that it was worse behind the closed doors at practices, during half-time talks, or at the end of tournaments.

The coaches were passionately defended by some parents and school Alumni which fits the pattern of charismatic bullies. Likewise, there were students who defended Mike Rice and said that he was not a tyrant.[226] This is an important aspect to understand about abuse victims: they often "love" their abuser and thus they defend him or her to the end. As the *World Heath Organization* advises adults who take testimonies from children who report being abused, "Avoid expressing disapproval of the alleged perpetrator, as this individual may be loved or cared for by the child even though abuse or neglect may have taken place."[227] Therefore, it is crucial that authorities do not mistake the child's devotion to or admiration for the abuser as an indicator that all is well and that the child has not been exposed to harmful behavior. One abuse victim expressed this dynamic in a 2014 article published in the *Ottawa Citizen*:

> "I was only 10 years old but make no mistake I loved him very much. I love him still," said McMillan, who is one of three victims who had the publication ban on their names removed. "That love was and is very real. I know how hard that is to hear." Despite his love for Jones, McMillan said the court proceedings forced him to re-live the "toxic" experiences, some of which he

---

[226] http://espn.go.com/mens-college-basketball/story/_/id/9135440/two-rutgers-players-defend-fired-coach-mike-rice

[227] Alexander Butchart and Tony Kahane, *Preventing Child Maltreatment: A Guide to Taking Action and Generating Evidence*, World Health Organization and the International Society for the Prevention of Child Abuse and Neglect, 2006. http://whqlibdoc.who.int/publications/2006/9241594365_eng.pdf?ua=1

had not yet faced. McMillan also called the abuse he suffered and its aftermath "horrific," but said he has forgiven Jones.[228]

This victim is now middle-aged and has had an adult's lifetime of experience to draw on in expressing his understanding of the conflicted nature that exists for the victim and abuser. The student testimonies from my former school express comparable confusion about their feelings due to the loyalty-binds they feel to the team, their teammates, and their coaches.

Note the complete disconnect between the abusive conduct and the student's admiration for the teacher in the following quote from a basketball player at my former school:

> *Frank was the most skilled on the team at the beginning of the season. But because all the plays were for Simon and Greg, he couldn't shoot and then he got worse because his confidence was hurt. [The teacher] has the potential to be a great coach because he is knowledgeable, loves the game, and can relate to players.*

This is a familiar pattern of favoritism: Frank is blocked from "plays" despite his skill, and this is juxtaposed with the student's admiration for the teacher who "loves the game" and "relates to players." The student giving the testimony appears unaware of the disconnect. Comparably, when Mike Rice's abusive techniques were exposed, many former players leapt to his defense:

> Justin Haas, a former student manager at Robert Morris, where Rice previously coached, said the image of Rice in the montage of Rutgers practices was at odds with the coach he knew and admired. Haas said that Rice had a "fiery approach" to the game and that his practices were intense for a reason: to bring out the

---

[228] http://ottawacitizen.com/news/local-news/hockey-coach-kelly-jones-gets-8-12-years-for-abusing-children

best in his players. Robert Morris's three conference championships and two N.C.A.A. tournament appearances were proof that his methods worked. "His style is nothing out of the ordinary across collegiate sports," Haas said. "Any player, current or former, that played for Coach Rice and knows Coach Rice will have nothing but positive things to say because they understand his method. They became a better man and better player from their experience."[229]

Rutgers University fired Mike Rice for his coaching methods; they did not read testimonies like the one above and decide that this student was the best judge of whether or not harm was being inflicted on Scarlet Knights players.

• • •

Abuse victims, whether they are beaten women, sexually abused children, or emotionally abused athletes, struggle to separate out their admiration and "love" for the abuser. They often believe that the abuse was "for their own good" and that they *deserved* to be treated with disrespect and humiliation because it was meant to make them better; it was meant to motivate them. In a 2009 study about coaching abuse, Gretchen Kerr and Ashley Stirling discover exactly this emotional confusion in abuse victims:

> The participants in this study who described their relationship with their coach as similar to that of a father-daughter or mother-daughter relationship also expressed feelings of admiration and respect for their coach. The authority of the coach in the coach-athlete relationship and the finding that athletes often do not question their coach's actions or directions is also supported by

---

[229] Joe Drape and Nate Taylor, "Question Arises as Scandal Unfolds: Where's the Line?" April 2013: http://natetaylorsports.wordpress.com/2014/07/10/question-arises-as-scandal-unfolds-wheres-the-line/

previous research. It may be that the coach's power advantage over athletes during their careers precludes them from thinking more broadly about their relationships. Furthermore, young athletes may lack the psychological maturity necessary to think critically about these relationships.[230]

Tom Perry, an abuse victim in Britain, who now campaigns for mandatory reporting of abuse in schools, explains why my former school's use of Alumni letters to put in doubt students coming forward with abuse testimonies is a faulty approach and ignorant about how abuse works: "'The dynamics of abuse have not changed,' he says. 'It may be deeply uncomfortable to acknowledge, but the child mistakenly believes themselves to be in a relationship with the abuser, and will therefore feel they are committing a betrayal by speaking out.'"[231] Likewise, in a position paper in the *Canadian Academy of Sport and Exercise Medicine* that advises doctors how to take abuse testimonies from athletes the following is recommended: "Do not speak poorly about the perpetrator. The perpetrator can be a person that the victim truly cares for. Some victims may feel the need to protect their abusers, and any threats against this person may lessen the athlete's willingness to report and/ or allow for further investigation of the issue."[232] At my former school, Administrators, lawyers and even the Commissioner decided that because Alumni and students supported the allegedly abusive teachers, and the

---

[230] Ashley E. Stirling and Gretchen A. Kerr, "Abused Athletes' Perceptions of the Coach-Athlete Relationship," *Sport in Society* Vol.12.2, March 2009: 227-239.
[231] Louise Tickle, "Britain's Elite Boarding Schools Are Facing an Explosion of Abuse Allegations," *Newsweek*, September 2014: http://www.newsweek.com/britain-elite-boarding-schools-facing-explosion-abuse-allegations-267201
[232] Ashley E. Stirling, Eileen J. Bridges, E. Laura Cruz and Margo L. Mountjoy, "Canadian Academy of Sport and Exercise Medicine Position Paper: Abuse, Harassment, and Bullying in Sport," *Clin J Sport Med* 21.5, September 2011: 385-391).

ones reporting were conflicted, the teachers need not be held publicly accountable.

The second lawyer hired at my former school to produce a report, wrote that the students did not use the word "abuse" to describe what happened to them and therefore it was not abuse. This kind of circular logic is problematic as the whole way in which abuse works is to ensure that the victims believe, on one level at least, that it is their problem: the victims worry they are blowing their experience out of proportion; they worry that others think what happened was okay; they believe that it's normal; they think they're soft; besides, they think, who are they to say what is abuse and what is not? As explained in the position paper on abuse in sport for the *Canadian Academy of Sport and Exercise Medicine*, it is vital to acknowledge the risk the athlete has taken in speaking up about their suffering:

> Assure the athlete that the maltreatment is not his/ her fault. Tell the athlete that you are glad that he/ she told you about the maltreatment. There is often a culture of silence around experiences of abuse, harassment, or bullying. Especially in sport, where mental toughness is ingrained in many young athletes, individuals may feel that they are weak in asking for help. The athlete needs to be assured that the maltreatment is not his/ her fault and that you are aware of the courage it has taken him/her to come forward.[233]

In contrast, at my former school, the Administrators, lawyers and Commissioner appear to have decided that if multiple students were alleging abuse, it was because they lacked ego development, were misinterpreting, and not only was the treatment essentially deserved, but

---

[233] Ibid.

they should have remained silent, as should the adults who tried to support them and care for them.

There are clear definitions of what constitutes bullying, harassment, and abuse; thus, to ask students if *they* think that what they went through was "abuse" clouds the issue and is unlikely to give the sought after facts of what has happened. According to the position paper for the *Canadian Academy of Sport and Exercise Medicine*, written in 2011 and therefore available as a resource for those investigating the circumstances described in the student testimonies, abuse is "a pattern of physical, sexual, emotional, or negligent ill-treatment by a person in a caregiver capacity (e.g. parent, coach) resulting in actual or potential harm to the athlete." If this is still confusing to someone in the second lawyer's position in assessing abuse, he could consult the table Stirling and Kerr supply that lists behaviors such as yelling, swearing, blaming, humiliating, shunning, grabbing and so on; behaviors that are recorded in fourteen student testimonies. Notably, the experts do not advise those investigating these situations to turn to the athletes and ask them if what they experienced was "abuse." The last person one should consult with, in terms of defining abuse, is the confused and conflicted victim.

In a 2012 article about Canadian Olympic rowing coach, Mike Spacklen, Teddy Katz quotes one of the Olympic team rowers who quit the team rather than continue under such abusive conditions. Even though he was an adult at the time, it still was not until later that he could articulate that he had suffered "abuse."

> Dan Casaca at one point thought he might be rowing at the Games in London. But in November the rower, who at one time was considered one of team's bright young prospects, retired and walked away from his Olympic dream. He says he couldn't take any more of what he says had become a barrage of negative comments directed his way from Spracklen.

"I was the whipping boy," he says and adds if this was Spracklen's way to motivate him it had the opposite effect. No matter what he did, he says he was told he wasn't good enough, he was lazy. This happened in front of the whole team. "Telling them I was no good...I didn't care about anything, that's verbal abuse. That's the definition of verbal abuse. Did I take it like that at time? No. Do I see that it is now? - Yes.' [234]

According to student testimonies, our son was spoken to in near identical terms and he too appears to have been the Head Coach's whipping boy. The only difference was that he was a teenager not an adult. Rowing Canada did not renew Mike Spacklen's contract regardless of the many rowers who sent in letters of praise and regardless of his stunning track record in terms of winning Olympic medals. [235] Brian Richardson was Rowing Canada's head coach at the 1996 Olympics where the team won six medals and he coached alongside Spracklen during the 2004 games in Athens. Richardson does not question why *he* is not credited with the team's success; instead, he praises Spracklen but also offers a caution:

"As a coach he is second to none if you want to win the gold medal ... [in the men's eight] there is probably no one better in the world to do that for you," Richardson says. But he adds: "You have to be aware there will be a lot of destruction and fallout because of it." He says Spracklen's tactics have had the Canadian team close to self-destructing over the years. [236]

---

[234] Teddy Katz, "No Middle Ground with Mike Spracklen," *CBCSports*, August 2012: http://www.cbc.ca/sports-content/opinion/olympics2012/2012/08/there-is-no-middle-ground-with-rowing-coach-mike-spracklen.html
[235] Allan Maki, "Mike Spracklen, Rowing Canada Part Ways," *Globe and Mail*, October 2012: http://www.theglobeandmail.com/sports/more-sports/mike-spracklen-rowing-canada-part-ways/article4582601/
[236] Teddy Katz, "No Middle Ground with Mike Spracklen," *CBCSports*, August 2012: http://www.cbc.ca/sports-content/opinion/olympics2012/2012/08/there-is-no-middle-ground-with-rowing-coach-mike-spracklen.html

At my former school, the students reported on the destruction and fallout; the only difference was the coaches had not won a high-school championship in over twenty years, let alone Olympic medals.

The second lawyer hired by the School, who positioned the students as liars who came forward, wrote extensively in his short report about how the basketball program at the School was exceptional and used this as a way to argue that the coaching must be motivational and abuse-free. However, according to an expert like Ashley Stirling the coaching practices described in student testimonies do not produce winning teams: "These poor coaching practices have been described by athletes as being distracting, engendering self-doubt, demotivating, dividing the team, and can potentially lead to dropout from sport."[237] While there are vocal supporters of "old style coaching" like the lawyer the School hired to write the second report, based on research there are no studies indicating that a bullying approach leads to athletic success.

Dr. Roland C. Summit describes and deplores the approach used by the second lawyer, who discounted student suffering because the victims were unable to identify and define what they were suffering as abuse:

> The normal coping behavior of the child contradicts the entrenched beliefs and expectations typically held by adults, stigmatizing the child with charges of lying, manipulating or imagining from parents, courts and clinicians. Such abandonment by the very adults most crucial to the child's protection and recovery drives the child deeper into self-blame, self-hate, alienation and revictimization. In contrast, the advocacy of an

---

[237] Ashley E. Stirling, "Understanding the Use of Emotionally Abusive Coaching Practices," *International Journal of Sports Science & Coaching* 8.4, 2013: 625-638.

empathic clinician within a supportive treatment network can provide vital credibility and endorsement for the child.[238]

When students speak up about abusive conduct, it's crucial that adults in caregiver positions listen. We are well aware that reporting abuse is extremely difficult and thus when a child or a teenager finds the courage, we owe it to him or her to listen, record, identify if other students suffered in comparable ways, reach out to them, and create a safe environment so others will find the courage to come forward. When we find out that the answer to the question, "Are you being harmed?" is a resounding "yes" from even one other student who corroborates the complaint, we must *act* to protect them. If it's fourteen students detailing systemic bullying by teachers, there is likely a serious problem and there is a good chance that many others are likely to have also been harmed, even if, like the majority of abuse victims, they are unable to speak up because they are too afraid or because they have normalized the conduct.

Adults constantly ask, "Why don't children speak up when they're being abused?" At the same time, adults constantly doubt them when they do speak up with the phrase: "but so many children like the teacher or so many players like the coach so he mustn't or she mustn't be bullying anyone." Dr. Alan Goldberg offers an informed reason as to why abuse victims, specifically athletes, do not speak up. He argues that it is because coaches ensure that their athletes are brainwashed to believe that the fault lies with them:

> Deep down, the abusive coach is a damaged human being. He/she is emotionally stunted and immature. The abusive coach usually

---

[238] Dr. Roland C. Summit, "The Child Abuse Accommodation Syndrome," *This article appeared in Child Abuse & Neglect Vol 7, pp. 177 - 193, 1983*: http://www.secasa.com.au/sections/for-students/the-child-abuse-accommodation-syndrome/

suffers from deep seated feelings of inadequacy and he/she unknowingly acts these feelings out on his/her athletes. Unlike healthier human beings, the abusive coach is not able to take an honest look at his/her own behaviors. This individual is too busy defending him/herself and blaming others. The abusive coach is a pro at playing head games and manipulating others. He/she is able to convince his/her players that his/her frustration, yelling, anger and bad behavior are all their fault.[239]

This psychological assessment of how abusive coaching works might even be intensified when it is a teacher-to-student relationship. Students are well aware that their job is to learn and listen to teachers, not set the parameters around their educational experiences. They may well believe that it is presumptuous for a student to write the rules on what a teacher should be doing. And saddest of all, students generally tend to be protective of their teachers. Often, they do not want to see their teachers in trouble or harmed or suspended or fired. These feelings are hallmarks of the abuser-abused dynamic.

At my former school, some students admired the coaches at my former school about whom they gave testimonies. The Assistant Coach is well known for having an absolutely legendary knowledge of basketball and a near-photographic memory for plays. Off the court, these coaches are popular and funny. They are intelligent and express care in a whole variety of ways for students. However, one will find this profile when one looks at schoolyard bullies too. It doesn't mean that there isn't a target. It doesn't mean there aren't victims who are suffering in serious ways. One only has to look as far as US university coaches who are paid multi-million dollar salaries to coach sports teams; these people are brilliant and

---

[239] Dr. Alan Goldberg, ""Coaching ABUSE: The dirty, not-so-little secret in sports." http://gazette.teachers.net/gazette/wordpress/dr-alan-goldberg/coaching-abuse-the-dirty-not-so-little-secret-in-sports-by-dr-alan-goldberg/

charismatic. They land highly desirable jobs and can at times produce amazing results. It doesn't mean they aren't bullies or abusing students.

For many reasons at my former school, the students found it difficult to come forward and report what was happening. They tried to downplay what happened. Initially, they wanted different coaches, but some didn't want to see the adults in trouble. A victim's caring, sympathetic nature is one of the greatest weapons in the arsenal of abusers. In Malcolm Gladwell's article on sexual predators he draws on the Freeh report completed following Penn State's coach Jerry Sandusky's trial. The report describes one of Sandusky's first victims, whose mother became concerned when she learned he had showered with her son. The mother, Alycia Chambers, was a psychologist who reported that her sense was Sandusky was grooming and quite possibly a pedophile:

> Later that day, Chambers met with the boy who told her about the prior day's events and that he felt "like the luckiest kid in the world" to get to sit on the sidelines at Penn State football games. The boy said that he did not want to get Sandusky in "trouble" and that Sandusky must not have meant anything by his actions. The boy did not want anyone to talk to Sandusky because he might not invite him to any more games.[240]

Children are, in a most terrible irony, protective of the adults who abuse them. Plus, they are aware that adults have the power to give and to deny. Adults communicate this to children in so many different ways: keep quiet; you'll get playing time. Don't report, and defend me if someone does, you'll get awards, maybe a job at the gym, your photograph in the

---

[240] Malcolm Gladwell, "In Plain View: How Child Molesters Get Away With It," *The New Yorker*, September 2012: http://www.newyorker.com/magazine/2012/09/24/in-plain-view

newspaper, status at school, praise in my reviews on the school website, access to the NBA player I coached, time on the court to hone your skills and get noticed, best of all, you won't be humiliated. As recorded in the testimonies from the students at my former school, they weighed the cost of speaking up like the boy described by Gladwell who doesn't want to miss the chance to go to football games. At this school, it wasn't just about losing playing time or being put in a position where you couldn't succeed; it wasn't just about not being chosen for coveted awards, or, not being written up in reviews, not being chosen for newspaper articles. It was about having peers turn against you, or worse faculty and Administrators, or worst of all, being targeted for more bullying by the teachers. One student told me she didn't want to give a testimony about her teacher because then the School might simply shut down the team and she needed to play. It was what kept her going in high school. She needed her sport.

The moment students came forward and reported to the Headmaster what was happening at my former school, the teachers began reaching out to them, phoning university students and asking them out to dinner or calling parents at home. Coming up to students on campus, they were saying things like, "hey buddy let's go for a coffee." The flip back to kindness and the grooming phase was nothing short of emotionally shocking and painful for our son and possibly others. These same teachers had let the students publicly be called liars and now it seemed they wanted to start the cycle all over again. It made the students more confused and conflicted, reinforcing a sense that they could not trust their own perceptions. The Headmaster's decision not to suspend the teachers, or tell parents or the School community the facts about what was actually going on, made it highly stressful for students and their parents. Equally confusing, after the second lawyer's report was published, that positioned the students who came forward as liars and uncommitted athletes, the

Headmaster tried to initiate a Restorative Justice process. The families involved wrote scathing notes to him and the Board of Governors stating their children, publicly humiliated by them, would not be participating in such an unhealthy process. The Restorative Justice people, contracted to work with the School by the Headmaster, were informed more fully about what had happened to the students who came forward and they also withdrew from the process.

• • •

Instead of any further participation in the Headmaster and Board's processes, I fulfilled my Duty to Report and filed the complaints with the Teacher Regulation Branch. The four teachers, Headmaster, and Chaplain were informed of the complaints against them in December 2012; however, as far as I know, they did not share this information with the parents at the School or with the School faculty. Likewise, at Rutgers University, those in charge hoped to quietly fine and suspend Mike Rice without the rest of the faculty discovering the full extent of what had happened. As an article in the *New York Times* by Steve Eder and Kate Zernike discusses, when the faculty did find out, they were furious that the University President had not shared the information with them about the abuse going on at the university:

> At least 10 faculty members, including the dean of the Graduate School at Rutgers in Newark, signed a letter calling for Dr. Barchi, just seven months into his term, to resign for his "inexcusable handling of Coach Mike Rice's homophobic and misogynist abuse of our students." The faculty members accused Dr. Barchi of covering up the coach's behavior by neglecting to tell them and the student body about the extent of it in the fall. "In

the meantime, in December, President Barchi reviewed Coach Rice's $700,000 contract — and renewed it," the letter said.[241]

The faculty and parents at my former school were not informed about multiple student reports of homophobic or misogynist slurs thrown at them by their coaches. It is intriguing in this context to once again compare the decision *not* to hold teachers accountable at a high school in contrast to the outrage at Rutgers University in response to Mike Rice not being *instantly* fired. As reported on *ABC*,

> Gay rights organization Garden State Equality is also calling for a full investigation into Rutgers' administrators, saying that they knew about this video and the anti-gay harassment for months and did nothing. 'Homophobia, harassment, intimidation and bullying have no place at Rutgers or in our society today,' the group said. 'And that changing a culture of bias and hate must begin with leadership at the top.'[242]

In this same climate with as many government documents saying zero tolerance for bullying, it is remarkable that the Headmaster and Board at my former school appeared completely secure in their knowledge that the Commissioner for Teacher Regulation would not discipline with even the mildest reprimand the Headmaster, Chaplain, or teachers and therefore no information would enter into the public realm. Therefore, the Headmaster and Board did not need to suspend certificate holders under investigation; they did not need to inform parents; they appeared to have no worries about liability. During the six-month investigation and the year and a half deliberation on the Commissioner's part, the Headmaster and Board

---

[241] http://www.nytimes.com/2013/04/04/sports/ncaabasketball/rutgers-fires-basketball-coach-after-video-surfaces.html?pagewanted=all
[242] Kevin Dolak, "Fired Rutgers Coach Mike Rice to Receive $100K Bonus," *ABC News*, April 2013: http://abcnews.go.com/US/fired-rutgers-coach-mike-rice-receive-100k-bonus/story?id=18879500#.UV3b33BGjgo

appeared utterly confident that the students' concerns would be dismissed. This speaks volumes about the way students reporting on abuse are treated.

In *Boy Smarts: Mentoring Boys for Success at School*, Barry Macdonald, founder of MentoringBoys.com advises that:

> Along with families, our schools construct much of boys' social and cultural environment and are intimately connected with many of their fears and anxieties. Our schools set the criteria for success and failure, socially as well as academically, and create a world in which individuals are accepted or rejected on an almost daily basis. While I recognize that discussions about homophobia may be uncomfortable amidst conflicting community opinions, we must forge partnerships to provide the guidance and support boys so desperately need. At the very least educators and parents are charged to provide harassment free schools and communities where both boys and girls may develop their self-concept without unnecessary stress and anxiety.[243]

Hearing from multiple students about their stress and anxiety caused by teacher conduct, the Commissioner decided that none of them needed to be held accountable and the public did not need to be informed.

• • •

When the Acting Commissioner received the information in August 2012, the file was expedited due to the seriousness of the allegations and the fact that the students were still in jeopardy. The unusual decision was made *not* to inform the teachers of the student complaints even though, as was explained to me by the Intake Officer, administrative law says the teachers have the right to know about the

---

[243] Barry Macdonald, *Boy Smarts: Mentoring Boys for Success at School*, Mentoring Press, Surrey, 2005: 53.

267

complaints against them and it should occur within six weeks of the branch receiving them. I was told that because the Headmaster had not suspended the teachers, the Teacher Regulation Branch had made the unusual decision to protect the students from any further repercussions and thus the teachers and Administrators were not informed. In October, the Acting Commissioner had the file examined at a meeting as one of the most egregious files requiring immediate attention. However, the permanent Commissioner was then appointed and the investigation slowed down to a glacial pace so that two years passed before he made his decisions *not* to discipline teachers, *not* to protect students, and *not* to inform the public or even the families whose children reported they had been harmed.

At the start of the whole ordeal with the Teacher Regulation Branch, when I explained to the Intake Officer that for a year the Assistant Coach had on his team a player who became a NBA superstar and was powerful because of it, she assured me that they had six excellent investigators who were highly experienced. Besides, she said that when they receive reports of charismatic teachers, it's often a red flag to them that they are dealing with a potential abuser. For adults who work with children to get away with repeatedly bullying conduct, they need to be pillars of the community and highly popular to cover their actions, the classic Jekyll and Hyde dynamic referred to in recent coaching abuse scandals. Although there were six experienced investigators at the Teacher Regulation Branch, the new Commissioner did not send any of them to investigate at my former school. Instead, he contracted out and hired the retired former Head of Commercial Crime for the RCMP who was also a lawyer. The investigator worked for a company called the Investigative Research Group that describes itself as follows:

The Investigative Research Group's (IRG) *Special Investigations Unit* is a highly skilled and experienced group of former law enforcement senior executives and experts which can be deployed proactively to protect corporate assets, market share and public reputations through the discreet and effective investigation of the most serious or exceptionally sensitive corporate situations at the executive level.[244]

The investigator did not appear to have experience with children, abuse, or the education system. In 2002, the *Globe and Mail* described him as "An RCMP officer with connections to top-level B.C. Liberals" as he had worked on two high-profile cases for the present government that had to do with financial corruption, but we were not sure how this made him an appropriate candidate to work with allegedly harmed, vulnerable students.[245] He also had worked with the Lawyer/ Board Member on at least one occasion, the same Board Member who had told us not to transfer our son to another school. The Board Member had asked us to gather information from other parents; he asked us to allow our son to be interviewed by the second lawyer, and then finally approved the publication of the lawyer's report that positioned our son and all those who came forward as liars. Neither the Board Member nor the Commissioner's investigator disclosed their prior working relationship to the families involved.

The other surprise for students and involved families was the length of time the Commissioner took to make his decisions. We had hoped that he would suspend the teachers so that our son could continue at school cleared of the label of liar and able to play basketball, but the Commissioner chose not to suspend the teachers. In terms of delay, the

---

[244] http://www.zoominfo.com/CachedPage/?archive_id=953402703&page_id=-190102802&page_url=//www.irgcanada.com/special-investigations-unit&page_last_updated=2011-12-05T02:14:36&firstName=Bill&lastName=Ard
[245] http://www.theglobeandmail.com/news/national/trial-probes-rcmp-conflict/article1020873/

269

Commissioner himself has stated in the government issued *Learn Magazine* that one of his top priorities is to "reduce the delay in the regulation process." As he says in no uncertain terms, "Delay is the cancer of adjudicative processes."[246] While he has adhered to this goal recently with his archived decision on public school teacher, David John Macdonald, he failed to reduce delay with the four teachers, Headmaster and Chaplain from my former school as his decisions took over two years to render. In stark contrast, Macdonald's file took approximately nine months from the District's suspension of him on September 25, 2013 until June 26, 2014. Surely at a school where students are not protected, parents are distraught, students have been positioned as liars without any apparent evidence, but with the weight of the Headmaster's position behind the insinuation, the Commissioner could have expedited his process and decisions.

In terms of child abuse situations, there are checks and balances at public schools that keep student safety as a key priority; however, some independent schools may lack similar checks and balances depending on the Appointed Official in charge. I imagine the system works fine when the Appointed Official is an administrator with integrity, having child health and safety as a priority, but what if that's not the case? As the Ministry of Education's *Supporting Our Students: A Guide to Independent School Personnel Responding to Child Abuse* states:

> The critical difference between the public and independent
> systems is the requirement that independent school authorities
> nominate an 'Appointed School Official' who is responsible for
> working with child care workers to determine whether a child has

---

[246] http://www.bcteacherregulation.ca/documents/Learn/2013/LearnMagazine_Spring_2013.pdf

been harmed by someone who works or volunteers at the school, or works on contract for the school.[247]

The Appointed Official's responsibility is to see if a child has been abused in any way. At my former school, fourteen students spoke up to say they were being harmed, or had been harmed, by the same teachers over a five-year span. They were clear and detailed in explaining what had happened and how it made them feel. Many of the students did not know each other and yet the testimonies corroborated one another. Nowhere in the Ministry of Education's guide did I find a directive to consult with other students or their families to determine if they experienced harm too. Nowhere did I see the Appointed Official being advised to bring in lawyers. According to the *B.C. Handbook for Action on Child Abuse and Neglect,* all it takes is one child being hurt, one student suffering abuse and the Appointed Official is expected to protect the child who reported the abuse, and has become especially vulnerable as a result, and to also ensure no other students are harmed.[248]

However, in October of 2012, the Acting Commissioner was aware that no one was protecting students and was also aware that the Headmaster, as Appointed Official to deal with child abuse reports at the School had been informed in 2011 of "child abuse" and had *not* protected students. She was aware that throughout the year, the Headmaster had received further reports from parents about teacher bullying. She knew that a full year later in 2012, the Headmaster had fourteen student testimonies that detailed teacher bullying. The Acting Commissioner was aware that he had exposed some of these students to one of the bullying teachers described in the student testimonies, resulting in peer bullying. She knew that he had then published a lawyer's report insinuating the

---

[247] http://www.bced.gov.bc.ca/independentschools/is_resources/SOS_guide.pdf
[248] Ibid.

students who reported on the bullying were liars and babies. With all this knowledge, the Acting Commissioner for Teacher Regulation put the file on hold.

In an environment where top Administrators like the Headmaster, Chaplain, and Board of Governors were implicated in a hostile environment and public humiliation of students, the Acting Commissioner did not act. The files were left for the new permanent Commissioner to attend to and then, even more harmful, the process took on a painfully slow timeline.

Public school teacher David John Macdonald had already been suspended and undertook a six-week course on anger management and psychological counseling to address his issues. The Commissioner may have been assured of the safety and wellbeing of students in this teacher's care. In contrast, he was also well aware, due to multiple messages of concern from parents, that the teachers and Administrators at my former school were continuing bullying conduct directed at highly vulnerable students who had come forward with abuse allegations. The police had to come twice to the School and speak to the Head Coach and the Administration about his continuing aggressive conduct toward students. Moreover, as discussed the young coaching intern who felt humiliated and bullied by the Director of Athletics, and then felt bullied by the Director of the Senior School and Head of Residence, attempted suicide in his residence room at the school. He too had reported to the police over the course of two hours how he was treated and what he witnessed at the school. The Commissioner also had this information at his disposal. Nonetheless, the Commissioner did not suspend the teachers or Administrators, nor did he accelerate his decision-making process to protect students and staff; rather he extended his process by a year and a half after having contracted out to an investigator with expertise in protecting corporate assets and company brands.

272

This is surprising, because the Commissioner has justified the use of expensive investigations because they have allowed him to act swiftly and decisively in subsequent cases. In his July 2013 *Annual Report*, the Commissioner stated that having an investigation allows him to act immediately upon its completion.[249] In an article by Janet Steffenhagen for the *BC Confederation of Parent Advisory Councils*, the Commissioner is quoted as saying, "Delay destroys the fairness of the process." In this same article, he specifically addresses teachers who coach: "The line between vigorous coaching practices and conduct that emotionally harms students is a difficult one to draw. However, it must be drawn." Steffenhagen adds, "Although he provides no details, [the Commissioner] says some of the most troubling complaints he's reviewed since becoming commissioner involved coaches, and drafting guidelines will be one of his priorities this year."[250] If the Commissioner finds drawing a line between vigorous coaching practices and emotionally harmful ones "difficult," he is in the wrong job. Universities *fire* coaches who are bullies, who use obscenities, favoritism, and humiliation under the auspices of training athletes. Universities have no problem drawing the line. While the Commissioner did draft yet more guidelines to add to the many that already exist, he also decided that the coaches' bullying described in testimonies by students at my former school did not require even a reprimand, or any public scrutiny.

After almost two years spent deciding on teacher and administrative conduct, the Commissioner's decisions were released over a six-month period. The only recourse an individual has to question his decisions is to request a judicial review. It costs anywhere from sixty to

---

[249] http://www.bcteacherregulation.ca/documents/FormsandPublications/AnnualMeetings/CTR_annual_rpt_2012_2013.pdf
[250] http://bccpac.bc.ca/news-blog/guidelines-planned-teachers-who-coach-sports

eighty thousand dollars. The decisions rendered about certificate holders at my former school are entwined; they would all need to be reviewed so it would cost approximately four hundred thousand dollars to have the Commissioner reconsider his decisions. However, none of the families were allowed to read or assess his rationale as to why he decided to not hold the teachers or Headmaster and Chaplain accountable so a judicial review was never a possibility even if families could afford such a colossal expense.

In his 2013 *Annual Report*, the Commissioner explained that inappropriate conduct in a professional role "typically refers to cases in which a teacher has failed to respect the professional boundaries between teacher and student, or failed to maintain an emotionally, intellectually and physically safe learning environment."[251] By not issuing a reprimand for bullying, he has cleared four teachers, the Headmaster, and the Chaplain of the students' allegations that their learning environment was not emotionally, intellectually, or in some cases, physically safe. In the *Annual Report,* the Commissioner also includes in the category of professional misconduct those cases that are "related to breaches of confidentiality, fraudulent documents or inappropriate publication (e.g. Posting information or referencing students on a social media site.)" [252] As discussed, the Headmaster breached student confidentiality by telling the Assistant Coach which students had come forward with complaints. He breached confidentiality in allowing Alumni to be contacted. He breached confidentiality in publishing the second lawyer's report in September 2012. And because of his earlier breach of confidentiality, certain students' names were clearly associated with the second lawyer's

---

[251] http://www.bcteacherregulation.ca/documents/FormsandPublications/AnnualMeetings/CTR_annual_rpt_2012_2013.pdf
[252] Ibid.

report, as was mine. The Headmaster was well aware that students had already been bullied by peers after his initial breach several months earlier in June 2012. Nonetheless, the Commissioner did not find any of these actions worthy of even a reprimand.

• • •

Dr. Alan Goldberg was brought in to speak at the *Champions for Children and Youth Summit 2013* in BC as an internationally renowned expert on bullies who coach student-athletes. He also read, and assessed in a written report submitted to the Commissioner, six of the fourteen student testimonies. The key points are as follows:

> (a) "The situation at [the school] is NOT one of these situations where the parents are the problem! I have never seen such detailed, well-documented, and consistent testimony from so many athletes (combined with my own observations from work with one such student) that confirm and validate the existence of a very serious and damaging problem."
> (b) "The following complaints from six testimonies and my individual work with one student-athlete indicate the presence of very real and significant emotional abuse."
> (c) "I completely disagree with the premise and conclusions that [the second lawyer] reached in his independent investigation… If a group of athletes have gotten to the point of launching a formal complaint, there is good reason for it and I am deeply concerned and dismayed that [the second lawyer] completely minimized and explained away their complaints of emotional abuse."
> (d) "These coaches, both male and female, named in the complaints should be immediately released from their duties, both as coaches, athletic directors and teachers. Their continued presence at [the school] creates an intense atmosphere of intimidation and fear for the targeted male and female students….If a teacher in a classroom repeatedly called his/ her students 'a fucking retard,' 'a fucking pussy,' or 'a fucking idiot,' would you let him continue to work with your students?"

275

In the spring 2015 edition of *Learn Magazine*, the Commissioner himself is in clear agreement with Dr. Goldberg that the kind of conduct the students describe is unacceptable. He explains as follows:

> Standards for the Education, Competence & Professional Conduct of Educators in British Columbia require teachers to foster the emotional, intellectual and social development of students. The Standards state that educators treat students with respect and dignity. Educators respect the diversity in their classrooms, schools and communities. Educators have a privileged position of power and trust [. . .] Sexual and/or gender identity must not be the subject of other than respectful comment.[253]

And yet, the Commissioner did not publicly discipline the teachers for repeatedly breaching these standards. Once again, it is relevant to compare the Commissioner's decision on public school teacher, David John Macdonald. This teacher was disciplined with a two day suspension without pay by the District on September 25, 2013. This was almost a year after the complaint was lodged against the six certificate holders at my former school and still the Commissioner had not made his decisions. The District had already reprimanded MacDonald in 2010 for "speaking inappropriately and disrespectfully to a student by yelling and using profane and derogatory language." The Commissioner considered his situation on "February 3, 2013" which one assumes is actually February 3, *2014*. This is four months after the District disciplined the teacher. The Commissioner issued a "reprimand" to Macdonald that meant the matter then became public. The teacher's conduct that resulted in a suspension by the District and reprimand from the Commissioner was this:

---

[253] https://www.bcteacherregulation.ca/documents/Learn/LearnMagazine_Current.pdf

276

(a) spoke to students in a demeaning way and used derogatory and profane language, by calling students "dumb asses," referring to students who were short as "midgets," and telling students to "get their fingers out of their asses"

(b) on occasion told students that if they "don't know what you are doing, go play cricket or volleyball"

(c) kicking basketballs or throwing down his whistle to the floor in a way that students perceived as frustration or anger at their failure to perform to his expectations.[254]

Macdonald agreed in a consent resolution agreement that he had breached two of the four standards by which teachers must conduct themselves in schools in BC. These two standards are:

Educators value and care for all students and act in their best interests. Educators are responsible for fostering the emotional, esthetic, intellectual, physical, social and vocational development of students. They are responsible for the emotional and physical safety of students. Educators treat students with respect and dignity.

Educators respect the diversity in their classrooms, schools and communities. Educators have a privileged position of power and trust. They respect confidentiality unless disclosure is required by law.

Educators do not abuse or exploit students or minors for personal, sexual, ideological, material or other advantage.

Educators are role models who act ethically and honestly. Educators act with integrity, maintaining the dignity and credibility of the profession. They understand that their individual conduct contributes to the perception of the profession as a whole. Educators are accountable for their conduct while on duty,

---

[254] https://www.bcteacherregulation.ca/documents/FormsandPublications/ ProfConduct/DisciplineDecisions/MacDonald_CRA_20140703.pdf

as well as off duty, where that conduct has an effect on the education system. Educators have an understanding of the education system in BC and the law as it relates to their duties.

In the testimonies of the students at my former school, in multiple complaints by many parents, in two videos, one by a parent and one by a local TV station, these two standards appear to be breached repeatedly. Moreover, every single behavior of the public school teacher who was disciplined is documented in the student testimonies. Some of the teachers at my former school were ejected from tournaments by referees for the conduct for which Mr. Macdonald was reprimanded and this is on record. However, the Commissioner states that although the teachers at my former school breached standards, he is not going to reprimand them, let alone suspend them.

I believe there are significant policy gaps that allow the wellbeing of independent school students especially to be at risk. Students are at risk in universities that also may strive to protect their program's prestige and their institution's reputation. This conflict of interest may lead to keeping the voices of abused students, courageous enough to speak up, silenced and ultimately re-victimized because, at the very least, their suffering is minimized and dismissed.

# CHAPTER NINE

# WORKPLACE BULLYING AND THE BRAIN

> The predominant governance structure of public
> education dictated by law is seriously flawed. What
> thousands of citizens and educators strongly desire for
> their schools can be discarded and replaced with the
> unscrupulous will of one individual. Exploitive school
> board members must be understood and stopped. The
> governance structure of public education must be
> changed.
>
> – Dr. Matt Spencer, author of *Exploiting Children:*
> *School Board Members Who Cross the Line* [255]

The chapter headings of Dr. Matt Spencer's book sound familiar in my
experience dealing with my former school's Board of Governors over the
last three years. Spencer's chapters revolve around maintaining silence
and ousting teachers who speak up. Although focused on education
governance, Spencer works in conjunction with the *Workplace Bullying*

---

[255] Dr. Matt Spencer is a veteran educational leader who has served in public
education in Missouri and California for thirty-four years. As the Senior Consultant
with the Workplace Bullying Institute of Bellingham, Washington, Dr. Spencer
champions efforts to ensure American schools are safe, productive and abuse-free
environments for students to learn and employees to serve. His book is a powerful
argument for the need on school boards to have independent watchdogs as the
safety and wellbeing of children is at stake.

*Institute* and examines the disastrous effects of bullying among adults. When I contacted the Institute to see if they had ever looked at bullying from teacher to student or coach to athlete, they were surprised because, in fact, they had not studied or researched bullying in either of these contexts. Nonetheless, in the same way that peer-to-peer bullying on the playground can offer key insights, examining adult-to-adult bullying is also helpful. We simply need to understand how much it is all magnified when the bullying has the most significant power imbalance: coach to student-athlete and teacher to student. The fact that the stereotypical phrase for a bully to say to a kid is "I'm going to teach you a lesson!" suggests that bullying may well be learned behavior, and may well be learned at school, not from peers but from a particular teacher or coach or administrator.

In the influential 2007 study, *The Bully at Work*, co-authored by two American psychologists, Drs. Gary and Ruth Namie, who head up the *Workplace Bullying Institute*, a survey of over seven thousand U.S. workers was conducted. The researchers discovered that nearly half of them had been impacted by workplace bullying in one form or another. This is not just an American issue. In an article for *Canadian Living*, Emily Kimber writes, "Awareness about **workplace bullying** is growing in Canada. In a 1999 International Labour Organization report, researchers warned that physical and emotional violence are becoming some of the biggest issues facing the workplace going into the 21st century."[256] The loss in productivity this causes is enormous. Yet there are detractors who say a workplace of "Bullies and Targets" is simply a part of how companies and employers operate to be productive and meet their quotas. In the International Labour Organization report, the authors

---

[256] http://www.canadianliving.com/life/work/dealing_with_workplace_bullies.php

explain that critics of anti-bullying will be quick to say, "strong words do not harm people. The notion is that Targets just need to grow a thicker skin to withstand the inevitable assaults that are a routine part of working."[257] This is the argument used at my former school by the teachers reported on by students, but more surprisingly by the Headmaster, Board, and the lawyer who wrote the report they published: they argue that students who react to a teacher's insults or swearing or yelling are simply students who are too sensitive; they are "soft" and so teachers and coaches must work on them to toughen them up, thicken their skin so that they can survive in a harsh world. Repeatedly in the testimonies, the students pride themselves on not crying and on not getting broken down by the teachers. One student reported in his testimony on how painful it was to watch the teacher coaching his own son: "*[The Assistant Coach] is incredibly hard on him. Sometimes he catches himself. [The son] breaks down. He has a long history of being broken down. I can't imagine my dad being like that with me. He swears at him and yells at him.*" As soon as any student is putting their energy into not being "broken down," rather than learning or developing skills, a bullying dynamic is likely at work.

• • •

In a powerful statement about coaching abuse, University of Minnesota Gophers' wide receiver, A. J. Barker lashed out publicly at his coach, Jerry Kill: "As a master manipulator, you misunderstood one thing about me: I have an extremely strong mind and **you never had the power to break me**." A. J. Barker, like so many student-athletes, ended up

---

[257] See p. 12, Dr. Gary Namie and Dr. Ruth Namie, *The Bully at Work: What You Can Do to Stop the Hurt and Reclaim Your Dignity*. Napier: Sourcebooks, 2000; 2nd edition, 2009.

quitting his university football team. In his parting letter, he details the techniques used by bullying coaches or teachers to maintain power over students; all these same techniques can be found described in the student testimonies from my former school. [258] Barry Macdonald comments in *Boy Smarts* on the destructive code of masculinity that limits and harms boys rather than strengthens and develops them. He alludes to the shaming concept of softness: "This particular code of masculinity, which has been a dominant force in western male culture for a long time, glorifies war and marginalizes males who are going *soft*."[259] This homophobic, humiliating concept has been around for a long time. The students, who asked for protection from alleged abuse, boys and girls, were seen to be "soft" or overly sensitive rather than *strong* for effectively speaking up against berating, humiliating, homophobic, insulting conduct.

The BC government agency, *HealthLinkBC* defines child abuse based on the very fact that children are "sensitive" to caregivers; teachers and coaches could reasonably be included in that definition. *HealthLinkBC* states, "The behavior of an emotionally abusive parent or caregiver does not support a child's healthy development and wellbeing— instead, it creates an environment of fear, hostility, or anxiety. A child is sensitive to the feeling, opinions, and actions of his or her parents."[260] If we know about this sensitivity as it applies to caregivers, why do we see it as a fault in students when they come forward and report that the yelling, swearing, and demeaning language used by their caregivers is harmful to them?

---

[258] Nate Sandell, "Gophers receiver A. J. Barker blasts Jerry Kill, says he's transferring," *ESPN*, November 2012: http://www.1500espn.com/sportswire/ Gophers_receiver_AJ_Barker_blasts_Jerry_Kill_says_hes_transferring111812
[259] Barry Macdonald, *Boy Smarts: Mentoring Boys for Success at School*, Mentoring Press, Surrey, 2005: 55.
[260] http://www.healthlinkbc.ca/healthtopics/content.asp?hwid=tm5075

The social and clinical psychologist team that wrote *The Bully at Work* disagrees with this belief system that would see sensitivity and softness driven from students and employees and they draw on neurological research to make their point. They considered the work of Professor Kip Williams and his colleagues at Purdue University who studied the physical effect on the brain of bullying in the workplace with the use of real time MRI scanners:

> ...people were insulted while being scanned. It turns out that insults, a form of verbal abuse, trigger neuronal pain pathways. It literally hurts to be insulted. Furthermore, when people in a social experience are inexplicably, and without warning, excluded from a fun activity with others, the brain responds in ways that mirror trauma and pain. Social exclusion is painful; it's real.[261]

I think we are at a time in society where we need to re-think the words "literally hurts" and the pain is "real." What this experiment shows is that verbal abuse is in fact physical abuse, except rather than target the body, it targets the brain.

As recorded in student testimonies, the teachers ignored or shunned certain students. The Purdue University study shows that these kinds of exclusions appear in the brain as "trauma" and "pain." Brain research shows that even ignoring harms the excluded individual. It's so subtle; it seems so minor; it's too petty really to even talk about, let alone report. However, if it is harmful to an adult at work, consider what it could do to a teenager's developing brain, and so maybe we do need to start reporting on these behaviors and the impact they have. Bullying flourishes with exclusions, small gestures, facial expressions, whispered or muttered comments so often meant for the target alone.

---

[261] See *The Bully at Work* (p. 13).

In BC, the Ministry of Education and the government of the day, particularly the Premier, are vocal about zero tolerance when it comes to bullies. The government went as far as to produce the *Safe School* report that lays out the qualities they want to establish for schools ensuring that they are safe for all students, not just the majority. Moreover, the advisory report repeatedly stresses that all students must be given fair chances. One of the disturbing powers that teachers have who bully students is to limit their opportunities: they can sit an athlete on the bench game after game; they can give the role in the school play to the student who never spoke up against them; they can give awards to students who haven't deserved them; they can award high marks to students who didn't earn them and grade harshly students they target. The Ministry of Education's report mandates that a community safe from bullying is one that "foster[s] respect, inclusion, fairness and equity."[262] Although the report is intended for students, considering the power and influence teachers and coaches wield, it makes sense to apply these same rules to their conduct as well.

"The Voice on Harassment: BC Student Voices" publication produced by the BC government turned to students to find out what their advice would be to teachers and administrators to reduce bullying, intimidation, and harassment in schools. Among several responses, one is particularly relevant: "treat all students equally." [263] The students vocalized this as a primary concern: for students, equal treatment appears to be a significant issue in schools. Rather than dismissing a request for equal opportunities with classic "sour grapes" or "disgruntled parents," perhaps administrators should listen and monitor fairness and equity in classrooms, sports, and extracurricular activities. A single complaint, maybe even two, could be dismissed as parents too invested in their

---

[262] https://www.bced.gov.bc.ca/sco/guide/scoguide.pdf#page=15

[263] http://www.bcpvpa.bc.ca/downloads/pdf/SVHarassment2006.pdf

children's futures, or students who have a sense of entitlement or believe they are due special privileges. However, when fourteen students provide detailed testimonies and give multiple interviews that outline concerns with how some students are given privileges and are exempt from insults, safe from public humiliation, never exposed to shunning, while others are denied opportunities, sidestepped for awards they earned, blocked from having chances to develop, while at the same time are repeatedly yelled at, sworn at, penalized, insulted, or simply ignored, then it's difficult to deny teacher bullying is at work.

The Ministry of Education's *Safe Schools* report, when it focuses directly on bullying itself does *not* take the stance that minor infractions are to be dismissed as part of students being too sensitive or needing to learn to toughen up for a harsh world. In fact, as the report states in regards to bullying, harassment, and intimidation:

> Safe schools make a "big deal" about "small" incidents of this type. All staff and students are educated about these serious behaviors and work together to prevent them from occurring. Students understand the critical role that bystanders play and take appropriate actions (including getting adult assistance) to stop such incidents.[264]

The problem with this document is, it assumes that teachers and administrators assist students in jeopardy from bullying, but it does not advise a student what he or she should do when the teacher, coach, or administrator is the bully. It does not direct them to people they can turn to for assistance and support when adults in powerful positions are the source of the harmful behavior. And while it is true that at my former school there would be presentations for students on bullying, and staff room discussions of incidents where peer-to-peer bullying had occurred, I

---

[264] https://www.bced.gov.bc.ca/sco/guide/scoguide.pdf#page=15

285

cannot recall in my nine years at the School that there ever was a discussion about teacher bullying or a discussion about the importance of not being a bystander when one teacher observes another acting in a harmful manner toward students. If my former school had a Human Resources person, let alone department for its hundreds of employees, it would make reporting on teacher or coach bullying much safer. However, despite requests for years from teachers, my former school does not have a Human Resources person.

• • •

In the articles I have read about Assistant Coach and whistleblower Eric Murdock, whose contract was not renewed after he went public with his concerns about basketball coach Mike Rice's abusive conduct, there is no mention of a safe complaint process or whistleblower protection. Perhaps these safeguards could have protected the Athletic Director, Tim Pernetti, from losing his job as well. It appears that in the workplace and in educational institutions, bullies are difficult to contain. Eric Murdock, Tim Pernetti and others were aware of Mike Rice's abusive conduct, but they seemed unable or unwilling to bring it to a halt. Although Rice yelled in apparent fury and disgust when coaching games, it was actually his conduct at practices that got him fired. As Steve Eder reported in the *New York Times,* there were all kinds of warning signs that abuse was occurring and the administrators were already aware prior to video footage hitting the news:

> There was the upperclassman who earlier in the year had come forward to say that he felt bullied. There was an outburst during a game that led to Mr. Rice's ejection. And there were the months of allegations from a former assistant, who repeatedly claimed that Mr. Rice was abusive.
>
> Tim Pernetti, the athletic director, knew all of that and had repeatedly tried to rein in Mr. Rice, according to a 50-page report

286

that Rutgers commissioned outside lawyers to prepare. He personally reprimanded him, attended Mr. Rice's practices and even assigned the university's sports psychologist to work with the team, the report said.[265]

At my former school, the Senior Boys Head Coach wasn't issued a technical foul or ejected just once, but *multiple* times from the Provincial Championships and from tournaments. There wasn't just one student who came forward to say he was feeling bullied; there were many. There was the Lawyer/ parent's report on child abuse in 2011. There were multiple parent complaints. There were many warning signs. It seems that at best, institutions like Rutgers and my former school lack the necessary processes for handling abuse situations; at worst, they have significant conflict of interest in themselves investigating student concerns. There is clearly work that needs to be done in terms of Human Resources, record keeping, anonymous reporting, proper oversight and so on.

For bullying to flourish, there must be an institution that enables it. To return to the definition in the *Health Agency of Canada* about psychological abuse and how it works, authors Deborah Doherty and Dorothy Berglund discuss two other techniques used by abusers especially institutionalized ones; these seem to be consistent with those described by the students as having been employed by the Headmaster and Board at my former school: the first is "minimizing and trivializing" and the second is "denying or forgetting."[266] Minimizing and trivializing, the authors specify as "refusing to validate the other person's feelings of

---

[265] http://www.nytimes.com/2013/04/07/sports/ncaabasketball/rutgers-officials-long-knew-of-coach-mike-rices-actions.html?pagewanted=1&_r=1&smid=tw-nytimes&partner=rss&emc=rss
[266] Public Health Agency of Canada: "Psychological Abuse: A Discussion Paper" by Deborah Doherty and Dorothy Berglund. http://www.phac-aspc.gc.ca/ncfv-cnivf/sources/fv/fv-psych-abus/index-eng.php

hurt" as well as "suggesting that nobody else would be upset by the same treatment."[267]

The Headmaster announced to the School community that some boys had had "unhappy experiences" and now he wanted to hear from students and apparently Alumni who had had "good experiences." He did not publicly validate the students' hurt; the way he proceeded, implied that others were not upset by the same coaching. This caused the situation to spin around until it focused on the bullies' targets and asked, what is it about them that led to their misperception that they were being abused? Why can't they be happy like everyone else? No longer were people focused on teacher conduct. Now, the Headmaster had people focused on the victims and their "issues," which he positioned as if *they* were what caused the crisis. If the Headmaster had actually informed faculty of the students' allegations, I believe they would have been appalled. But he shifted attention away from teacher accountability and focused it on students' "unhappiness." Ill-informed teachers were quick to assume students were "whining" and "complaining about playing time" and their parents were being "demanding." The Headmaster's failure to publicly state the facts of the matter allowed for these kinds of skewed perceptions to flourish. Likewise, it appears that when Alumni were contacted, the attention wasn't on the teachers' conduct and the students' testimonies; instead, it was on the parents who were depicted as acting aggressively to take over the Athletics Department as if this would somehow benefit their children. Without knowing my involvement, various Alumni talked to me about how they had been called to write in and support the teachers. There was no mention of student testimonies. They were told several parents

---

[267] Deborah Doherty and Dorothy Berglund, "Psychological Abuse: A Discussion Paper," Ottawa: Public Health Agency of Canada, 2008: http://cdn.timurkaripov. netdnacdn.com/readonline/5a6c4a43645142385633782b44486c73566b593d

288

were complaining. It is important for the Alumni of my former school to know the full story, rather than to have been given vague statements encouraging their defense of the teachers and the School. Some of them might feel they were asked to write in and support something under false pretenses.

The other technique Doherty and Berglund see as being used by institutionalized abusers is "denying that any abuse has ever taken place," which results in "forgetting promises or agreements."[268] It has been remarkable to watch a Headmaster, Chaplain, Lawyer/ Board Member we initially contacted and Chair of the Board acknowledge teacher bullying and make a series of promises to heal its terrible scars, come full circle to deny the harm ever happened and to renege on their agreements made with students and parents. The Headmaster promised different coaching, then reinstated the teachers about whom students had given testimonies. The Headmaster promised to pay for psychological counseling for all harmed students. He paid for a couple of sessions for our son and then stopped without discussion, despite us continuing to submit receipts for recompense. As discussed, in the spring of 2012, the Headmaster wrote my husband and me an email:

> I have spoken with both [one teacher] and [the other teacher] and they have committed to addressing all the issues I have put on the table, and all the issues I have put on the table are the ones you have mentioned.

The teachers' commitment to address all the issues was forgotten and instead transformed into denial that any harm had taken place; the Headmaster and the teachers then came full circle to publicly positioning the students as liars. When teachers and Administrators deny or "forget"

---

[268] Ibid.

previously made promises and agreements, it is extremely difficult to protect students. The students' only recourse was to quit the sport they loved. One student-athlete noted in her testimony the pattern of previously passionate athletes quitting the team in their final year:

> *In grade 10, [Juniors] Andrea and Sylvia were playing up on the Senior Team, because almost every senior girl had quit. It was in the Provincials and [the coach] launched into her attack on them:*

> *You call yourself a basketball player*
> *You go to basketball camps*
> *You buy basketball shoes and clothes*
> *You're not a basketball player*
> *You let us down*
> *You were nervous*
> *You wrecked it for the senior girls.*

Called up as grade tens to compensate for the lack of senior players who gave up their sport rather than continue to suffer, they are bullied for their inexperience. It hardly seems fair. On the boys' team, three senior players quit in the 2011-2012 season. In the 2012-2013 season, six boys who had played every year previously refused to try out for the Senior team once the coaches they'd reported on were reinstated. Quitting is a well-documented reaction to abuse among athletes from high school, to university, to Olympic athletes. They give up the sport they love in order to survive. Investigative journalist Robert Cribb in a *Toronto Star* article on abusive coaching consults experts who measure an athlete quitting a team as the ultimate statement about how much they are suffering: "[Nicole] LaVoi has co-authored several studies into egregious behavior in youth sports. 'Whether or not they're being directly yelled at, the indirect effect is much more potentially impactful than the direct abuse of one parent or coach. It could ultimately be contributing to athletes dropping out of sport.'"[269] Considering the research on the exceptional athletes being the ones abusive coaches tend to target, teams and countries may well be losing their greatest athletes.

In the *Public Health Canada* report on abuse Doherty and Berglund's definition of psychological abuse offers an explanation for how parents made a terrible mistake in believing that the Board of Governors and the Headmaster had their children's wellbeing at the forefront of all other concerns. As Doherty and Berglund explain:

> Psychological abuse can occur in relationships in which the abuser holds a position of trust and authority over the victim. In some instances, an individual may perpetrate the abuse in environments where the organizational structure fosters power imbalances that perpetuate the situation. This abuse is referred to as "systemic abuse" or "institutional abuse" because the system itself silences the victims (Simmons 2002).[270]

Adults in positions of "trust and authority" have effectively silenced the students who came forward at my former school. There is nothing more important in this book than finally allowing the students' voices to be heard.

In a June 2013 article in the *Guardian*, a teacher argues that the education system, if based on results, is structured to enable bullying and thus students and teachers pay a terrible price:

> As adults we recognise that the children who bully others are often damaged, with low self-esteem in large part moulded by

---

[269] Robert Cribb: http://www.thestar.com/sports/hockey/2010/07/08/outofcontrol_amateur_coaches_mentally_abuse_players.html

[270] Public Health Agency of Canada: "Psychological Abuse: A Discussion Paper" by Deborah Doherty and Dorothy Berglund: http://www.phac-aspc.gc.ca/ncfv-cnivf/sources/fv/fv-psych-abus/index-eng.php

their environment and their formative experiences. Government constantly criticises unfairly, makes personal attacks on the teaching profession and idolises an environment where results come first. In this hugely pressured and critical environment is it not inevitable that bullying in schools has become commonplace? In the same way, my self-esteem was battered and my abilities constantly questioned by the bullying member of the senior leadership team: she herself is pressured by the environment the government has helped to create. This climate of fear, stifled creativity, and little regard for the individuality of children and staff does little to encourage a nurturing, supportive approach to management or mentoring.[271]

Bullying is a significant issue in sports, schools, and the workplace, and we are all aware how linked it is to "formative experiences"; however, we have yet to fully address the bullying teachers or coaches may do to students and their developing brains. This is clearly one area in which as a society we can educate administrators, teachers, parents and most important, students, so that this kind of bullying is quickly identified and remedied rather than covered up or condoned. Chances are very good that if we eliminate so much bullying in the formative years in classrooms and on courts, on fields and on ice-rinks, we are less likely to see bullying harm adults in the workplace.

---

[271] http://www.theguardian.com/teacher-network/teacher-blog/2013/jun/08/bullying-education-overdose-secret-teacher

# Chapter Ten

## Homophobic Culture Keeps Students Silenced

> Like it or not, Rutgers' failure to stop Rice when it could have has invited the rest of the country to be its judge and jury. There is a collective shock that anyone who had seen the snippets did not fire Rice immediately. That we are now caught in the endless cycle of finger-pointing, backtracking and blame doesn't change the fact that Rice was retained despite video evidence that included more f-bombs than an R-rated movie, his use of gay slurs and his repeated physical contact with his players. "I literally could not watch that video," Hall of Fame Syracuse coach Jim Boeheim said from his Atlanta podium. "Honestly, I couldn't watch it anymore."
>
> – Tara Sullivan, Associated Press [272]

When a teacher in a position of trust and authority bullies a student or students, it is officially categorized as "emotional abuse" and measured by the "significant harm" it causes young people. It is not supposed to be

---

[272] Tara Sullivan, "Sullivan: Rutgers Taking the Spotlight from National Champions," *Associated Press*, April 2013: http://www.northjersey.com/sports/college-sports/college-basketball/sullivan-rutgers-taking-the-spotlight-from-national-champions-1.571658

measured by intention. It is not supposed to be measured according to majority rules. In other words, it should not matter if the adult meant to cause harm. Nor should it matter if the victims number fewer than those who normalize, deny, or simply did not experience the abuse. However, it appears that because emotional abuse is not in the Criminal Code, a teacher can say "I didn't know" or "I didn't realize" that what I was doing was harmful, or my goal was to *toughen up* players, or my behavior was to *motivate* athletes.

None of this makes sense when studies show that emotional abuse is as equally damaging as physical abuse; comparably, neglect has been found to be worse than active abuse. In interviews conducted by Ashley Stirling and Gretchen Kerr with retired elite athletes, they found that "Participants reported that the denial of attention and support had the most negative effect, followed by the experience of verbal emotionally abusive behaviors. Interestingly, the physical behaviors used had the least negative effect."[273] It would appear that the legal system in Canada has not caught up to many years of research into emotional and psychological abuse; its absence from the Criminal Code is a clear indication of that. If an adult has committed sexual or physical abuse, it is irrelevant whether or not he or she thought it would help the child in some way. It should also be irrelevant whether or not coaches believe that it motivates athletes when they scream incoherently, yell or mutter obscenities, shun or grab a student for in the face scenes of public humiliation. Corporal punishment used to be permitted in schools. That changed. It's now time for laws to change again to include in the Criminal Code emotional, psychological, and verbal abuse or "bullying" from teacher to student and coach to

---

[273] Ashley E. Stirling and Gretchen A. Kerr, "Defining and categorizing emotional abuse in sport," *European Journal of Sport Science*, July 2008: 8 (4): 173-181.

student-athlete. It may actually transform the way our society functions.[274]

In a September 2014 article in *The Guardian*, Lauren Laverne argues that emotional abuse in intimate relationships should be in the Criminal Code. She notes that in France "psychological violence" has already been criminalized. If advocates recognize that emotional abuse needs much more serious consequences in adult-to-adult relationships, surely it is even more vital with our most vulnerable population: children.[275] If emotional abuse was in the Criminal Code, teachers and coaches could no longer use the excuse that their conduct was meant to motivate.

In this process with my former school, stretching out over three years, the teachers have repeatedly used the excuse "I thought it would motivate" or "I was teaching a lesson" or "that term is not harmful" or that gesture that was felt as intimidating and threatening was meant as "intense and passionate." Yelling and screaming, gesticulating wildly, frenetic conduct seemed to be repositioned by these teachers and those who investigated the crisis as indicative of the teachers' commitment and success. They were all just signs of just how much these teachers "cared about" the students. Universities do not think this is what *caring* looks like in sports; instead, coaches are fired.

As long ago as 1983, psychiatrist Dr. Alice Miller exposed a poisonous pedagogical approach as having devastating effects on children. Her study, *For Your Own Good: Hidden Cruelty in Childhood*

---

[274] Louise Tickle, "Britain's Elite Boarding Schools Are Facing an Explosion of Abuse Allegations," *Newsweek*, September 2014: http://www.newsweek.com/britain-elite-boarding-schools-facing-explosion-abuse-allegations-267201
[275] Lauren Laverne, "It's time to make emotional abuse a crime," The Guardian, September 2014: http://www.theguardian.com/lifeandstyle/2014/sep/07/time-to-make-emotional-abuse-a-crime

*and the Roots of Violence* has been so influential that a new edition was released in 2002. Essentially, Miller argues that caregivers who use abusive approaches, whether physical or emotional, harm children in significant ways even though they claim to have "the child's best interests" in mind.[276]

Poisonous pedagogy underpins the argument that coaches need to yell, swear, humiliate and demean athletes to get the best out of them and for them, or their team, to be successful. With this in mind, imagine, out on the court in the middle of a game, in front of both teams and the spectators, the Head Coach rushes up to a student and yells in his face, while shoving his finger in his chest: *"That is soft! That is fucking soft!"* The student recorded this incident in a written testimony requested by the Headmaster. The student then discussed this incident along with other ones in the Headmaster's office with him and the Chaplain. The student tried to explain away the teacher's behavior even in the written testimony: *"I must have made a mistake I guess but I don't know what I did. I never did find out."* Then in teenaged terms he described the harm it caused: *"That reduced my confidence and confused me. It put my head in a different place. I felt emotional. I had no idea what to do differently."* He then added a crucial piece of information without realizing how important it is in the bullying cycle: *"[The Assistant Coach] probably heard it and the other players because [the Head Coach] yelled it at me."* The other teacher, acting as a bystander, is potentially doing more harm, in this circumstance, because the bystander-teacher is giving a de facto stamp of approval which makes the student believe that the abuse is normal and deserved. In his mind, the Head Coach was treating him this way for *his own good.*

---

[276] Alice Miller, *For Your Own Good: Hidden Cruelty in Childhood and the Roots of Violence*, trans. Hildegarde and Hunter Hannum, New York: Farrar, Straus, Giroux, 2002.

As these incidents happened over and over again, the impact would be substantial: other teachers, and in the case of the female coach named in the testimonies, her father, the Assistant Coach, would act as bystander during those times when a student or the whole team were yelled at aggressively and publicly humiliated. The teachers' initial claims to the Headmaster were that they did not know that their conduct was harmful. Keeping in mind the outdated pedagogical belief system that appears to cling to some sports cultures, namely that it is good for students to be yelled at, insulted, sworn at, and called obscenities because it hardens them, teachers who coach may not know when they have crossed the line. However, for teachers to privately admit to the Director of the Senior School and then to the Headmaster that they participated in this conduct, without knowing the harm it was doing, but then publicly turned around and denied they did it creates a whole other category of harm being done to students.

One of the four teachers sent an email out to School faculty that criticized the whole team as "soft" during the Provincial Championships in Kamloops: "Boys lose by 11 with a soft second half performance." Just as devastating then as the teacher that yells "fucking soft" at a student are the teachers who either remain silent or reinforce the message that the abuse is deserved because, in this case, the boys are failing to achieve masculine *hardness* (with all its sexual overtones likely not lost on adolescent boys or in sports culture in general). The Assistant Coach would yell at students that they were as "soft as butter"; according to Google's online urban dictionary, "soft as butter" is an "expression to describe an absolute pussy who makes the most cowardly person look like a hero."[277] The students stated time and again in their testimonies just how harmful this messaging was to them.

The use of misogynistic or homophobic terms to humiliate teenage boys is both widely discussed and well documented in sports journalism and abuse literature. However, as the teachers themselves said in their responses to the student allegations of bullying, in a school culture where using this language is seen as "normal" it was difficult to know when they've crossed the line. And far more insidious and poisonous are the students' beliefs, when exposed to repeated humiliation as they record in their testimonies, that perhaps they deserve it because they *are* "soft." And to bring it full circle, the worry that they are in fact soft stops them from asking for help or protection.

In an article that responded to the Mike Rice scandal, T. F. Charlton examines the phenomenon of athletes not reporting on abusive coaches:

> We should hardly be surprised, then, that players don't speak up about abuse — and even, as in Rice's case and many others, actually defend abusive behavior. Male and female players alike model the message they receive: that coaches who violate their emotional and physical boundaries do so for players' good, and players who don't handle this stoically aren't up to snuff.[278]

At my former school, it was difficult to hold the teachers accountable when the Headmaster appeared to believe that this kind of humiliating conduct is deserved as if it's the School's responsibility to eradicate student "softness." A little less than two years after listening to the

---

[277] http://www.urbandictionary.com/define.php?term=Soft%20as%20butter
[278] T. F. Charlton: "Why do athletes tolerate abusive coaches? In locker rooms, insubordination is a worse crime than abuse of authority. Unless that changes, nothing else will." *Salon.com*: http://www.salon.com/2013/04/05/why_do_athletes_tolerate_abusive_coaches/

students detail their suffering, in February 2014, while awaiting the Commissioner's decision whether to publicly hold accountable the teachers, the Chaplain and himself, the Headmaster published on the School website the following blog entry that revolves around the idea of "soft." He begins by noting that the ground is frozen in Victoria:

> It sounds kind of soft, I imagine, to anyone from central Canada [...] to read such an observation. This reaction is understandable especially among those (the vast majority) who think an essential part of education should be challenges that test not only the intellect, but also the character and the physical self. I would put myself in that category. Our students are indeed tender plants, sheltered from the worst and kept appropriately safe, but they do need on occasion to be put out into the weather, to harden them in preparation for the world they will enter after [high-school]. Otherwise, they will suffer some unhealthy shocks.

He seems to suggest that the students are "soft" and the School needs to "harden them," because the world is a tough place. This is comparable to the poisonous pedagogy argument: I am going to treat you in a harsh way so that you can get stronger and therefore be better prepared to face adversity at university or in the world. If students are *shocked* now, they will be better prepared for "some unhealthy shocks" in the world after high school. The suggestion is that being shocked now will make later shocks seem par for the course; they will be normalized and therefore lessen the impact of their harm. The popular catch phrase for this kind of thinking is "what doesn't kill me makes me stronger." It is easy to follow along and be lulled into thinking that tough teachers make tough kids. They get rid of the "tender" and the "soft" qualities of students and therefore make them more resilient and able to withstand the harshness out in the world. Sounds like a good lesson, but the experts have produced significant research, documented throughout this book, that shows it doesn't work. In fact, they argue, it has the opposite effect.

The Headmaster continued his blog with some questionable history to make his point: "It is worth remembering that schools like ours were founded, in the nineteenth century, not to refine the intellect, but rather to provide an environment for the children of the upper classes where they would not be spoiled." I have not been able to find any documentation of any school founded for this purpose; to my knowledge, there are not any schools in England, Canada, or America that were founded on this principle. The founding principles behind schools, whether public or private, were not to take rich, privileged students and ensure by harsh treatment they were not spoiled; in fact, the founding of schools was often inspired by just the opposite idea. However, the Headmaster's blog went on to articulate that giving upper-class children harsh treatment supports the real lesson he wants to teach: "Thus began various abandoned habits such as cold showers, the cane, miserable food, and a rather tribal set of hardships deliberately created to prevent students from getting soft." Once again, he uses the word "soft." It is clearly an important cultural word at the School and the Headmaster has now tied it to educational practices, such as corporal punishment, that was rendered illegal in Eastern Canada in 1971 – the land of hard weather lessons that opens the blog. The Headmaster seems to be quite committed to ensure that his audience understands that the "character" and the "physical" aspect of students have a tendency to get "soft" unless teachers harden them. If corporal punishment is no longer allowed, then public humiliation, derogatory terms, raising the voice, shoving a finger in a student's chest, and yelling at him that he is "soft," may well have to be used in its place. It's for the students' own good after all. In his February 2014 blog, the Headmaster says corporal practices have been "abandoned," but he does not deplore them; rather, he celebrates the idea that nowadays there are different methods to eradicate the softness found in students.

The blog continues with more questionable history such is his apparent desire to send his message home: "This experience [namely the caning, bad food, and cold showers that toughened up students] justified the words of the Duke of Wellington, that 'the battle of Waterloo was won on the playing fields of Eton.'" The Headmaster's blog implies that Eton was one of those schools founded to eradicate spoiled upper-class students, but it wasn't. In fact, it was founded long before the 19th century to educate impoverished students. Furthermore, this famous statement was made *not* in reference to school brutality; rather, it was said while the Duke was watching the boys play sports on the field.

One may more readily assume the comment about winning the Battle of Waterloo had to do with recognition that the bonding, the teamwork, the joy in physical exercise was what contributed to a strong battalion. It is harder to see the statement being tied to a student being caned or put in a cold shower. This kind of educational ethos, articulated by the Headmaster's blog, may well act as an example of what Dr. Alice Miller refers to as poisonous pedagogy. Students must suffer because we don't want them to be "soft."

• • •

In May 2014, in an article in *The Guardian*, Alex Renton writes about his abuse at Ashdown School where he attended before going on to Eton. Renton is a writer, and he explores his reaction to the systemic abuse he suffered and that is now being exposed in such a way as to rock the foundations of several esteemed British schools. He initially speaks of the experience in intellectual terms:

> Besides, the sexual abuses were, in my version of the story, just detail: the real narrative was of five years of deliberate crushing of our individuality, the suppression of emotional freedom. Sexual bullying seemed just a part of the violence and cruelty that was the basic currency of the school and hundreds like it; the tools with which it squashed our little forms into the mould. Out

of it would come upper-class Englishmen and women – ready to go and run an Empire or, at least, take charge of lesser mortals with normal feelings. So went my thinking. Nothing unfamiliar: it has been said by British liberals from George Orwell onwards. Psychiatrists I have spoken to agree that, yes, while sexual and physical abuse is the headline grabber (and what makes criminal cases), real damage is done to children and adults by long-term psychological abuse. A child may recover from a blow, but not from the withdrawal of love and the denial of safety – the "complex trauma" child psychologists talk of.[279]

Along with many experts and confirmed by neuroscientists, we are reminded once again that the mind does not recover as well as the body. The scars on the victim's sense of self and on the victim's brain sometimes do not ever heal. Regardless of years of research, our laws protect the body, but not the mind.

Renton recounts how, as a middle-aged man, he sent his parents an article about how his contemporaries were seeking compensation for their suffering as children at Ashdown. His mother's reaction, which was to tell him that when he was a child, he had informed her of a teacher's abuse, suddenly made him cry at the loss of who he was before he attended such an abusive school. He wept at his childhood loss of trust in adults. Only years later, as a middle-aged man was he able to piece together what actually happened to him at Ashdown. He realized that having told his mother the truth about his abuse led to the targeting he suffered at the hands of the Headmaster. His mother did what our son repeatedly begged us *not* to do: she went and spoke to the School Administrators who removed the teacher who had abused him. They "retired" him and sent him on to abuse other children at another school to

---

[279] Alex Renton, "Abuse in Britain's Boarding Schools: Why I decided to confront my demons," May 4, 2014 in the *Observer / Guardian*: http://www.theguardian.com/society/2014/may/04/abuse-britain-private-schools-personal-memoir

remove any liability; however, Alex Renton, the child who spoke up, was punished for telling his mother in a way that parallels the way students at my former school have paid a terrible price for daring to tell what their coaches were doing to them. Renton writes:

> Ashdown had broken me, as you do when you train an animal, and then drilled me until I was a suitable citizen. But my mother's revelation showed I had kicked back. In fact, I had broken the most important of all of [the headmaster's] rules. I had told tales out of school. I specifically said a teacher was touching me in a way I didn't like and that I "hated" him. And she had gone straight to the school to raise hell with the headmaster's wife. That may explain Mr. X's disappearance shortly after (to teach at another school, according to the Ashdown School Bulletin of that year). It may explain the way the headmaster targeted me in the following years, singling me out in front of the school as a fraud, a failure and a perpetrator of "filthy behavior." But it gave me a new vision of the brave little boy who wouldn't be cowed by Billy Williamson: the boy who spoke out.[280]

Our son also told us "I hate those guys" in reference to his coaches. This strong word shows up in other student testimonies. Just like the boy Alex Renton, the students at my former school "kicked back." There's nothing more powerful or tough than that. The Headmaster at my former school thinks it's caning that removes softness, but actually it's independent thinking and the strength to stand behind one's own convictions. Toughness comes from speaking up when you have a lot to lose.

A tough person is one who does not remain silent when another is being harmed, even though it means quite likely becoming the lightning rod for the bully. Toughness comes from a deep-seated belief in equality, meritocracy, and respectful treatment for all and the courage to fight for it. In almost every testimony, the students commented on how awful and hard it was to watch other students suffer at the hands of their coaches.

---

[280] Ibid.

303

Frightened people choose to be bystanders; people normalize bullying because it's safer and easier than speaking up and "kicking back" at abusers. When those in power are the bullies, the hard path requires fighting for the softness, the sensitivity that all people have, especially children, and it is an aspect of humanity that must be protected and allowed to flourish. That is a lesson that schools should teach.

Alex Renton examined the disturbing fact that the influential and powerful adults who govern Britain now may well have been victims of teacher and administrator abuse in childhood. He recognizes this fact is worrisome because this kind of training serves to foster individuals who lack "softness." He worries that schools like Ashdown actually foster an inability to have empathy and an inability to think independently. Commitment to the team, devotion to the school, may well outweigh in these abuse victims' minds, commitment to the health and wellbeing of themselves and all others:

> And so it is interesting that so many senior politicians in government went to boarding schools, places that, by definition, practice on young children the techniques of "attachment fracture" – a psychiatrist's phrase – that are key to removing early emotional ties and building esprit de corps. [281]

The students at my former school who spoke up about coach and administrative bullying refused to have their emotional ties fractured. They did not put devotion to the school ahead of students' rights to a healthy and safe environment in which to learn.

Ironically, in the "real world," that the Headmaster at my former school believes we must train our students to survive in, the term "soft" is considered homophobic and highly offensive. It is such a harmful insult that Jevon Tyree, a football player on scholarship at Rutgers University,

---

[281] Ibid.

quit because his coach "called [him] soft." As recorded by sports writer, Ryan Dunleavy, in *USA Today*: "Rutgers' player quits after coach's verbal abuse." The word had such devastating implications for this young football player that he walked away from a Division I team and his scholarship. In the article referenced previously on why athletes tolerate abusive coaches, T. F. Charlton explains:

> ...male athletes in particular are held up as and expected to be paragons of a certain kind of masculinity, seen as the rejection of all that is coded "feminine." Exhortations that male athletes 'be a man' or 'not act like little girls' are even more pervasive in sports than they are in general culture. So it's little surprise that a coach would use insults that imply his players are less than men to shame, humiliate and control them.[282]

It's one thing to speak this way as a coach at a university; it's quite another to speak this way as a high-school teacher. Especially when the Ministry of Education has specifically stated in their *Safe Schools* report that people:

> ...associated with safe, caring and orderly schools assume responsibility, in partnership with the wider community, for resolving critical safety concerns. They work together to better understand issues such as bullying, intimidation and harassment, racism, sexism and homophobia, and to learn new skills to respond to them.[283]

At a School where students report that they were called "soft," "pussies," and told to "grow some balls," one would assume that an informed

---

[282] T. F. Charlton: "Why do athletes tolerate abusive coaches? In locker rooms, insubordination is a worse crime than abuse of authority. Unless that changes, nothing else will." *Salon.com*: http://www.salon.com/2013/04/05/why_do_athletes_tolerate_abusive_coaches/
[283] https://www.bced.gov.bc.ca/sco/guide/scoguide.pdf#page=15

Headmaster who may have been uninformed before these students spoke to him would have learned in reading the testimonies and conducting interviews that this language was harmful to adolescent boys; it offends, humiliates, and hurts them. If he did not understand then, one would reasonably expect he would have learned what constitutes humiliating and destructive behavior through the media about the variety of scandals that have swept American university athletic programs: Rutgers, Penn State, Indiana State, University of Iowa, Notre Dame, and the University of California, Berkeley. The tough love approach has not been proven to get results as evidenced by the track record of the basketball teams at my former school. One of the greatest misconceptions in the sporting world is the belief that being hard on athletes makes strong teams. As argued by University of Toronto experts in the use of emotional abuse in sports: "One of the barriers to the implementation of an athlete-centered approach is the assumption, held by many sport practitioners, that holistic development comes at a cost to athletic performance." However, there is "no empirical evidence" to back this belief up.[284]

A number of the students who reported being bullied in their testimonies were at university, and there was no benefit to them in speaking up. It is such a sign of their character that they spoke up to ask for protection for future students, not for themselves. When one has suffered years of programming that says "you deserve it," it is incredibly difficult to maintain a sense of one's own worth. Among children, be they school-aged or university students, the ones who speak up are the ones who exemplify toughness, not the kind that will have them as adults yelling at and humiliating people in their power, but the kind of toughness

---

[284] Ashley E. Stirling and Gretchen A. Kerr, "Abused Athletes' Perceptions of the Coach-Athlete Relationship," *Sport in Society* Vol.12.2, March 2009: 227-239.

that comes from *not* believing your abusers and refusing to be a bystander while others suffer.

T. F. Charlton exposes the use of the "for your own good" argument that appears to dominate sports culture at some schools and universities. She says athletes are taught that abusive practices are for their own "benefit and edification."

> Such behavior is often framed as — to use Sean Hannity's words — a coach 'running a tight ship' and providing players with needed structure. Players who chafe under or object to a such 'discipline' risk not only getting in trouble for questioning the coach's authority, but also being painted as 'soft,' not mentally tough enough to take whatever the coach dishes out. That is to say, they become exactly the "sissy" or "fairy" the coach suggests they are.[285]

According to student testimonies, the coaches at my former school used exactly the attacks most feared by students to make them believe they were "mentally soft" and if they reported then they would be "pussies." Students rarely speak up while under the control of the teacher; sometimes they come forward in later life, but more often they never speak up at all in their defense, or in defense of others. Perhaps this is why we continue to see so much drug and alcohol dependency, low self-esteem, depression, self-harm, and eating disorders, as well as a remarkable number of suicides in our adolescent population. These may well be silent expressions of pain from emotionally and psychologically being beaten into believing one is worthless and deserving teachers' or coaches' disgust and anger.

---

[285] T. F. Charlton: "Why do athletes tolerate abusive coaches? In locker rooms, insubordination is a worse crime than abuse of authority. Unless that changes, nothing else will." *Salon.com*: http://www.salon.com/2013/04/05/why_do_athletes_tolerate_abusive_coaches/

Neuroscientist Dr. Frances Jensen, in her book *The Teenage Brain,* notes that now in 2015 suicide has moved from the third to the second leading cause of death in teenage populations. She advises us that "because adolescence is already a time of mood swings and behavioral irregularities, it is even more important for parents, guardians, and teachers to be aware of the emotional needs of adolescents, especially in times of crisis and stress, when adolescents' vulnerability to mental disorders is at its highest" (183).[286] Jensen wants parents and teachers to be aware that "even minor, and definitely major, psychiatric problems need to be addressed early since they put the person at higher risk for mental illness later in life" (188). The students at my former school who demonstrated a variety of mental disorders in response to the emotional abuse they reported are now at risk, not just during adolescence, but for the rest of their lives. Jensen says "we have an epidemic of anxiety and related disorders" and she emphasizes that "anxiety disorders have a strong connection to environmental stressors" (189). One remedy for this epidemic is to protect and then support, rather than re-victimize, students who report emotional abuse when experienced at the hands of their teachers or coaches.

According to Dr. Jensen, girls are at greater risk than boys for anxiety disorders (189). Female athletes suffer their own kind of bullying from coaches and respond in distinct ways. Dr. Alan Goldberg paints a disturbing picture of what emotional abuse does to young women:

> Abusive coaches use threats, FEAR and intimidation to scare athletes into submission. They BULLY their athletes into keeping silent OR ELSE, (incurring my wrath, loss of playing time or

---

[286] Frances E. Jensen with Amy Ellis Nutt, *The Teenage Brain: A Neuroscientist's Survival Guide to Raising Adolescents and Young Adults,* Toronto: Harper Collins, 2015 (183). All subsequent quotes are from this text, page numbers follow the quotations.

athletic scholarship, etc!) They destroy an individual's self-esteem and seriously undermine their confidence. They teach their athletes to be passive and tolerate abusive behavior in relationships. This is a particularly insidious and disturbing lesson to teach anyone, especially young women! And I have an even harder time when you have a female coach, reinforcing these 'lessons' in young female athletes.[287]

Perhaps female coaches also feel they must toughen up their athletes, ensure that the girls aren't "soft." However, Goldberg argues that these kinds of abusive practices have the opposite effect: "A coach doesn't EVER need to be abusive and demeaning to prepare athletes to perform at the highest level! Instead, this behavior undermines mental toughness and makes athletes vulnerable to poor performance and repetitive performance problems."[288]

Based on the responses of elite athletes they studied, Ashley Stirling and Gretchen Kerr identified "shunning" or "ignoring" as the worst form of physical and emotional coaching abuse and then they linked it to the techniques female bullies use when targeting a victim: "The social isolation and exclusion often used by girls to bully is similar to the denial of attention and support found in this study. Abuse in the coach-athlete relationship, however, is unique given the critical nature of the relationship between the coach and the athlete." It was particularly striking in the girls' testimonies how frequently they reported their female coach used this type of bullying during games. Stirling and Kerr's survey of former elite athletes reveals how harmful this conduct can be:

> According to the athletes, denying attention and support is used
> by the coach as a form of punishment that compromises the

[287] Dr. Alan Goldberg: "What abusive coaches teach female athletes," January 3, 2014: https://www.facebook.com/DrGsportspsych/posts/585669734834454
[288] Ibid.

closeness of the coach-athlete relationship and tells the athlete that she is not worthy of attention. This has the result of degrading the athlete's sense of self-worth and reducing her ability to cope with the emotional abuse.[289]

According to the student testimonies at my former school, the coaches used the "ignoring technique" frequently and from one year to the next. Moreover, in the student testimonies, even the same phrases occur year after year directed at different target students or the team as a whole. The same actions where the coach threw down her clipboard, the same storming out on the team and saying the team is an "embarrassment," the same in the face yelling, the same grabbing, the same swearing at particular students or the team in general, the same demeaning comment that a particular student is the "worst shooter" on the team can been seen in the testimonies of players from different years. It's a script for a play that is performed over and over again. As one student said to the next after seeing her targeted by the coach, *"I guess you're the new me."* According to the testimonies, the students saw the pattern and were aware that someone was going to be the bullying coach's next target. In emotional abuse, there is often a targeted student or small group of students who especially suffer while other teachers and students block the trauma, normalize the abuse, consciously take bystander roles or simply deny it's occurring. Yet at the same time, we tell our young men and women, we even tell very young children, "you deserve respect and to be treated with dignity as do all people; therefore, you must never be a bystander when you witness bullying."

Unfortunately, there are unspoken rules in some schools, universities, or on certain sports teams that include these messages: if the

---

[289] Ashley E. Stirling and Gretchen A. Kerr, "Defining and categorizing emotional abuse in sport," *European Journal of Sport Science*, July 2008: 8 (4): 173-181.

bully is the teacher or the coach, keep quiet; protect yourself; protect your younger siblings who are at the school; protect your family's social standing in the community; protect your parents' jobs; this is an influential group of people; don't make waves; don't be a complainer; don't show that you are soft or weak or can't handle what is being said and done to you. The reason adults may say this to children is because unlike playground bullies, teachers and coaches have the power to negatively impact a student's present *and* future.

Just like on the playground, the bully often has an entourage of those who benefit by not being the victim and who invest the bully with power and popularity. If at times the majority feels uncomfortable about the suffering they witness, they rationalize it by saying it's deserved, it's meant to motivate, or they recognize their own survival hinges on keeping quiet. In a classroom, there's more chance to escape abuse because one can transfer classes, but when it has to do with athletics, students can't transfer teams. Therefore, reporting on teachers or coaches is very difficult to do. There are significant barriers to speaking up. In *Yahoo Sports* in April 2013, sports reporter Erik Adelson argues that the real motivator for keeping quiet, even more than trying to protect a teacher or coach's reputation, is fear. He says that when the video of Mike Rice abusing players was aired, "social media exploded with horror and one resounding question: Why didn't anyone fight back?" He looks beyond Rutgers University to multiple athletics programs for his answer and concludes that the question of why athletes tolerate abuse has "a one-word answer: fear."[290] If Division One university-aged athletes are unable to overcome their fear to speak up against an abusive coach, students

---

[290] Erik Adelson, "Why do College Athletes Tolerate Abuse?" *Yahoo Sports*, April 2013: http://sports.yahoo.com/news/ncaab--why-don-t-college-athletes-call-out-abusive-coaches--222535612.html

being emotionally and physically abused by teachers or coaches in high school are even less likely to speak up. Adolescent boys in particular do not want to be seen needing their parents on any level, let alone asking for protection. And so silence reigns and the longer a student is abused, the more he or she believes it's *deserved* and perhaps worse, *normal*. In this kind of environment, with adults who are explosive and unpredictable – one minute they're a good friend, next minute they're screaming and humiliating you – a student's anxiety level rises so high and so consistently that he or she is no longer clear on what is acceptable and what is not, what's doing damage and what's not. Moreover, this terrible syndrome is reinforced by actual physical damage to the brain.

It is not only my former school where teachers were investigated and no disciplinary action occurred. In March 2013, in the *Deseret News*, Amy Donaldson, a thirteen-year veteran of sports writing, recorded how shocked she was that swim coach, Greg Winslow, had been investigated for his abusive coaching practices, and yet the University of Utah did not take action to protect its athletes:

> After reading the allegations, it seems baffling that an independent investigation, like the one Utah athletics director Chris Hill said the Office of Equal Opportunity conducted, could find nothing that required disciplinary action. In fact, if the OEO did talk to 50 people, including current and former athletes, how on earth did Winslow retain his job?[291]

Eventually Winslow was fired. Still, there appear to be unfortunate parallels between the Winslow incident and those that took place at my former school: specifically the ten-page lawyer's report that concluded

---

[291] Amy Donaldson: "Why do We Tolerate Abuse in Coaching?" *Deseret News*, March 2013: http://www.deseretnews.com/article/865575390/Why-do-we-tolerate-abuse-in-coaching.html?pg=all

the teachers' conduct, while troubling at times, had not risen to the level of abuse which contradicted the police and sport psychology assessments. Likewise, the Commissioner's decisions also concluded none of the four teachers' bullying or the administrative enabling of it, as described by students, required any disciplinary action or public transparency.

A slightly different but equally problematic response occurred with Mike Rice: money and time were invested in a fifty-page report, which stated in fact that Rutgers could fire Rice without running the risk of an unfair dismissal suit because of his abusive conduct; however, the university did *not* initially fire him and protect their athletes, until Rutgers Administration was exposed in the media. In other words, it seems that certain educational institutions perhaps value their reputation, or in the case of universities the exorbitant financial gains from their teams, more than the safety and health of their students. They will not tolerate abusive teaching practices if they are exposed and receive negative media attention; however, if not, they allow abuse to continue with a vague promise that the coach has toned it down or has had professional development or is adhering to a new code of conduct.

Sports reporter Amy Donaldson offers yet another example, from the U. S. Speed skating team, of an investigation that led to the discovery of "disturbing" behavior on the part of Coach Jae Su Chun that included allegations of verbal and physical abuse, but were dismissed and not addressed until he was accused of cheating. Donaldson writes:

> Consider briefly, the independent investigation initiated by U.S. Speed skating into allegations of emotional and physical abuse against two coaches who were subsequently fired and banned for an unrelated allegation of cheating. The investigators found the

coach's methods "disturbing," but in the end, said they did not rise to the level of abuse.[292]

In an article in *The Toronto Star*, Lynn Debruin reports that Coach Jae Su Chun instructed Simon Cho, a member of the American speed-skating team, to tamper with the skates of his Canadian rival. She too acknowledges the larger issue that was swept under the carpet until he was accused of cheating: "these allegations are part of a larger scandal involving Chun, also accused by a dozen national team members of 'unchecked' verbal, psychological and physical abuse. The coach denies any wrongdoing, but has been suspended during the investigation."[293] Cheating is taken seriously, whereas it appears that reports of psychological and physical bullying are once again minimized and dismissed; they too do not reach the level of "abuse." At least the coach was suspended during the investigation so that a safe environment is created for athletes to come forward. This never occurred at my former school.

Amy Donaldson foregrounds in her article on coaching abuse the sad fact that quitting the team is often the only recourse for athletes in institutions that condone their abuse: "For all the athletes who overcome these incidents, who succeed because — or in spite — of these types of coaches, there are as many athletes who leave sports because they don't

---

[292] Ibid.

[293] Lynn Debruin, "Speed skating scandal: Simon Cho says American coach pressured him to tamper with Canadian rival's skates," *The Toronto Star*, October 2012: http://www.thestar.com/sports/olympics/2012/10/05/speed_skating_scandal_simon_cho_says_american_coach_pressured_him_to_tamper_with_canadian_rivals_skates.html

want to be harassed, berated or humiliated."[294] Having witnessed for years a wide range of coaching styles, Donaldson is able to draw a clear line between the amazing coaches who "teach," whom she puts in a radically different camp from those who "taunt." In contrast, the Commissioner for Teacher Regulation and apparently many others appear unsure where to draw this line. In her article, Donaldson raises questions about the point we have reached as a society whereby we condone abuse, especially in athletics: "Maybe calling someone names isn't illegal, but should it be the way we try to inspire greatness? Maybe embarrassing someone in front of their teammates isn't against the law, but should it be the way we motivate people that we care about?"[295] Her questions contribute volumes to my belief that we are long overdue for including emotional, psychological, and verbal abuse in the Criminal Code.

In reference to the alleged abuse of swimming coach, Greg Winslow, at University of Utah, Donaldson ends her article with the following challenge: "I would like to know what the OEO [Office of Equal Opportunity] investigation found and what university administrators knew. Because while they might need a panel of experts to tell them what is and isn't legal, they shouldn't need anyone to tell them what kind of behavior is and isn't moral."[296] I would also add that they shouldn't need anyone to tell them that conduct not tolerated on a playground, in a classroom or office, conduct that has been shown in extensive studies to do permanent damage to students' and athletes' brains, should not be tolerated *anywhere*.

---

[294] Amy Donaldson: "Why do We Tolerate Abuse in Coaching?" *Deseret News*, March 2013: http://www.deseretnews.com/article/865575390/Why-do-we-tolerate-abuse-in-coaching.html?pg=all
[295] Ibid.
[296] Ibid.

Using BC, Canada as a case study, herein lies the problem: the Ministry of Education has a zero tolerance policy for peer-to-peer bullying and the Independent School's Association has clear guidelines on what constitutes emotional abuse and what teachers and administrators must do to protect students, especially the highly vulnerable student who speaks up and reports the abusive acts. BC School Sports has a strict code of conduct for coaches that leaves no room for emotionally abusive practices. The Ministry of Children and Family Development says emotional abuse is against the law.[297] The Ministry of Education's Teacher Regulation Branch, headed up by the Commissioner, has clear standards for teacher conduct. All these authoritative bodies have published guidelines that outline that emotional abuse is either not tolerated or illegal in civil court. However, what fourteen students and their families discovered over three years is that not one of these publicly funded agencies would enforce these laws and rules. How many others hit the same wall when trying to protect students? Ashley Stirling and Gretchen Kerr believe that abusive conduct by coaches would never be tolerated if teachers acted similarly in the classroom: "The coaches behaved in ways that would not be allowed in other instructional settings – teachers, for example, would incur serious consequences for name-calling and throwing objects at students."[298] At my former school, what we learned was that teachers do not incur even the mildest of consequences, such as a reprimand, for abusive conduct reported on by many students.

---

[297] http://www.mcf.gov.bc.ca/child_protection/keeping_kids_safe.htm
[298] Ashley E. Stirling and Gretchen A. Kerr, "Defining and categorizing emotional abuse in sport," *European Journal of Sport Science*, July 2008: 8 (4): 173-181.

The failure of codes of conduct and guidelines is not unique to BC, it is also seen in boarding schools in Britain. According to freelance writer Beth Morrissey:

> In 1999 all schools in the United Kingdom were required to implement an anti-bullying policy, but most research since then has confirmed that levels of school bullying have either remained the same or got worse. Unfortunately bullying by other pupils just won't seem to stop, even when schools try to tackle the problem head on. This often leaves pupils who are being bullied feeling frightened, frustrated and powerless.[299]

Clearly, whether it is at universities or high schools or the workplace, bullying is becoming more and more out of control even though the effects parallel, if not go beyond, the harm caused by sexual and physical abuse. This must change.

In his article "Message to Coaches: Stop Screaming and Start Teaching" for *Sports Illustrated* on the Mike Rice scandal, sports writer Austin Murphy examined University of Utah swim coach Greg Winslow's case to show that emotional abuse, because it is not in the Criminal Code like sex abuse, may well be tolerated by educational institutions. Keeping in mind the fifty page report that exonerated him, as discussed by Amy Donaldson, Winslow's methods included:

> . . .taping PVC pipe to swimmers' backs, and forcing them to swim laps underwater. In another instance, he forced a swimmer to complete underwater laps with a mesh bag over her head. The abuse was repeatedly brought to the attention of Utah athletic

---

[299] Beth Morrissey, MLIS "How to Stop Bullying by Other Pupils," *Teen Issues*, February 4, 2013: http://www.teenissues.co.uk/HowToStopBullying ByOtherPupils.html

department officials. Yet Winslow was never disciplined until he became the target of a police investigation for sexual abuse.[300]

The complaints against Winslow went on for five years, but until there was something other than emotional or psychological abuse, it was tolerated. Students, teachers, parents and administrators need to have zero tolerance for emotional abuse because it can do lasting harm and physical damage. When athletes and students come forward, at great personal risk, to report abusive behavior on the part of their coaches or teachers, the fault for the abusive acts must not be laid at their feet. It is time to end the re-victimization of students and athletes who speak up and instead support their right to pursue their education without abuse, whether it's on the court or in the classroom, whether it is in high schools or university programs.

Just like the legal changes that have occurred in the realm of sexual and physical abuse, it is important to consider the same for emotional, verbal and psychological abuse. While the Toronto Board of Education abolished corporal punishment in 1971, it wasn't until a 2004 Supreme Court Ruling, that it was stopped in all Canadian schools. We have been educated for so many years as a society that corporal punishment does not toughen students up or eliminate their softness so that they become better thinkers or artists or athletes. Lawmakers finally decided that physically disciplining children results in people who don't think clearly or confidently, who don't develop artistically, and who fail to achieve their potential in athletics. Long before 2004, there were many psychological, psychiatric and educational studies done, based on solid research, that taught that corporal punishment was failing our youth. We

---

[300] Austin Murphy, "A Message to Coaches: Stop Screaming and Start Teaching," *Sports Illustrated*, April 2013: http://www.si.com/college-basketball/2013/04/24/college-coaches

have the same kind of long-term, well-researched, scientifically documented studies that argue that we are failing our students when we allow emotional abuse to occur in our schools.

Ever since the Rutgers-Mike Rice scandal, sports commentators, university officials, athletic directors, professional athletes, psychologists and educators have expressed opinions about how athletes are taught or how students are coached, what constitutes abuse and what inspires development. In his article for *Sports Illustrated*, Austin Murphy defers to Dr. Alan Goldberg whose area of expertise lies in examining "what causes athletes to have performance problems, why they choke, why they get stuck in repetitive performance blocks." Dr. Goldberg argues that the usual culprit is:

> ...the kind of hidebound, ossified coaching that got Rice fired – 'the old-school, abusive model,' says Goldberg, 'where you yell and scream and when people screw up you shame them and punish them and make them run wind sprints.
>
> It's supposed to build mental toughness. It does the opposite. It doesn't prepare athletes to be peak performers. It makes them afraid to mess up. It gets them in their heads, thinking, and you can't perform well in any sport if you're thinking.
>
> It makes them feel badly about themselves, and it creates performance problems.[301]

Dr. Goldberg goes on to explain that abusive coaching:

> ...isn't just stupid and counterproductive. The screaming, saliva-spritzing, profanity-laced method made famous by Woody Hayes and Bob Knight and imitated by countless dime-store dictators

---

[301] Ibid.

through the decades is borderline sociopathic. It's incredible, with the profusion of anti-bullying programs in schools across the country, that this sort of coaching is still tolerated.[302]

One might reasonably assume that Dr. Alan Goldberg would be exactly the kind of expert who would be listened to in terms of how harmful the behavior of the teachers was while they coached high-school students. His many books and articles are readily available to any educational institution that wants to address coaching abuse; yet none of the universities under discussion, or my former school, tried to assess harm; instead, their concern appeared to be with their legal position. Dr. Goldberg wrote an assessment of six testimonies that was sent to the Commissioner for Teacher Regulation that advised the teachers should be instantly relieved of their duties. However, the Commissioner ruled that the teachers' bullying conduct, as recorded in student testimonies, did not deserve even a reprimand. I believe that it is incumbent upon the Commissioner for Teacher Regulation to let families read his decisions, not just the families whose children were harmed and who have been blocked from reading his reports, but anyone interested in reading the findings and coming to their own conclusions. Parents need to make informed choices about whether they want their child exposed to teachers who swear, use obscenities, make derogatory comments, yell in the face of students, shove their fingers into students' chests, shun students, target for personal attacks, humiliate students, grab them, and so on. Parents have a right to this information.

When the Mike Rice story first broke, professional athletes spoke about how badly the trust was broken between parents who handed over their children to a coach and a university with the belief that they would

---

[302] Ibid.

320

receive exceptional instruction and training; never for a moment would they have allowed their children to go into such a program if they knew they would be bullied day in, day out by their coach. NBA player LeBron James did not respond to the video of Mike Rice by saying the student-athletes appeared *too sensitive* or that Rice's coaching tactics would harden his players and remove their softness. He did not say those were the methods that had made him a great player. Instead, he tweeted: "If my son played for Rutgers or a coach like that he would have some real explaining to do and I'm still gone whoop on him afterwards! C'mon."

# Chapter Eleven

# PTSD and Student Safety

> I have been treating [a student] for PTSD, (Post Traumatic Stress Disorder) as a result of a two year, on-going abusive situation that he experienced as a member of the basketball team. As a result [this student] has experienced excessive anxiety and a loss of self-confidence whenever he is in a pressured performance situation. He suffers from an inability to concentrate on task and can also become physically ill.
>
> – Dr. Alan Goldberg's letter to excuse our son from writing AP exams

At my former school, which runs a lecture series on brain research and features experts on professional development days for teachers, there does not seem to be awareness that bullying can scar a student's developing brain. And yet, one of the eight standards for teachers according to the Teacher Regulation Branch is being aware of student development:

> **Educators understand and apply knowledge of student growth and development.** Educators are knowledgeable about how children develop as learners and as social beings, and demonstrate an understanding of individual learning differences and special needs. This knowledge is used to assist educators in

making decisions about curriculum, instruction, assessment and classroom management.[303]

To my knowledge, at my former school, there were never any professional development workshops or presentations to address this seeming lack of knowledge that screaming and humiliating students may well be causing physical brain damage. Our son's individual learning differences were not factored in when his coach called the team "retards."

At Penn State University, the way the administration behaved with their knowledge of Sandusky's abuse is relevant to the way my former school responded to multiple student reports that they were being abused and suffering. According to the legal investigation that produced the Freeh report, the "most powerful leaders" at the university "in order to avoid the consequences of bad publicity [. . .] repeatedly concealed critical facts relating to Sandusky's child abuse from authorities, the University's Board of Trustees, the Penn State community, and the public at large." At my former school, there were reports written by lawyers, but the details recorded in fourteen student testimonies have never been disclosed until now. The anguished words from those who lived in that environment have never been shared with the school community or public at large. It is possible that not every member on the school's Board of Governors even fully knows what students endured on and off the basketball court at the school. Certainly the staff, faculty and families with children at the school have not been fully informed. To my mind, this is an example of repeatedly concealing critical facts relating to harm reported by multiple students. To my knowledge, the Headmaster did not even share the testimonies with the police. The police would not have known about them without the Lawyer/ parent and I forwarding them on.

---

[303] http://www.bcteacherregulation.ca/Standards/StandardsDevelopment.aspx

The Freeh Report on Penn State established "bad publicity" as the concern that caused those in power to conceal Sandusky's abuse, but it also highlighted other causes which may be relevant to how my former school handled students coming forward with detailed reports of the bullying they were suffering: "A striking lack of empathy for child abuse victims by the most senior leaders of the University"; "a lack of awareness of child abuse issues"; and "a culture of reverence for the football program that is ingrained at all levels of the campus community."[304] The Headmaster, the lawyers who were hired, the Commissioner for Teacher Regulation dismissed students' pleas that the abusive coaching be stopped. Experts in child abuse or abuse in sports were not brought in to assess student testimonies. If they had been, perhaps empathy for what students were suffering may have been followed by swift and effective action.

John O'Sullivan, author of *Changing the Game: The Parents' Guide to Raising Happy, High Performing Athletes, and Giving Youth Sports Back to Our Kids* has written an article entitled "The Enemy of Excellence in Youth Sports." O'Sullivan deplores coaches who don't develop *all* athletes on their teams and instead serve their own egos with short-term wins being the focus rather than long-term athlete development. Moreover, he advises parents: "Please demand that your schools and youth sports clubs hire transformational coaches who value your child and treat him or her with the respect and dignity they deserve in victory and defeat, and then support those coaches!"[305] Treating a child

---

[304] Report of the Special Investigative Counsel Regarding the Actions of The Pennsylvania State University Related to the Child Sexual Abuse Committed by Gerald A. Sandusky: 16-17. http://deadspin.com/5925386/here-is-the-official-report-of-louis-freehs-investigation-into-penn-state-discuss
[305] https://stevenashyb.wordpress.com/2015/01/12/the-enemy-of-excellence-in-youth-sports/

with respect and dignity will allow him or her to fulfill his potential; anything less than that, as documented by countless experts, has the power to limit and hurt children in serious and lasting ways.

Although the law does not protect students from emotional abuse on the court or in the classroom, like it does sexual abuse, research shows that emotional abuse may well be more damaging. According to research included in an article by Ashley Stirling and Gretchen Kerr in the *International Journal of Sport and Exercise Psychology*, emotional abuse has "debilitating developmental effects and life-long implications"; moreover, it has "serious implications for the child's mental health and psychosocial functioning [. . .] and has been suggested to correlate more strongly with depression and anxiety compared with other childhood traumas including physical abuse, sexual abuse, and neglect."[306] With this in mind, it makes sense that the Canadian Bar Association discusses the importance of protecting children and the duty to report abuse; it states: "The protection of children is considered one of society's greatest obligations." The Canadian Bar Association statement lists what abuses are against the law and includes "emotional abuse"; however, when it refers to the laws that govern abuse under the *Child, Family and Community Service Act*, only physical and sexual abuse are listed. Emotional abuse falls through the cracks. The document specifies how the laws govern abuse: "In addition to the normal rules of criminal and civil law that apply to everyone, there's also specific provincial legislation called the *Child, Family and Community Service Act*, which is intended to protect children from sexual and physical abuse and neglect. The Act defines a 'child' as any person under 19." It then poses the question:

---

[306] Ashley E. Stirling and Gretchen A. Kerr, "The perceived effects of elite athletes' experiences of emotional abuse in the coach–athlete relationship." *The International Journal of Sport and Exercise Psychology* 11.1, 2013: 87-100.

"How is abuse and the neglect of children defined?" One expects a definition of sexual and physical abuse, as well as neglect, because they are specified above; however, it also includes a definition of "emotional harm" which is not listed as something from which children are protected. It is this gap that seems to leave students at risk.

This is how emotional harm is specified in the Act: "This is defined as a child having serious anxiety, depression, withdrawal or self-destructive/aggressive behaviors due to persistent emotional abuse by a parent, such as scapegoating, blaming, rejection, threats, insults or humiliation. Emotional harm can also happen to children who witness violence in their homes." Yet another significant gap: notice how this is all directed toward parenting and there is no mention of caregivers, coaches or teachers.[307]

One of the ways in which certain teachers get away with emotional abuse is in the vague area of active and passive abuse: when it's active then it's considered premeditated; when it's passive, then it's considered part of the caregiver's incompetence. The police liaison officer who read the student testimonies and continued to monitor the situation at my former school, went repeatedly to Crown Counsel as he became more concerned that the teachers may have crossed the line into criminal conduct. However, he could not press charges because, as he explained, the emotional abuse would be seen in court as "passive." He wrote an email to us to explain:

> Before we recommend a criminal charge, we need both 'mens rea' (mental element of the offence or guilty mind) and 'actus reus' (guilty act). In this case, we have the act, but not the mindset. All the coach would have to say is in regards to the

---

[307] http://www.cba.org/bc/public_media/family/156.aspx

grabbing of the jacket and/or shirt is "I was trying to grab his attention in the heat of the moment."

Bullying coaches may well exploit this distinction as a way to get away with abusing their athletes: the intensity of the competition means nothing can be premeditated. However, the grabbing of our son was not done at games except once. It happened over and over again at practices. Nonetheless, it was excused. This is why emotional abuse needs clear legal lines drawn so that the laws, unlike the apparently pointless guidelines that currently exist, cannot be manipulated to serve adults who repeatedly harm children in their care, marshaling the argument that it's about sports or winning or they didn't know it was causing harm.[308]

At my former school, the report drafted by the lawyer hired by the Board compared in notable ways to the report written at Rutgers on Mike Rice. As recorded in the *New York Times*:

> On Friday, the university also released a 50-page report that John P. Lacey, an outside lawyer, prepared last year in response to the abuse allegations. It made clear that Rutgers officials were aware that Mr. Rice's outbursts "were not isolated" and that he had a fierce temper, used homophobic and misogynistic slurs, kicked his players and threw basketballs at them. But it described Mr. Rice as "passionate, energetic and demanding" and concluded that his behavior constituted "permissible training." It found that he aimed to "cause them to play better during the team's basketball games." His methods, "while sometimes unorthodox,

---

[308] Jane Barlow and Anita Schrader-McMillan, "Safeguarding Children from Emotional Abuse – What Works?" June 2009: https://www.gov.uk/government/uploads/system/uploads/attachment_data/file/222093/DCSF-RBX-09-09.pdf

328

politically incorrect, or very aggressive, were within the bounds of proper conduct and training methods," the report said. [309]

The lawyer responsible for the report at Rutgers resigned for his involvement in this assessment of abuse, but only when it became public. The culture at my former school was to accept the lawyer's report paid for by the School and published by the Headmaster even though it defamed students by means of anonymous quotes from other students. To my knowledge, none of my colleagues raised any concerns about it. Eight months after Mike Rice was fired amid a media firestorm, the TV sports clips highlighting the Assistant Coach's comparable conduct aired and, rather than be concerned for student safety and health, the sports casters seemed amused. This speaks to the way certain communities normalize abuse under the auspices of sport. Unfortunately, as is widely documented, student-athletes who are being abused are sometimes forced to quit or self-destruct when their community and society excuse the conduct. It is tragic when they quit their sport, but it makes sense when one realizes that they have to constantly relive the trauma when they play.

Dr. John Schinnerer concludes in his article "Help, My Coach is a Bully!" that "Rather than helping them to 'toughen up,' 33 percent of verbally abused children suffer from significant levels of post-traumatic stress disorder (PTSD). This is the same disorder that haunts many war veterans and victims of violent assault."[310] New research into the adolescent brain's vulnerability offers neuroscientific reasons as to why.

---

[309] Kate Zernike and Steve Eder, "Rutgers Tries to Calm Furor as More Officials Quit," *New York Times*, April 2013: http://www.nytimes.com/2013/04/06/sports/ncaabasketball/athletic-director-tim-pernetti-is-out-in-rutgers-abuse-scandal.html?_r=0

[310] John Schinnerer, Ph.D, "'Help, My Coach is a Bully!': The Consequences of Verbally Abusive Coaching": http://www.selfgrowth.com/articles/Help_My_Coach_is_a_Bully_The_Consequences_of_Verbally_Abusive_Coaching.html

As discussed, our son has been diagnosed with PTSD by Dr. Alan Goldberg, and according to Dr. John Schinnerer asking him, an adolescent, to go back on the court competitively is like asking a traumatized solider to return to active duty. Regardless that basketball is his passion and ultimate joy, he won't go back on the court. As documented, much of this has to do with the adolescent brain's developmental vulnerability.[311]

I am hopeful that teachers, just like coaches, can change and stop the cycle of abuse and the way it has been normalized in sports. In a recent article in the *International Journal of Sports Science and Coaching*, the researcher offers an example of positive change. A coach of elite athletes explains, "I remember this one kid – I called the kid to ask why he hasn't signed up for the next season and the father said to me, 'Because of you he doesn't want to play soccer anymore.' It was one of the most devastating comments I have heard. I can honestly tell you I was in tears.'"[312] This coach goes on to say that from that point forward, he changed.

At my former school, parents wanted to give the coaches a chance to change, but instead, the process flipped: teachers, reported on by multiple students, were treated as if their conduct was fine, and it was the students who had issues. Likewise, I instantly went from being a valuable contributor to the School to being a problem employee. Some educational institutions do not seem to want teachers or coaches who speak up on behalf of the rights of student-athletes to play in a safe and healthy environment. Due to my treatment, there was a clear message issued at

---

[311] Tamsin McMahon, "Inside Your Teenager's Scary Brain," *Maclean's Magazine*, January 2015: 48-53.
[312] Ashley E. Stirling, "Understanding the Use of Emotionally Abusive Coaching Practices," *International Journal of Sports Science & Coaching* 8.4, 2013: 625-638.

my former school that if you report on abuse, you may suffer consequences that even affect your career.

I have subsequently met another former teacher from this School. This teacher reported to the Middle School Director about sexual misconduct directed at grade six girls by another teacher. From that point on, *the teacher who reported on the abuse* was closely monitored by the Director. Repeatedly the Director would arrive unannounced in class and take notes, which the teacher found understandably disconcerting. He would call the teacher into his office and say that the teacher said "um" too often when teaching, along with highlighting other errors. After seventeen of these surprise visits during one month, the teacher so hated going to work that the teacher quit during spring break. The teacher reported on was subsequently "retired." I have heard from another colleague that there is yet another teacher who went through a comparable crisis and quit after suffering immense stress. Both teachers work elsewhere in the city and neither will speak up, because my former school has such influence in this community. I believe this kind of information is vital for parents, but from my experience, I have sympathy for teachers who can't afford to put their job on the line to stand up for students.

In this context, it is interesting that there is debate about whether or not the British school system should make reporting abuse mandatory, and a lawyer who specializes in child abuse highlights the risks of putting students first:

> It's difficult to gauge public schools' position on whether they consider it necessary to strengthen their safeguarding with criminal sanctions for failure to report, as those asked were not willing to be interviewed. But with two decades of experience representing victims of abuse, Peter Garsden says that without such a law, the system is always going to fail. "Human instinct will always be with selfish considerations," he says. "For staff, that's their jobs and their security of livelihood. Unless they're

331

brave, they're not going to report it. They'd be bringing the whole pack of cards down."[313]

It takes bravery for students who may suffer consequences. It takes bravery for teachers. To report on abuse, the person reporting must put selfish considerations aside. It's not easy to do. I have found it remarkable the price the students have paid for reporting, the price their families have paid, as well as the price I have paid as a teacher. And now I've learned about the price paid by two other teachers before me. I randomly stumbled upon this information; there may well be other teachers who reported on abusive conduct and were penalized for it.

The Assistant Coach, Eric Murdock who exposed Mike Rice's abusive conduct was still cut from Rutgers' University. And the coaching intern at my former school who attempted suicide also lost his contract. The coaching intern initially considered his position at this school to be a career-establishing job where he especially hoped to develop his skills as a basketball coach. However, he was treated like an unwanted witness, told not to attend practices, and penalized for offering to coach a B-Team for boys who wouldn't play for the A-Team's coaches. The school's police liaison officer interviewed the coaching intern for two hours. However, as discussed, the police could do nothing. Because emotional abuse is not in the Criminal Code, the police could not intervene and establish any protection for students.

A comparable issue is raised by sports reporters in terms of Mike Rice's abusive conduct as they examine the potential criminality of his behavior. In the *New York Daily News*, April 2013, sports journalist, Tom

---

[313] Louise Tickle, "Britain's Elite Boarding Schools Are Facing an Explosion of Abuse Allegations," *Newsweek*, September 2014: http://www.newsweek.com/britain-elite-boarding-schools-facing-explosion-abuse-allegations-267201

Harvey, titles his article with the pressing question for this study: "Does Mike Rice Belong in Jail?"

> In New Jersey, a person commits an offense if, with purpose to harass another, he subjects another to striking, kicking, shoving, or other offensive touching, or engages in any course of alarming conduct or of repeatedly committing acts with purposes to alarm or seriously annoy such other person. Anyone who has watched the disturbing video would have to agree that coach Rice crossed the line of acceptable behavior [. . . ] Worse, if any of those students were 17 or younger, the behavior would fit the definition of child abuse under a state statute, and anyone who failed to report the abuse may have also violated the law. The fact that Pernetti and Barchi are still allowed on campus shows a complete lack of perspective and common sense among Rutgers' Board of Trustees.[314]

According to student testimonies, the teachers at my former school behaved in comparable ways to Mike Rice: according to students, they engaged in a "course of alarming conduct" that certainly felt as though they had "purposes to alarm or seriously annoy" the players. In BC, like New Jersey, emotional abuse is against the law, but it is not in the Criminal Code and therefore it is disciplined within schools and universities by educators and administrators or in civil court for those who can afford enormous legal fees. However, there is an inherent conflict of interest in an independent school: as in a university, they have to keep one eye on attracting students and their tuition payments. This may make it difficult to keep the other eye fully focused on student health, safety, and wellbeing. This is why they should not investigate or regulate themselves; they need to have independent oversight on the

---

[314] http://www.nydailynews.com/sports/college/harvey-mike-rice-belong-jail-article-1.1306712

333

Board and within the school itself. Students should have the ability to report teacher or peer bullying in a safe environment and know that a record will be kept, so that if a pattern emerges, appropriate action can be taken and students will be protected.

# Conclusion

# Call to Action

> The mentality in hockey is that people are afraid to say anything about the coach or the organization or the league because they're afraid of repercussions against their kid. But you have to take a stand when you see something that isn't right.
>
> – Father of son allegedly abused by his coach [315]

What happened at my former school appears to be part of a larger societal problem, one that Stephen Goldstein, Associate Chancellor of the Newark Campus of Rutgers, referred to in April 2013 as a "bullying epidemic."[316] A great deal is known about the way bullying infects and harms; yet despite all the research and knowledge, the contagion of bullying seems to be on the increase. Maybe this is because we continue to study and analyze its proliferation among children on the playground, and among adults at the workplace, when we should extend the paradigm to focus on adults bullying children, teachers bullying students, and coaches bullying athletes. These models represent the most significant power imbalances.

---

[315] Robert Cribb, "Coaches Facing Allegations of Abuse," *The Star*, July 2010: http://www.thestar.com/sports/gthl/article/842193--coaches-facing-allegations-of-abuse

[316] http://blog.nj.com/njv_guest_blog/2013/04/opinion_a_plan_to_end_the_bull.html

Suffering from insomnia in the fall of 2012, our son wrote us a letter that highlights this: "When I lie in my bed all I can think about is images on and off the court seeing friends humiliated and embarrassed. I hate this, because I didn't do anything at the time. That's the worst part, not being able to stick up for what's right, because you are a child and not an adult."

I would love to read studies done by the experts on the harm done to children forced into the position of bystander because the bully is a teacher. I wonder what that would look like on an MRI machine. Seventeen years old, and suffering from insomnia yet again, our son wrote a letter that typifies exactly why it is that teacher bullying is the most damaging of the abuses: "I knew from the beginning that I was good enough to start and that I'm not a 'fucking retard.'" He adds that if his teenage brother had issued the insult, it wouldn't have been so bad, but that coming from a teacher he once respected, "it hurts more than you can imagine."

We can't imagine the hurt, but we did witness it in the form of his not playing the sport he loved for the first time since grade four and in the hole it left in his life; we witnessed it in the depression he suffered, having lost all interest in his future, lying on the couch watching TV and essentially giving up for a period of time; we witnessed it in the educational assessment that measured a significant decline in his ability to learn, concentrate and remember; we witnessed it in his panic attacks and anxiety around any kind of performance, from taking a math test to attending a social event. However, our son has fought back in remarkable ways and so can many students who have been abused. He was quite likely saved a great deal of further suffering by working with Dr. Alan Goldberg. Fortunately, we were able to pay for his sessions, and we educated ourselves about emotional abuse so we were better informed about what he needed, and we knew what to do to support him. But what about families that can't afford counseling for their children? What about parents who aren't trained to access the key information on emotional abuse and what it does? For our son, the scars will always be there, but his steely comportment carried him through the hell of grade twelve at a School where he was labeled a liar for speaking up about his teachers' bullying.

We need to stop drawing up guidelines, and instead hold teacher-bullies accountable. We need to shift our approach from an abuser-sensitive one to a victim-sensitive one. If we want teachers to report on abuse by colleagues, and parents and students to speak up when teachers are bullying, then we need a far better system to record and assess allegations in schools. We need legislation and courtroom protocol changed so that it supports and protects abused children rather than re-victimizes them. We need informed and educated authorities to enforce the rules around safe and healthy schools.

My research for this book has revealed that these issues are not limited to one School, one province or one country. I have heard from parents and advocates from California to Florida that they too are fighting to have emotional abuse put into the Criminal Code to better protect children. The following comments therefore apply in a variety of ways to a much larger movement than just the Canadian one I have focused on: there is a great deal of excellent research and government documents on the effects of bullying from one child or teen to another, but there are no research projects or documents or government reports, as far as I can discover, that address teachers who bully students. While there are strict rules for coaches who bully athletes, it appears no one keeps records when they're breached, and no one enforces these rules. My hope, therefore, is that this book acts as a catalyst for psychologists and government policy writers, lawmakers, educators, neuroscientists and psychiatrists to open up and explore this extremely important issue that has the potential to harm students' developing brains, hurt their sense of self in profound ways, and to limit them throughout life.

There's a significant amount of excellent, well researched, well-documented material on the subject of emotional abuse; however, it does not appear to form a part of widespread student, teacher, or administrator education. This could be because the studies tend to focus on parent to child rather than teacher to student.[317] When I was forced to resign from my former school due to the toxic atmosphere created around me, I was hired to work at another independent school. For the first time, I attended a faculty event at the start of the year and the Principal handed out booklets produced by the Ministry of Education that outlined sexual, physical, and emotional abuse. He informed us that it was accessible online. He also drew all teachers' attention to the Ministry of Education's Codes of Conduct that are clear on what our professional duties are in terms of the students in our care. Furthermore, my new school has created an anonymous reporting system on any and all bullying. Hopefully, this school's approach will be a model for other schools that are not presently foregrounding the expectations for teacher conduct and the types of behaviors that are abusive and harmful. My experience has been that this kind of crucial education, for those who have power over children, is not taught often enough. My experience has also been that the Commissioner for Teacher Regulation may have clearly articulated standards, but he also has the power to ignore them in certain cases and not hold teachers accountable or share his decisions with the public.

---

[317] See Reinert, D., & Edwards, C. (2009). Childhood physical and verbal mistreatment, psychological symptoms, and substance use: sex differences and the moderating role of attachment. *Journal of Family Violence*, 24, 589-596 or Vissing, Y., Strauss, M., Gelles, R., & Harrop, J. (1991). Verbal aggression by parents and psychosocial problems of children. *Child Abuse and Neglect*, 15, 223-238.

In an article about Dr. Wendy Craig, a bullying expert based at Ontario's Queen's University, the lack of teacher-education about bullying is discussed:

> Since most traditional bullying takes place at schools, it seems logical that teachers would be equipped with professional knowledge and skills to nip bullying in the bud or handle ongoing cases. Not so. Bill Beasley, an Alberta teacher and Queen's alumnus, who hosts a much-visited website at www.bullying.org, notes that bullying is one of the biggest non-academic problems for teachers, yet they get virtually no formal training for dealing with it.

Along with Dr. Alan Goldberg, Dr. Wendy Craig was also brought in to speak at the *Champions for Children and Youth Summit 2013* in BC. In the article about her, entitled "Battling Childhood Aggression," Alec Ross looks at the work she specifically does with teachers to remedy their lack of knowledge or understanding of bullying:

> For her part, Craig lectures about bullying to teacher candidates at the Queen's Faculty of Education, but admits that this is not enough. "Addressing this lack is another PREVNet signature project: an online magazine called *MyHealth*. Schools can subscribe to it so that teachers and students can read articles, written by youth, about health topics including bullying. PREVNet's role is to provide the evidence-based background material to the writers. The idea is that the magazine will reach every youth and educator across the country so that they'll have a sense of how to recognize bullying in their classroom, what strategies will work, which ones don't, and how to pick bullying prevention programs for your classrooms that do work," says Craig. [318]

---

[318] Alec Ross, "Battling Childhood Aggression," *(e)Affect* Issue 1, Spring 2012.

The more teachers and administrators are informed about bullying, the better. However, it seems that there is more and more information being generated, but the problem persists or worsens. As stated, I believe it's time to change the focus and look at the way in which teachers bully students and coaches bully athletes. The more we keep examining childhood bullying, the less prepared we are to address teacher or coach bullying when students report it.

Setting strict rules, enforcing those rules and educating teachers, administrators, coaches, and students around emotional abuse would constitute significant steps forward and may avert future tragic and expensive problems. According to the 2006 *World Health Organization's* study: "In addition to the health and social costs associated with it, child maltreatment has a huge economic impact. The economic costs include: direct medical costs, lost earnings and tax revenue due to premature death, special education, psychological and welfare services, protective services, foster care, preventive services, and adult criminality and subsequent incarceration related to child maltreatment."[319] Along with sexual and physical abuse, emotional abuse is very costly in a whole variety of ways.

In situations where teacher bullying is covered up and enabled, it would appear that there are two "stories" that struggle to coexist in educational institutions: the first narrative is zero tolerance for bullying among children, as well as an expectation that even child bystanders would find the courage to stand up and redress or at least report what is happening. This narrative is widely published in government issued

---

[319] Alexander Butchart and Tony Kahane, *Preventing Child Maltreatment: A Guide to Taking Action and Generating Evidence*, World Health Organization and the International Society for the Prevention of Child Abuse and Neglect, 2006. http://whqlibdoc.who.int/publications/2006/9241594365_eng.pdf?ua=1

documents and articulated at public forums. The second narrative is unspoken; however, it is the narrative that rules the day in schools where teachers are permitted to bully students. This narrative influenced students, teachers and parents at my former school and it appeared to be this: normalize bullying behavior, don't ask questions, don't raise concerns, certainly do not report, especially not in writing, do not intervene at any cost, keep quiet and if you're lucky, the behavior will never come close to you or your family. Teachers who bully, and the administrators who turn a blind eye or worse, support them, are masters at penalizing those who dare to speak up.

I have discussed at length abusive coaching behaviors, but what does the alternative look like? What are the behaviors that are exhibited by good coaches so that teachers and administrators are able to recognize those as well? According to Dr. Alan Goldberg:

THE GOOD COACH....

- NEVER uses humiliation or embarrassment as a coaching tool
- Genuinely cares about the welfare and well being of each athlete
- Is a pro at catching athletes doing things right
- Rarely raises his/her voice
- Is supportive and encouraging
- Builds healthy relationships with his/her athletes
- Is honest and trustworthy
- Creates a feeling of personal safety on the team
- Is able to celebrate his/her athletes' successes/accomplishments
- Is a positive person
- Understands that coaching is about doing what's best for the kids
- Has winning in perspective and defines success in appropriate ways

341

- Tends to be flexible, yet still able to set good limits
- Is open to constructive feedback from players and parents
- Is friendly, non-defensive, and approachable
- Uses hard physical conditioning appropriately
- Is NEVER physically abusive!
- Communicates displeasure directly and appropriately to athletes
- Coaches by generating mutual respect
- Maintains an open mind
- Is a good communicator
- Leaves his/her athletes feeling good about themselves
- Fuels the athlete's enjoyment and enthusiasm for the sport
- Is a wonderful role model
- Earns respect from players and parents
- Does NOT act out his/her feelings/insecurities on his/her athletes[320]

This is an effective list for a teacher in a math or language class, or a teacher on an outdoor education trip, or in a theater or the school parking lot. We shouldn't need special guidelines for every activity when we are entrusted with the care of children.

The title, *Teaching Bullies*, suggests that bullying teachers can be taught not to harm the students entrusted to them and I do believe this to be true. This is exactly why the original parent group initially hoped when this crisis began that the teachers would be given time to get better while off campus and on salary. Meanwhile, the students could continue to learn and play sports in a safe, supportive environment. I think it is vital that we step outside the abuse cycle and put a plan into action so that while this kind of harmful conduct is not tolerated in schools, it is nonetheless

---

[320] Dr. Alan Goldberg, ""Coaching ABUSE: The dirty, not-so-little secret in sports." http://gazette.teachers.net/gazette/wordpress/dr-alan-goldberg/coaching-abuse-the-dirty-not-so-little-secret-in-sports-by-dr-alan-goldberg/

treated as an illness that can and should be treated. Most individuals do not want to bully. It's an infection that one catches from someone else. It's an infection a child may catch from a parent, a coach, a teacher, or other significant adult in a child's life.[321] I believe that bullying is learned behavior. Thus, teachers who bully students are not "bad" people; they are people who aren't well and need help. Therefore, as a society, we need to talk about it and put in place remedies.

However, the title *Teaching Bullies* is also a terrible reminder to us that abusive teachers hold powerful positions that can actually teach bullying to children. Although parents, children, and school administrators sometimes believe that by covering up a teachers' bullying behavior, they are protecting teachers, in fact they are simply reinforcing the bars of the cage they already inhabit. The whole paradigm has to shift if we are ever going to move forward in the education system and in the workplace and eradicate bullying behavior. We are never going to teach our children not to bully on the playground when we do not address the much more serious issue of teachers who bully students and coaches who bully athletes.

The conclusion of the Freeh report written about Jerry Sandusky and the legacy he has left at Penn State is a call to action. It is addressed to all educators, all teachers, and all administrators who have the responsibility for teaching children and caring for them:

> The release of our report today marks the beginning of a process for Penn State, and not the end. It is critical that Old Main, the Board and the Penn State community never forget these failures and commit themselves to strengthening an open, compliant and

---

[321] Ibid. As Dr. Alan Goldberg explains: "Many abusive coaches were abused as children by either their parents or coaches. The only way to stop this insidious cycle is to directly work on the issues with a trained counselor."

victim sensitive environment—where everyone has the duty to "blow the whistle" on anyone who breaks this trust, no matter how powerful or prominent they may appear to be. [322]

This book is dedicated to the fourteen students who gave testimonies in an unsafe environment. It is dedicated to fourteen students whose lives will be forever changed by being strong enough to step up, be truthful, share their experiences on and off the court and withstand the onslaught that followed. They served the school in ways that should never be forgotten. They showed courage of an extraordinary kind, courage that the esteemed adults in their world could not muster. They were honest in an atmosphere that praised and privileged falsehood. They signed their names to testimonies that were clear in communicating the need for respect from teachers and their refusal to participate on the basketball teams unless things changed. They said *no* to abuse, knowing they might be punished for it. The fourteen students further exemplify service, courage, honesty, and respect, the four pillars upon which my former school claims to be founded.

Dr. Alan Goldberg has this impassioned message for all student-athletes and the fourteen students at my former school are models of this kind of bravery:

> Sometimes abusive coaches will manipulate you into believing that if you tell parents or anyone else about what's been going on, then that's a sign that YOU are weak. Actually the opposite is true! Standing up to an abuser and reporting him/her is a sign of great strength! In essence you are making the healthy, self-protective statement, "I will no longer allow you to mistreat me

---

[322] Report of the Special Investigative Counsel Regarding the Actions of The Pennsylvania State University Related to the Child Sexual Abuse Committed by Gerald A. Sandusky: 16-17. http://deadspin.com/5925386/here-is-the-official-report-of-louis-freehs-investigation-into-penn-state-discuss

this way because I value myself too much!" This is a very important statement for you to make to any individual who is physically or emotionally hurting you. Do not try to "tough it out" when it comes to this kind of abusive behavior.[323]

The more students stand up and speak out about teacher bullying and coaching abuse, the more they should be supported by their parents, school administrators, and educational authorities and the less bullying we will have in our society, the fewer suicides, less depression, fewer failures to fulfill potential, less addictive behavior, less aggression, less bullying in the workplace, less quitting of teams.

Everyone should have the right to learn in a safe, fair and healthy environment so they can fulfill their potential separate from the vicious cycle of bullying.

---

[323] http://gazette.teachers.net/gazette/wordpress/dr-alan-goldberg/coaching-abuse-the-dirty-not-so-little-secret-in-sports-by-dr-alan-goldberg/